What People Are Saying About Joshua Mills and *Light Warriors*...

Light Warriors by Joshua Mills is an extraordinary revelation of the power and presence of God's glory, which can saturate the earth with *light*. In this book, Joshua takes readers on a journey into supernatural realms of understanding, equipping believers to operate as "light warriors" in a time when *"darkness covers the earth and thick darkness is over the peoples"* (Isaiah 60:2 NIV). His profound, Spirit-led insights help readers understand how to carry and release the glory of God in their everyday lives, transforming situations and advancing the kingdom. I highly recommend *Light Warriors* to anyone desiring a greater understanding of the glory and of how to brilliantly walk in its fullness with boldness and authority.

—Patricia King
Founder, Patricia King Ministries

Joshua Mills's book *Light Warriors* is more than just a guide to spiritual warfare—it's a key to understanding, unlocking, and weaponizing the light of heaven in your life. Ready to light things up?

—Darren Stott
Senior Leader, Eden Church, Seattle, WA
President, Renaissance Coalition
Host, *Making Light of It*

Light Warriors, the newest book by my friend Joshua Mills, firmly introduces believers to the realm of freedom and authority over all darkness. This is the realm of signs, wonders, victorious living, and intimacy with God; most important, it is a realm that is accessible to all of the church! Romans 8:19, 22 tells us that creation groans, awaiting the revealing of the sons of God. Joshua Mills shows us that all these sons of God are *light warriors*!

—Dr. James Tan
James Tan Ministries International

Light Warriors by Joshua Mills is not only a "now" title for a new book but also a "now" message for an unprecedented hour. Darkness is everywhere in our day, and it exists due to the absence of light. As the body of Christ, we must arise, put on the armor of light, and shine to fulfill our Isaiah 60 mandate. Light warriors are being summoned by the King and commanded to invade every dark space and place! From the Scriptures, the first thing we learn about God is that He is life. The second thing we learn about God is that He is light. Those who are alive *in* Him will shine *for* Him. Once again, Father, Son, and Spirit are declaring from the heavens, "Let there be *light!*" In this book, you will learn the ways of heavenly light and become a ray of light. Welcome to the dawning of the *light warriors*!

—Tim Beck
Evangelist, revivalist, missionary, and pioneer
www.harvestandrevival.com

Light Warriors is a pivotal guide for those yearning to master effective spiritual warfare and engage in triumphant living. As you immerse yourself in the pages of this book, expect to be transformed and prepared to disarm the enemy and fulfill your God-given destiny. Mills equips us with heavenly strategies, empowering us to shine the glorious light of God in a world shrouded in darkness. With scriptural depth and prophetic insight, he reveals how we can harness the radiant power of God's glory to break the chains of darkness and advance God's kingdom. Mills's revelations are not just teachings—they are a clarion call for us to rise as warriors of light in these perilous times. Embrace the call, and let the light of Christ illuminate your path to victory!

—Adam F. Thompson
Voice of Fire Ministries
Author of several books, including *The Elijah Invitation*
www.voiceoffireministries.org

Light Warriors is absolutely intriguing, carrying an unprecedented anointing. It captivated me, and I couldn't wait to read on! I believe Joshua Mills outdid himself in this book. He has always been known for living in the glory, but I believe this book exudes the greater glory. *Light Warriors* will stir a hunger in your soul and spirit.

—Kathy DeGraw
Author, *Healed at Last* and *Mind Battles*
kathydegrawministries.org

Light Warriors is not only a brilliant title from a magnificent writer, Joshua Mills, but also a must-read book to fully understand who you really are here on earth: a light warrior. Joshua is called to impart and strengthen the body of Christ to rise and shine for the glory of God. With this profound revelation, you will thrive, overcome, and be victorious in every battle you face!

—Desiree Ayres
Co-pastor and cofounder, In His Presence Church, Los Angeles, CA
Coproducer of multiple music projects, including *Witness*
Author, *Beyond the Flame* and *God Hunger*

As I read this book, my faith rose up to believe that the light of Jesus overcomes the darkness! I loved the teaching on the armor of light that we can put on daily. Thank you, Joshua, for teaching us about the light of the glory of God!

—Dr. Gaius Lawrence
Senior Pastor, Church of Praise International, Osaka, Japan
President and Founder, Kingdom Connection International (KCI) Network

God has given leaders like Joshua Mills to the body of Christ as a ministry gift for exactly such a time as this! For, only as we live from the higher dimensions of God's glory can we parry the enemy's intensified attacks and wiles and, at the same time, truly move forward for God and make a decisive difference in this end-time world. Only in the glory are the necessary insights, strategies, and divine secrets that make all the difference revealed. The keys that will be deposited into your spirit as you read Joshua's new book, *Light Warriors*, will make you effective and impactful in your life and ministry in a whole new way and on another whole level: as Jesus's "light warrior"!

—Dr. Georg Karl
Founder and president, Glory Life Network of Churches and Glory Harvest International Ministries
Author of several books, including *Journey into Glory* and *Sons of Glory*
www.glorylife.net

The apostle John had a significant relationship with Jesus during His earthly ministry. The two were so close that Jesus, from the cross, gave John the responsibility to care for His mother, Mary. If anyone could have given us a purely historical narrative of Jesus's life, it would have been John. And yet, in his gospel, he chose to introduce Jesus mainly from a theological point of view. *"The Word gave life to everything that was created, and his life brought light to everyone. The light shines in the darkness, and the darkness can never extinguish it"* (John 1:4–5 NLT). I'm grateful to Joshua for taking the time to unpack this revelation of "the Light of the World." You will receive a tangible impartation to walk in this truth.

—D. Karl Thomas
Lead Pastor, Impact Church Network, London, ON

It is a great blessing to read a book that leaves an impression on you when you are done. *Light Warriors* is such a book. Joshua Mills has done an excellent job of conveying the profound truth that every believer has authority and must walk in the light of God's presence. Through many illustrations and life experiences, Joshua reveals how to live in the presence of the Lord. Jesus is the light, and we can experience this light, or ability to bring change in our lives. You will immediately be able to connect to and apply this life-changing ability.

—*Jim Hockaday*
Jim Hockaday Ministries International
Author, *Until I Come*

The title of this book says it all: we are truly *Light Warriors*. When every believer knows who they are and *whose* they are, they walk as a child of light. Light is never afraid of the darkness, and light always expels darkness. In this book, Joshua Mills reveals the Word to show who we are and what we have in Christ: we are the ones who shine God's light in every sphere we influence!

—*Leo Nicotra*
Lead Elder, GGC Life (Glorious Gospel Church), Sydney, AU

Light Warriors by Joshua Mills is a truly transformative book that equips readers to live a life intimately connected to Jesus. Joshua's ability to articulate profound spiritual principles in an accessible and encouraging way sets this book apart. With his unique blend of deep spiritual insight and practical wisdom, he guides believers into a deeper understanding of what it means to be a warrior in God's kingdom. Not only are his teachings rooted in biblical truth, but he also shows how he has lived them out through his own experiences, making this book a powerful tool for anyone seeking a more vibrant relationship with Jesus. Whether you're a new believer or someone who has walked with the Lord for years, Joshua's message will inspire you to pursue more of Jesus with passion and purpose. I highly recommend *Light Warriors* to any Christian who longs to walk more closely with the Lord and to see His kingdom advance in their life.

—*Baldur Einarsson*
Author, *Ice and Fire: Thawing a Murderer's Heart*
Reykjavik, Iceland

In *Light Warriors*, Joshua Mills masterfully unpacks the realm of God's light. I remember meeting Joshua in person and seeing the light all around him. I believe this is a realm that he carries and is assigned by God to equip the church in. This book is enlightening and takes readers through a captivating journey on how to function in the light and destroy darkness. *Light Warriors* will flood readers with light.

—*Chazdon Strickland*
Founder, Ignite the Globe

"Let there be light" (Genesis 1:3)! These are the first recorded words of God in Scripture as He released luminescence across creation that caused it to assemble into its appropriate form. Today, we are in need of a fresh revelation of divine illumination, and Joshua Mills has done exactly that with his latest release, *Light Warriors*. This book contains a well of impartation for power, authority, and purpose. The revelation on these pages will awaken you to the victorious light God has created you to be and cause you to walk in your proper form—as a light warrior.

—*David Yancey*
Author, *Mantles of Glory*
Glory Culture International, Fresno, CA

Do you know you are a carrier of God's Spirit, love, and light? Many of us have been kept in the dark about this reality because we've believed the enemy's lies that we lack worth or are not strong enough to fight him. The enemy wants to keep us fearful and in the dark because he knows our great potential in Christ to counteract his schemes against us. *Light Warriors* by Joshua Mills breaks through the confusion and lies with the illuminating light of God's truth, showing us that *each of us* is a light warrior who can rest secure in God's love and overcome any attack of the enemy. In this liberating book, you will discover how to experience life, freedom, and healing in the Light and then convey Him to others in a powerful, transformative way.

—*Liz Wright*
Liz Wright Ministries
CEO and Founder, International Mentoring Community
Host, *Encountering God* television program and *Live Your Best Life* podcast

Light Warriors shows how to be on the offense with the light instead of cowering in the dark. A spiritual surgeon, Joshua Mills gives you revelation knowledge about God's light penetrating the darkness. Joshua has a unique anointing to describe God's glory. This book not only reveals how the glory is bringing light into your life, but it also shows how you can focus that light into a laser beam for healing, deliverance, and overall well-being. Your spiritual toolbox will expand as you read this work.

—*Keith and Mary Hudson*
Keith Hudson Ministries and Arise Conferences, Santa Barbara, CA

Joshua Mills, my dear friend, reminds me of one of the biblical prophets. The things that happen to Joshua cause people to see that the prophetic realm has not died out, and that the Holy Spirit is still very much alive, at work, and moving within us and among us. John 1:5 tells us that the light came into the darkness, and the darkness could not overcome it. You will be tremendously blessed as you read *Light Warriors* and receive the impartation that it releases.

—*Father Tom DiLorenzo*
In Season and Out of Season radio program, East Boston, MA
www.InSeason.net

OTHER WHITAKER HOUSE BOOKS BY JOSHUA MILLS

*Angelic Activations:
A Scriptural Look at the Modern-Day Ministry of Angels*

*Power Portals: Awaken Your Connection to the Spirit Realm**

*Moving in Glory Realms: Exploring Dimensions of Divine Presence**

*Seeing Angels:
How to Recognize and Interact with Your Heavenly Messengers**

*7 Divine Mysteries: Supernatural Secrets to Unlimited Abundance**

*Creative Glory: Embracing the Realm of Divine Expression**

The Miracle of the Oil: Receive the Power of God's Anointing

SOAKING PRAYER ALBUMS

A Revelation of the Glory

Activating Angels in Your Life

Creative Spark

Experience His Glory

Healing from the Psalms

Mind Freedom

Miracle Mindset Focus

Opening the Portals

Prayer Power

Receive Your Healing

Release the Light

You Are Blessed

*Available in study guide and audiobook format.

JOSHUA MILLS

LIGHT WARRIORS

A HEAVENLY STRATEGY FOR SPIRITUAL WARFARE

WHITAKER HOUSE

Publisher's Note: This book is not intended to provide medical or psychological advice or to take the place of medical advice and treatment from your personal physician. Those who are having suicidal thoughts or who have been emotionally, physically, or sexually abused should seek help from a mental health professional or qualified counselor. Neither the publisher nor the author nor the author's ministry takes any responsibility for any possible consequences from any action taken by any person reading or following the information in this book. If readers are taking prescription medications, they should consult with their physicians and not take themselves off prescribed medicines without the proper supervision of a physician. Always consult your physician or another qualified health care professional before undertaking any change in your physical regimen, whether fasting, diet, medications, or exercise.

Unless otherwise indicated, all Scripture quotations are taken from *The Amplified® Bible, Classic Edition*, © 1954, 1958, 1962, 1964, 1965, 1987 by The Lockman Foundation. Used by permission (www.Lockman.org). All rights reserved. Scripture quotations marked (AMP) are taken from *The Amplified® Bible*, © 2015 by The Lockman Foundation, La Habra, CA. Used by permission. (www.Lockman.org). All rights reserved. Scripture quotations marked (NKJV) are from the *New King James Version* of the Bible, copyright © 1979, 1980, 1982, by Thomas Nelson, Inc., Nashville, Tennessee. Used by permission. All rights reserved. Scripture quotations marked (NLT) are from the *Holy Bible, New Living Translation*, © 1996, 2004, 2007 by Tyndale House Foundation. Used by permission of Tyndale House Publishers, Carol Stream, Illinois. All rights reserved. Scripture quotations marked (KJV) are from The Holy Bible, King James Version, public domain. Scripture quotations marked (NIV) are from *The Holy Bible, New International Version*, copyright © 1973, 1978, 1984, 2011 by Biblica, Colorado Springs, Colorado. Used by permission. All rights reserved. Scripture quotations marked (ESV) are from *The Holy Bible, English Standard Version*, copyright © 2001 by Crossway Bibles, a publishing ministry of Good News Publishers. Used by permission. All rights reserved. Scripture quotations marked (MSG) are taken from *The Message: The Bible in Contemporary Language* by Eugene H. Peterson, © 1993, 1994, 1995, 1996, 2000, 2001, 2002, 2018. Used by permission of NavPress Publishing Group. All rights reserved. Represented by Tyndale House Publishers, Inc. Scripture quotations marked (NASB) are taken from the updated *New American Standard Bible®*, © 1960, 1971, 1977, 1995, 2020 by The Lockman Foundation. Used by permission. All rights reserved. (www.Lockman.org). Scripture quotations marked (TPT) are taken from The *Passion Translation,®* © 2017, 2018, 2020 by Passion & Fire Ministries, Inc. Used by permission. All rights reserved. (ThePassionTranslation.com). Scripture quotations marked (KJVER) are taken from the *King James Version Easy Read Bible*, KJVER™, © 2001, 2007, 2010, 2015, 2023 by Global Evangelism, Inc. Used by permission. All rights reserved.

The forms LORD and GOD (in small caps) in the Scripture quotations represent the Hebrew name for God *Yahweh* (Jehovah), while *Lord* and *God* normally represent the name *Adonai*, in accordance with the Bible version used. Boldface type in the Scripture quotations indicates the author's emphasis.

Back cover photo by Dustin Mitchell, Creative Dust Studios.

LIGHT WARRIORS:
A Heavenly Strategy for Spiritual Warfare

Joshua Mills
International Glory Ministries
JoshuaMills.com
info@joshuamills.com
PO Box 4037 | Palm Springs, CA 92263

ISBN: 979-8-88769-045-2 | eBook ISBN: 979-8-88769-046-9
Printed in the United States of America
© 2025 by Joshua Mills

Whitaker House | 1030 Hunt Valley Circle | New Kensington, PA 15068
www.whitakerhouse.com

LC record available at https://lccn.loc.gov/2024046747
LC ebook record available at https://lccn.loc.gov/2024046748

No part of this book may be reproduced or transmitted in any form or by any means, electronic or mechanical—including photocopying, recording, or by any information storage and retrieval system—without permission in writing from the publisher. Please direct your inquiries to permissionseditor@whitakerhouse.com.

1 2 3 4 5 6 7 8 9 10 11 **W** 32 31 30 29 28 27 26 25

This book is for the true "light warriors"—those who desire to shine bright with the light of Christ, dismantling darkness and contending for this world to be a better place, a habitation for heaven on earth.

"The path of the righteous is like the morning sun, shining ever brighter till the full light of day."
—Proverbs 4:18 (NIV)

CONTENTS

Acknowledgments 15
Foreword by Katie Souza 17
Introduction: Victorious Spiritual Warfare 19
    1. Living in the Light of Christ 22
    2. Becoming a Light Warrior 35
    3. Working with the Light 53
    4. Embracing the Joy-Light 75
    5. Releasing Healing Light 95
    6. Activating Angels and Disarming Demons 121
    7. Moving as Chariots of Light 144
    8. Ascending in the Light 161
    9. Entering Pathways of Light 175
   10. Shifting Atmospheres with Praise-Light 190
   11. Activate the Glory Light! 214
About the Author 224

ACKNOWLEDGMENTS

Although this book is ultimately the result of a dramatic supernatural vision that I received, the revelation within its pages has been accumulated over the process of many years through divine inspiration, exhaustive research, experimental trial and error (putting faith into action), and listening carefully as wise voices have spoken rays of light into my spirit.

Some of those anointed voices, which I must acknowledge here, include Patricia King, Renee Branson, and JoAnn McFatter. Their pioneering intrigue regarding the scriptural and practical truths of God's powerful light became a supportive portal for me to delve in deeper.

My wife, Janet, and three children, Lincoln, Liberty, and Legacy, continue to be my greatest supporters and sounding boards for every book that I write, and this one was no different. Thank you for your patience, influence, and willingness to sacrifice for this message to be extended around the world in book form.

I must acknowledge my faithful editors, Harold McDougal and Lois Puglisi, who have been committed to the spirit of excellence and glory concerning this message. Your scriptural, editorial, and creative input has enhanced this book to make it extremely accessible to those who will read it.

Katie Souza, thank you for writing the foreword. You have ministered over many years in the glory revelation of the light, and this message belongs to you as much as it belongs to me.

Thank you to Liberty Mills, Myles Milham, Victoria Milham, and John Mandoukos for your modeling talent for the chart diagrams, and to Kali Mock, Alicia Spiewak, Leza Milham, and Joseph Costa for your "hands of power." Also, to Katie Brown for your photography expertise! To Ken Vail of Prevail Creative in Charlottetown, PEI, for creating the diagrams, and to Becky Speer, Whitaker House art director, for the cover graphics and overall layout of this book.

To Christine Whitaker and the entire team at Whitaker House: I'm grateful once again for your trust and willingness to publish the "now word" of the Lord. It is always a pleasure partnering with you in this important work of the glory.

I must acknowledge our Miracle Worker partners, who sacrificially give of their time, prayers, and finances to support this ministry on a monthly basis. Your support has enabled another book to be written, and, in turn, countless lives will be transformed and changed.

There are always many people involved in the process of writing any book worth reading. I'm certain that there are many more names that should be mentioned in this acknowledgment, but it would be impossible to list them all. You know who you are, you know your impact upon my life and this message, and I am truly grateful for the divine connection that has brought this message forth.

May God receive greater glory and the people of God receive greater empowerment through this divine revelation of light warriors.

FOREWORD

When Joshua Mills told me he was writing a book about the light of Jesus Christ, I was thrilled. First, because I have known Joshua and his wife, Janet, for over twelve years, and I have witnessed firsthand their integrity and humility. I have seen the raw power and glory from God that resides on their lives and ministry. We have ministered together in many meetings, as well as on television broadcasts, and there has never been one occasion when the presence of the Lord didn't show up.

Second, I was so excited about Joshua's new book because, over the centuries, the church has tragically often been in the dark about the light of Christ, and that is true for the church today. This book is long overdue. There is so little understanding about the astounding power of God's light. The Lord birthed in me a forerunner revelation concerning the light of Christ over a decade and a half ago. We must realize that Jesus said, *"While you have the Light, believe in the Light [have faith in it, hold to it, rely on it], that you may become sons of the Light and be filled with Light"* (John 12:36).

A man in Minnesota suffered from a strange hearing disorder in which every time he took a breath, it sounded in his ears like a door slamming shut. Conversely, whenever he breathed out, it sounded like a door opening, followed by sounds of severe static. He had suffered from this condition for most of his life. The interference to his hearing was so bad that he became very proficient

17

at reading people's lips during conversations because it was extremely difficult for him to understand clearly what they were saying. However, he attended one of my meetings, and as I taught about the healing power of Jesus's light, he was totally healed of this condition. When he came up on the platform to testify, I asked him to test his hearing by breathing in and out. As he did so, he began to weep and cried out, "It's gone!"

Christ is the Light of the World, and His light brings life. What Joshua is about to reveal to you in *Light Warriors* must never be thrown to the side and forgotten after the closing chapter. As you receive the illumination contained within these pages, you will be infused with the life-giving power of the *"Sun of Righteousness"* as He arises on you with healing in His wings and beams of light. (See Malachi 4:2.)

When you read through the wealth of teaching and Scripture in this book, I encourage you to read it out loud over yourself. Psalm 119:130 says, *"The entrance and unfolding of Your words give light; their unfolding gives understanding (discernment and comprehension) to the simple."* As you follow along with Joshua, your voice will release the light of Christ that is in you; your decrees will be established because the Light is shining upon your ways.

I also encourage you to lay hands on yourself as you read along because the Bible says, *"He [God] covers His hands with the lightning and commands it to strike the mark"* (Job 36:32). As God's power flows through you, His lightning will strike its mark and drive out the darkness of sickness, disease, lack, affliction, and demonic oppression that is in your life.

Included in this book are activations to enable you to walk in this revelation in practical ways. I believe that you will be filled with the healing and delivering power of God's light, and be transformed as you sit in the presence of His illumination, reading and participating with the revelation.

Arise and shine, for your light has come! (See Isaiah 60:1.) Get ready for an encounter with God's life-giving light!

—Katie Souza
Katie Souza Ministries
Author, *Healing the Wounded Soul*

INTRODUCTION: VICTORIOUS SPIRITUAL WARFARE

"His brightness was like the light; He had rays flashing from His hand, and there His power was hidden."
—Habakkuk 3:4 (NKJV)

One night, not long ago, the heavy presence of God's glory filled the room where I was sleeping, and I was lifted into a heavenly nighttime vision. In this vision, I saw God's mighty right hand stretching toward me. Large, powerful pillars of light were shooting out from His hand as celestial beams reached down from the heavens. I could feel the radiating energy that flowed from God's hand vibrating directly into me. And, as I raised my hands to surrender to His power, I saw that this heavenly flow of brilliant light was not only coursing through me but also being released from my own hands. As these magnificent beams of heavenly light shot out, they illuminated the darkness around me, shifting the very atmosphere with their brilliance.

That heavenly encounter was the vision that birthed this book. It was not a mere dream; it was a supernatural revelation. I have never considered myself much of a nighttime dreamer. If I do remember a dream, it's always filled with deep spiritual significance, as this one was. Although I had taught about God's glory light for many years, that encounter released an abundance of oil to spark an explosive ignition of revelation to share.

I was already deep into working on a different manuscript when I had that extraordinary nighttime encounter with the Spirit. The vision affected me so dramatically that, the very next day, I reached out to my publisher, Christine Whitaker, at Whitaker House, and told her that I must switch gears and write a book about the light that had impacted me in such a supernatural way. Without hesitation, Christine and her team gave me the green light, and now this book is in your hands!

So, the journey that led me here was unexpected. I love the ways in which God leads us when our hearts are open to Him. It's still a mystery to me how perfect glory can flow through imperfect people, but it does. Jesus Christ is the *"hope of glory"* (Colossians 1:27, various translations) within us, and He is also the Source of supernatural light.

SPIRITUAL STEPPING STONES

My previous release with Whitaker House was a book entitled *The Miracle of the Oil*,[1] and, on its pages, I imparted truths that could help the reader to receive the power of God's anointing. I hope you have read that book and have received the impartation that was available from each chapter. If not, perhaps you'll choose to read it next on your spiritual journey. We need the oil for spiritual breakthrough and so much more, but one of the most important benefits of the anointing is that it allows us to tap into the light of God's glory.

There is a spiritual progression by which we move from the dimension of faith into the anointing and on into the glory realm. Faith acts as our foundation, the anointing as our passage, and the glory as our ultimate destination. These are the stepping stones that the Spirit has provided for us, and, when we approach the glory, we must understand that this is the realm of God's living light, a concept we will talk much about in this book. This realm is so awe-inspiring that it is beyond human comprehension. Without the oil (the

---

1. Joshua Mills, *The Miracle of the Oil* (New Kensington, PA: Whitaker House, 2022).

anointing), we cannot have spiritual light; but, with the oil of God, we can have all the light we need for ourselves, and enough to share with others as well.

NEW DAYS AND NEW STRATEGIES

Light is one of the manifestations of God's glory, and, in these last days, the Spirit is teaching us how to access the power of heavenly light for victorious spiritual warfare. This is not the way we have waged warfare in the past, but new days call for new spiritual strategies. God wants us to recover His original plan for spiritual warfare. He is providing us with a higher revelation, with better tools for overcoming, so we can release His powerful light. When the light shines, darkness *must* flee. As we stand on the precipice of new spiritual battles, we will be armed with unprecedented strategies, gifted to us by God Himself to ensure our triumph. He is giving us a new way to win the battle!

Throughout the Bible, we find references to the glorious light of God—each reference a key to unlocking a deeper understanding of our walk with Him, mastering effective spiritual warfare, shifting spiritual atmospheres, taking authority over diseases, successfully ministering healing, working with God's angels, and disarming enemy assignments while supernaturally advancing in the Spirit to fulfill God's end-time plan of bringing multitudes into the kingdom of God before the second coming of Christ. In this book, we will take a look at all these aspects of God's glory light. Again, in the glory light, we have access to everything we need to live a victorious life. The revelations in this book will enable you to release the light and help set captives free from their chains of darkness.

Are you positioned and ready, with your heart open and your hands raised, to receive these divine strategies? I believe that the content in this book was given to me as a gift from heaven, and now I give it to you. This is our moment to arise and shine as *light warriors!*

CHAPTER 1

LIVING IN THE LIGHT OF CHRIST

*"But if we walk in the light as He is in the light,
we have fellowship with one another, and the blood of Jesus Christ His
Son cleanses us from all sin."*
—1 John 1:7 (NKJV)

T he glory realm is the realm of God's light, and everything about His glory is brilliant.

The Psalms describe God in terms of glory light:

The LORD wraps himself in light as with a garment. (Psalm 104:2 NIV)

The prophet Ezekiel had a striking vision in which he saw the Lord as "gleaming amber" from the waist upward, and as fire from the waist downward:

I saw a figure that appeared to be a man. From what appeared to be his waist down, he looked like a burning flame. From the waist up he looked like gleaming amber. (Ezekiel 8:2 NLT)

When the apostle John described the face of Jesus that he had seen in a revelatory vision, he included this phrase: *"his eyes were like blazing fire"* (Revelation 1:14 NIV).

John also wrote:

God is Light, and there is no darkness in Him at all. (1 John 1:5)

In recent years, one of the principal things that has been missing among church leaders and members is a heavenly vision of the God of light. I mean a real, genuine, authentic vision of the Lord and His glory. Yes, we have a lot of vision for church building, church planting, expanding church campuses, "taking our cities for God," reaching more nations with the gospel, and distributing more Bibles. All of those visions are good, and, at their core, they carry the heart of the Lord. But what we really need is for spiritual leaders to have an encounter with the burning, passionate fire of God—the pure glory of Jesus.

Light warriors are those who live from the higher realms of God's glory. We need to see the Lord and be moved by His light in such a way that we can never be the same again. Ezekiel, John, and others in the Bible had this revelation, and I believe that the Spirit wants all of us to receive the same revelation: God is light. He is *the* light. Everything about God is illuminating.

Light is the primary manifestation that flows from the glory realm. In other words, when you enter into the glory, and the glory enters into you, your spirit is illuminated with divine truth that flows into your soul and even into your physical body. I believe that, in the coming days, as the glory intensifies for the people of God, this light will become more apparent in a very tangible way. The psalmist wrote, *"Let your face shine on your servant"* (Psalm 31:16 NIV), and *"Turn us again to yourself, O Lord God of Heaven's Armies. Make your face shine down upon us"* (Psalm 80:19 NLT). This same cry is in the heart of every light warrior today. We want to see the light, feel the light, hear the light, even as we walk in the light, for God is light. I believe that we are coming into days when God's visible light will shine upon our faces and flow throughout our entire bodies as a testimony that we are children of the light.

Human beings were made in God's image (see Genesis 1:26–27), and I believe Adam and Eve were originally clothed with His light, and that's why they were not ashamed of their "nakedness" in the garden of Eden. They were not naked; they were clothed, but their clothing was the finest that has ever been seen. They were clothed with the light of God's glory! God wants to restore His glory light in us and shine it through us.

This glorious manifestation of light will be revealed in conjunction with the greater glory that is being poured out over the earth. To a degree, we've already begun to see evidence of it in sparkles of golden glory—the shekinah glory—appearing upon us and around us in the atmosphere as we worship, but I believe we've only just begun touching the surface of what God desires to do concerning releasing His light.

Cindy, from Birmingham, Alabama, one of the students in the Bible college where I taught, shared a remarkable experience of seeing photos from her wedding day, where one photograph in particular stood out against all the others. In this extraordinary picture, she is in her elegant wedding gown, taking Communion with her husband, and there is a bright, ethereal glory haze surrounding them, bathing the moment in a heavenly light. When Cindy showed me the photo, it was clear that it had not been altered in any way, and there was no natural explanation for why this image would differ so significantly from the rest of the photos in the wedding album. The picture seemed to be a divine signature, a tangible sign of God's presence and blessing upon their union. The supernatural radiance captured in that instant symbolized the heavenly favor that would guide their marriage, serving as a visible reminder of God's hand actively working in their lives.

My wife, Janet, has recounted stories from her childhood about witnessing a remarkable phenomenon surrounding her mother, the Rev. Patricia Bechard, who was an evangelist. Even at a young age, Janet noticed the glory light shining around her. Despite often facing persecution for operating in the gifts of the Spirit—particularly in churches that did not embrace such manifestations—her mother ministered with unwavering authority. Janet vividly remembers seeing a glowing aura outlining her mother as she preached, a visible manifestation of the glory of God enveloping her. This radiant light was a testament to the divine presence that accompanied her mother's ministry, revealing the spiritual power and favor she carried.

Once, while I was ministering in Budapest, Hungary, a woman in attendance at one of the meetings was excited to discover that her feet began brilliantly shining (within her shoes), an unusual manifestation that was visible for all to see. This incident reminded me of Romans 10:15 (AMP): *"How beautiful are the feet of those who bring good news of good things!"*

Many times, when I minister, people tell me, "I can see a light around you." One time, while I was preaching in Bangkok, Thailand, someone captured a photo of this light, which looked like a bright orb hovering just behind my head. Another time, while I was ministering near Taipei, Taiwan, a bright shaft of light appeared in the middle of the auditorium where we were gathered. When the worshippers saw this light, they were instantly drawn toward it, and many stretched their arms to reach their hands into it. In that moment, there was a feeling of intense angelic activity.

The manifestation of light in my life has become so common that it doesn't surprise me anymore. The first few times that people saw it around me, I thought, "Oh, wow, that person has a special gift to see in the Spirit realm." But now I realize that this light is an impartation of the shekinah glory that I carry on my life. As I walk in the Spirit, I am revealing the kingdom of light. I am a light warrior, and God's glorious light can be seen on me.

People can also see the angels of light that surround my life, they are made aware of the healing light that emanates from my spirit, they can feel the warmth of God's light that I walk in, and they often describe it as a gentle peace. They'll say things like, "When I am around you, I just feel so much better." This effect really has nothing to do with my ability—it's Jesus, the Light of the World, shining through me. I am only a vessel, a conduit. Just as a lightbulb is a servant of the power of electricity, I am a servant of the King of Glory. I shine with *His* light. Jesus said:

> *I am the light of the world. If you follow me, you won't have to walk in darkness, because you will have the light that leads to life.*
> (John 8:12 NLT)

And to those who listened to and followed Him, Jesus also said:

> *You are the light of the world—like a city on a hilltop that cannot be hidden. No one lights a lamp and then puts it under a basket. Instead, a lamp is placed on a stand, where it gives light to everyone in the house. In the same way, let your good deeds shine out for all to see, so that everyone will praise your heavenly Father.* (Matthew 5:14–16 NLT)

A young man recently told me that he received a word from the Lord that I was a "radiant glory man." I think this term could be given to all of us as believers. We are all called to be *light warriors*, radiating the light of Christ everywhere we go.

MANIFESTATIONS OF THE LIGHT

God's light brings various manifestations of His power and glory.

GOD'S LIGHT CONVEYS HIS PRESENCE AND PROTECTION

When the Israelites traveled through the wilderness after their release from slavery in Egypt, God revealed Himself to His people as light, leading them by the luminous pillars of His glory.

> *The Lord went before them by day in a pillar of cloud to lead them along the way and by night in a pillar of fire to give them light, that they might travel by day and by night. The pillar of cloud by day and the pillar of fire by night did not depart from before the people.* (Exodus 13:21–22)

God, as light, became a supernatural protection for His people. This light separated the Israelites from the pursuing Egyptians as they came out of Egypt. (See Exodus 14:19–20.)

Just as the Israelites saw God's light within the pillars that led them in the desert, we can see and experience God's light within His glory cloud as it manifests today. Often, when people experience God's manifest presence for the first time, they will describe it in terms relating to light and its effects. For example, some might say, "I saw a very bright vision." Others might say, "It felt so warm and comforting." Still others may feel a sense of electricity or otherworldly energy. These are all indications of God's glorious light, which manifests His presence and protection.

GOD'S LIGHT BRINGS PURITY

In the beginning, when God created the world, He *"separated the light from the darkness"* (Genesis 1:4)—and this distinction is both symbolically and physically represented in the Bible. In Moses's time, during the plagues against Egypt, there was the type and "shadow" (prophetic figure) of Egypt in contrast to the type and shadow of the land of Goshen, the part of Egypt where the Israelites lived. It was totally dark in the majority of the land of Egypt. For three days, the Egyptians could do nothing. It was so dark for them that they couldn't even see their hands in front of their faces. But, during those same days, God's children in Goshen had light and were unhindered in their activities. (See Exodus 10:21–23.)

God intended for there to be a separation between light and darkness in our lives, too, and, in recent days, He has been dealing with the body of Christ worldwide to reveal the darkness within it and to bring His convicting, healing, and restoring light. Wherever the light shines, full exposure comes. For many people, this might at first seem like an uncomfortable process, but it is also a good thing. For too long, there have been things in the church that were never intended to be there because they are not from God and do not reflect Him. What commonality does light have with darkness? As the apostle Paul wrote, *"What do righteousness and wickedness have in common? Or what fellowship can light have with darkness?"* (2 Corinthians 6:14 NIV). God is now bringing a divine separation. You can't mix the holy with the profane. Why? Because it spoils the whole.

My friend Catherine Mullins, who is a consecrated worship leader, wrote a social media post directed toward those who are in full-time ministry, specifically worship leaders, and I totally agree with what she said:

> Don't expect to be effective for the kingdom when you're a good singer but not living a consecrated life. God doesn't just care about what we do on the platform; He cares about the movies we watch, the clothes we wear, the words we say, the books we read, the websites we visit, conversations we have, the food we eat, how we treat people we disagree with, the thoughts we think…all of it. He cares about all of it.[2]

According to the Scriptures, God demands a higher standard of spiritual leaders:

> *A church leader is a manager of God's household, so he must live a blameless life. He must not be arrogant or quick-tempered; he must not be a heavy drinker, violent, or dishonest with money.* (Titus 1:7 NLT)

---

2. Catherine Mullins, Instagram post, January 22, 2024, https://www.instagram.com/p/C2ahMYpPvrq/?igsh=NTc4MTIwNjQ2YQ%3D%3D.

In emphasizing these points, I'm not being "religious" or legalistic; I'm being biblical. Paul had to address these matters in his day too. (See, for example, 1 Timothy 3:1–15.) How much more should we address these things in our twisted society today? I would like to ask the question again, and I hope you will ponder it in your heart: "What does light have in common with darkness?" The truthful answer is that they have nothing in common. They are complete opposites.

When leaders are held to a higher standard, the purpose is so that the true leaders whom Christ has anointed and ordained can lead those who follow them in the same pattern of higher living and holiness. Spiritual leadership is a glorious calling, a call to rise up into kingdom light, the glory realm. The Spirit of God is calling us to walk in the light and not in darkness. As light warriors, we must be committed to this call.

GOD'S LIGHT BRINGS EMPOWERMENT

In many ways, the Old Testament account of the Israelites seeing the Lord manifested as a pillar of glory cloud by day and a pillar of fire by night was a foreshadowing of what happened on the day of Pentecost, as recorded in the second chapter of Acts:

> *And when the day of Pentecost had fully come, they were all assembled together in one place, when suddenly there came a sound from heaven like the rushing of a violent tempest blast, and it filled the whole house in which they were sitting. And there appeared to them tongues resembling fire, which were separated and distributed and which settled on each one of them.* (Acts 2:1–3)

For those early believers, God came into the atmosphere as wind and fire. Have you ever seen or heard a mighty forest fire? It roars! On several occasions, Janet and I saw and heard forest fires in Southern California. They are loud—and not easy to put out. My friend David Yancey, who is a fellow minister and author, is also a longtime professional firefighter in Visalia, California. He told me, "The bigger the flame, the louder it is. The big wildfires in the forest can move at a phenomenal rate of speed, and it can sound like a freight train. When there is wind present, it magnifies everything, making it burn hotter and move much more rapidly, and it definitely increases the volume of its sound."

Similar to forest fires being loud and ferocious, there was a loud heavenly announcement at Pentecost that ushered in the presence of the Holy Spirit (God Himself in Spirit form). As I have written elsewhere, I believe the angelic seraphim were present and active on the day of Pentecost, preparing the atmosphere for the arrival of the Holy Spirit. The initial wind of Pentecost was filled with the ministry of God's angels, His "spirit winds" and servant *"flames of fire"*: *"Referring to the angels He says, [God] Who makes His angels winds and His ministering servants flames of fire"* (Hebrews 1:7; see also Psalm 104:4). The angels prepared the atmosphere, but God Himself came into the room where those humble disciples were gathered, and He *"settled"* (Acts 2:3) upon them. His very Spirit went into them, and, through the Light, they received power.

The Greek word for this power is *dunamis*. It is miracle-working light, and it was what enabled these disciples to speak in "tongues," languages they had never studied. (See verse 4.) But, much more than that, this light activated the early believers to flow in the power of the Spirit, with supernatural gifts operating in their daily lives.

Jesus had prophesied and promised that this very thing would happen:

> *But you will receive power [dunamis] when the Holy Spirit comes upon you. And you will be my witnesses, telling people about me everywhere—in Jerusalem, throughout Judea, in Samaria, and to the ends of the earth.* (Acts 1:8 NLT)

This divine empowerment was given to enable each of Jesus's followers to be a light and a witness. The definition of the English word *witness* is "one that gives evidence" or "one who has personal knowledge of something."[3] When that fiery light came and rested upon those early believers, it was evidence that Jesus was alive and that He was the light that shines in the darkness. Likewise, when we allow the light of Jesus to shine through our lives, we become light warriors, blazing a path as we push back the forces of darkness so that the reality of the gospel can be witnessed now.

---

3. *Merriam-Webster.com Dictionary*, s.v. "witness," accessed November 5, 2024, https://www.merriam-webster.com/dictionary/witness.

GOD'S LIGHT OVERCOMES THE DARKNESS

God's light overcomes both the darkness that is around us and the darkness that is within us. In the Old Testament, we read about Eleazar, who was of the priestly lineage in Israel:

Eleazar son of Aaron the priest will be responsible for the oil of the lampstand, the fragrant incense, the daily grain offering, and the anointing oil.
(Numbers 4:16 NLT)

In those days, lamps needed oil in order to produce light and shine. Oil, therefore, was essential to the sacred lampstand, and there is a great revelation in its use in this way.[4] If you understand that sickness, disease, infirmity, and pain are all attached to the kingdom of darkness, then the greatest and most obvious solution to overcoming their ill effects is simply to release the light to cast them out—but you cannot release the light unless you've first yielded yourself to be filled with the anointing oil. This is a process that requires a deeper surrender to God and a willingness to submit to the Spirit's leading. A greater anointing comes with greater sacrifice. The degree of anointing that you are willing to permit will determine the amount of light that you are able to emit.

Years ago, when I was new to experiencing the glory, I saw the glory appear as a rainbow inside the church sanctuary of Emmanuel Christian Center in Spring Hill, Florida. It was miraculously stretching from one side of the platform to the other, displaying seven rays of brilliantly colored light, each ray prophetically reminding us of God's eternal covenant with humanity. (See Genesis 9:11–13.) God is still the God who keeps His promises.

Several years later, Janet and I were ministering as guest speakers in Gold Coast, Australia, and, late one night in our hotel room, we saw a rainbow shining in the darkened room. This didn't seem to make any sense in the natural, since it is impossible for a rainbow to appear in darkness. Scientifically, a rainbow is a refraction of light, and yet, there it was, a rainbow appearing in the darkness.

The next day, when we spoke to the other guest speaker about our experience, he replied, "Yes, I saw the same thing in my room!" This was a confirmation

---
4. As mentioned earlier, you can read all about the necessity of the anointing oil and what it means practically and prophetically in my book *The Miracle of the Oil*.

that God was speaking. He is the One who makes light shine into the darkness, for He *is* the Light. (See, for example, 2 Corinthians 4:6.) If you sense darkness all around you, invite God's glory to shine brilliantly into your dark world. Ask the Spirit to give you a revelation of His glory light.

About twenty years ago, Janet and I went on a missionary journey to Puvirnituq, Nunavik, in the Canadian Arctic region. We had been invited by Pastor Eliasi to minister at his annual Winter Bible Conference. One of the other ministers there was Renee Branson, a powerful woman of God from Houston, Texas. For many years, she had been the editor of Pastor John Osteen's written materials, but at that time she was the missions pastor at Lakewood Church. We instantly connected with her, as we had certain things in common: we had all been mentored by Charles and Frances Hunter in healing ministry, and we all shared a great love for the nations.

During the course of that week, we were very blessed by Renee's Bible teaching, and we absorbed every word of it into our spirits. She took a special liking to us—a young couple just getting started in the ministry. It was a divine connection. On the way back home from the conference, our seats were next to hers on the plane to Montreal. For hours, we shared testimonies with each other, and she really encouraged us and stretched our faith for miracles. In fact, it was our conversation that day that began to plant the seeds for the revelation I'm sharing with you in this book.

One of the most profound things that Renee said that day was this:

God told me years ago, "I'm not ashamed of your darkness." You know, everybody has dark areas in their life, places where the light has not yet shined, areas where the revelation knowledge of God's glory has not yet touched. But God said, "I'm not ashamed of your darkness."

I'll never forget what she said, and I've gone back to those words many times. If you believe them, you'll find yourself being freed from feelings of failure and shame because you will understand that God loves you, despite your mistakes and sins, and He wants to heal and restore you. Instead of running away from God, you'll begin running toward His glory light in pursuit of truth and increased freedom. God is not ashamed of you. He knows your past, but, even more than that, He has prepared a better future for you in the light.

(See Jeremiah 29:11.) His Word carries the power to penetrate any darkness in your life.

The psalmist wrote:

The entrance and unfolding of Your words give light; their unfolding gives understanding (discernment and comprehension) to the simple.
(Psalm 119:130)

Just as the sun rises in the morning, bringing light for a new day, the entrance of God's Word is bringing new spiritual light right now. As you're reading this book, and the prophetic Scriptures become more and more alive to you, the light will arise within you, and areas that have been captive to darkness will begin to see that light. You will experience new freedom—a new spiritual release—and the old ways and old patterns of the past will evaporate with the dawning of a new day. *Let there be light!*

But the path of the [uncompromisingly] just and righteous is like the light of dawn, that shines more and more (brighter and clearer) until [it reaches its full strength and glory in] the perfect day [to be prepared].
(Proverbs 4:18)

GOD'S LIGHT PROVOKES SPIRITUAL OPPOSITION

As carriers of God's light, we must be prepared for spiritual opposition. The enemy spirit, Satan, is threatened by you because you have within you the true Light that shines in the darkness. Why do you think he's been attacking you so much and trying to wreak havoc in your life? Don't give him an inch. Don't agree with his curses, his intimidation, or his lies. You carry the light, and that light dominates every form of darkness, no matter how powerful it may seem.

God's light in you is power-filled. It is so much more powerful than the forces of the enemy. I don't think we realize how much power God desires to release through our lives as we begin moving in His light. Isaiah prophesied,

Moreover, the light of the moon will be like the light of the sun, and the light of the sun will be sevenfold, like the light of seven days [concentrated

in one], in the day that the Lord binds up the hurt of His people, and heals their wound.... (Isaiah 30:26)

This verse says that the light of the moon will be as bright as the sun, but the sun will be concentrated with so much light that it will be like seven days' worth of light! That's the kind of brightness that God will lead His people into. Other people will fall on their faces before God, overwhelmed by His glory, and will repent before Him, all because of the light that is upon you and me. We will carry this degree of the light as we submit our lives to God fully and allow Him to work within us. In this way, we'll begin moving from glory to glory, just as the Scriptures have expressed:

And all of us, as with unveiled face, [because we] continued to behold [in the Word of God] as in a mirror the glory of the Lord, are constantly being transfigured into His very own image in ever increasing splendor and from one degree of glory to another; [for this comes] from the Lord [Who is] the Spirit. (2 Corinthians 3:18)

When God spoke through the prophet Isaiah to foretell of Jesus's coming, He talked in terms of light:

You will do more than restore the people of Israel to me. I will make you a light to the Gentiles, and you will bring my salvation to the ends of the earth. (Isaiah 49:6 NLT)

Jesus Christ was a Jew, not a gentile (representing every other culture or nationality in the world), but it was through the people of Israel that God birthed the message of salvation in the Messiah, who came to save and transform people of every nation and background. Just as God is light, He intends for us to be beings of light in this world who reflect Him and carry the message of His salvation. The disciple Matthew quoted Isaiah 9:1–2 when speaking of Jesus and His ministry:

The people who sat in darkness have seen a great light. And for those who lived in the land where death casts its shadow, a light has shined. (Matthew 4:16 NLT)

The same theme was expressed earlier by Zechariah, the father of John the Baptist, when he prophesied about the mission of the One for whom John would prepare the way:

> *To shine on those living in darkness and in the shadow of death, to guide our feet into the path of peace.* (Luke 1:79 NIV)

Bringing light, dispelling the darkness, and leading others into God's path of peace—this is the calling of a *light warrior*.

YES, LET THERE BE LIGHT! CAN YOU FEEL THE SPIRIT'S POWER FLOWING THROUGH YOU AND CAUSING DARKNESS TO FLEE? YOU'RE WINNING THE SPIRITUAL WARFARE BATTLE BECAUSE YOU'RE A *LIGHT WARRIOR*.

CHAPTER 2

BECOMING A LIGHT WARRIOR

"Rescue others by snatching them from the flames of judgment. Show mercy to still others, but do so with great caution, hating the sins that contaminate their lives."
—Jude 1:23 (NLT)

When we consider the responsibilities of a soldier or of a warrior in general, we usually think of their fighting battles, overtaking enemy armies, and even using weapons of mass destruction. So, I don't want you to be mistaken about the way in which I am using the word *warrior* in this book. I'm talking about being a warrior of light, which is very different from being a warrior at the natural level, facing a natural war, or dealing with natural enemies. There are inherent risks and dangers that come with being a warrior in the earthly sense. For example, because warriors engage in physical combat, they face the risk of sustaining physical injuries, including cuts, bruises, broken bones, or even more severe bodily damage (like loss of limbs and traumatic brain injuries). There is also the risk of emotional and psychological trauma, including the very real potential for post-traumatic stress disorder (PTSD). Warriors face the grave and ultimate danger of losing their lives in combat.

However, such elements of natural warfare do not apply to spiritual warfare. In most teachings that I've heard about spiritual warfare, there is a strong emphasis on the battle and the battle wounds or scars that we will need to endure in order to secure ultimate victory. But I don't believe that teaching is correct. If we properly understand our authority in Christ and the power we have in the Spirit realm, it will change both our perspective and our outcome.

THE NATURE OF OUR WARFARE

The Scriptures remind us:

> We are not wrestling with flesh and blood [contending only with physical opponents], but against the despotisms, against the powers, against [the master spirits who are] the world rulers of this present darkness, against the spirit forces of wickedness in the heavenly (supernatural) sphere.
> (Ephesians 6:12)

We are facing a *spiritual* war. Warriors of light shine and radiate with the manifestation of God's glory. Our warfare being completely spiritual in nature, we operate from the glory because our guidance and strength come from a higher dimension.

Still, being a light warrior isn't a gentle call. In the kingdom of God, one of our major roles is similar to a role the National Guard in the United States often fulfills: rescuing people from danger. We must learn how to pull people out of darkness into the kingdom of light by spiritual force.

The dictionary defines a *warrior* as:

1. a person engaged or experienced in warfare; soldier.
2. a person who shows or has shown great vigor, courage, or aggressiveness, as in politics or athletics.[5]

A light warrior is anyone who engages in spiritual warfare and shows great vigor, courage, and aggressiveness to bring divine illumination to those who have been trapped in darkness. We are not moved by physical or emotional shadows that attempt to challenge the truth, for we carry the light. We do not endeavor to wrestle and fight with a carnal mindset, using the plans

---

5. Dictionary.com, s.v. "warrior," https://www.dictionary.com/browse/warrior.

and methods of man, for there is no light in that. We are called to follow the higher way outlined for us within the Scriptures.

In the realm of the Spirit, *"the kingdom of heaven has endured violent assault, and violent men seize it by force [as a precious prize—a share in the heavenly kingdom is sought with most ardent zeal and intense exertion]"* (Matthew 11:12). We must learn how to use every tool and spiritual weapon that has been given to us by the Spirit of God. Note that our heavenly weapons are much different from the weapons soldiers wield in the natural:

> *For the weapons of our warfare are not physical [weapons of flesh and blood], but they are mighty before God for the overthrow and destruction of strongholds, [inasmuch as we] refute arguments and theories and reasonings and every proud and lofty thing that sets itself up against the [true] knowledge of God; and we lead every thought and purpose away captive into the obedience of Christ (the Messiah, the Anointed One).*
> (2 Corinthians 10:4–5)

It is in the Spirit realm that we find our identity as light warriors. As I expressed earlier, I'm becoming more and more aware of the light within me, the light that radiates from me, and the light that has power over every enemy assignment. I feel an intense call to release this light and dispel the deeds of darkness.

> *The night is far gone and the day is almost here. Let us then drop (fling away) the works and deeds of darkness and put on the [full] armor of light.* (Romans 13:12)

You are a *light warrior*. Maybe you haven't realized it, but, in a very deep way, you've felt the call to bring change into the world around you. You have the God-given ability to feel when others hurt; you recognize the pain, and you desire to help relieve it. You are called to carry and release God's light in a supernatural way. In the past, you may have felt bound by the presence of evil that has lurked in the shadows around you, but the light within you is making a new way. Don't look back—keep looking forward! You're being given the divine task of bringing light into a darkened world. This is the work that you've been called to. It's time to accept that call.

DEFINING THE CALL

In this world, we face a very real battle on a daily basis. It's a battle between the flesh and the Spirit. It's a battle for our time, our attention, our resources, our influence, and our anointing. It's a very real battle for souls. The reality of this conflict is an obvious call for the people of God—His light warriors—to arise into position. We must shine now as never before!

This reminds me of an old hymn we used to sing in church when I was growing up. It was a call to rise to this spiritual challenge before it's too late:

Onward, Christian soldiers!
Marching as to war,
With the cross of Jesus
Going on before;
Christ, the royal Master,
Leads against the foe;
Forward into battle,
See, His banner go![6]

According to this hymn, the idea is that the finished work of Christ goes before us, and we march behind His banner of victory. This should give us hope. We are not asked to fight this battle on our own or from an earthly mindset. (See, for example, Colossians 2:15; 1 John 4:3–4.) Instead, we must lift our vision higher and recognize that the battle has already been won in the light of heaven, and we're now simply called to march forward, advancing and occupying the territory that Christ has eternally secured for us. Remember, we're not fighting *for* the victory; we're fighting *from* the victory.

Does this mean that the march forward will be without challenge? Certainly not. There is a very real enemy of our souls, and he is active, attempting to deceive and bring confusion to our lives. That's why we are called to be light warriors. As such, we carry a strong motivation and tenacity for proclaiming the truth, creating peace, and bringing change into the world around us as we work miracles through the light of God.

Yes, I'm aware of the challenges that abound in spiritual warfare, but, in God's glory realm, nothing is too difficult. (See, for example, Matthew 19:26.)

---

6. Sabine Baring-Gould, "Onward Christian Soldiers," *Melodies of Praise* (Springfield, MO: Gospel Publishing House, 1957), 209. Public domain.

I've discovered that when I boldly face areas of darkness in my own life and allow the light to shine brightly on them, the darkness quickly flees, making way for me to receive the freedom of living in God's light, and for this new freedom to abound. Again, this process might initially seem intimidating, but you've been called to this challenge, and I believe that's why you're holding this book in your hands.

I've come up with an acrostic for the word *light* and another for the word *warrior*. The "light" acrostic highlights some of God's qualities that you must keep in mind and hold on to as a light warrior, some of which we have discussed above. Then, the "warrior" acrostic expresses additional qualities that define your call as a warrior of light.

God is…

- L: *Loving* (God is compassionate and caring, and you can rely on His love to protect and sustain you, no matter what is happening in your life and in the physical world. [See, for example, Psalm 46:1–3; 1 John 4:16–17.])

- I: *Illuminating* (God illuminates you by His truth, and you can trust Him to show you the way to fight the powers of darkness. [See, for example, Psalm 119:130; John 17:17.])

- G: *Glorious* (God's glory is magnificent, and His radiance brings light into the darkest places of your life, family, and community. [See 2 Samuel 22:29.])

- H: *Holy* (Holiness is an essential part of God's nature, and as you receive His forgiveness for sin, He cleanses you from all unrighteousness so you can be filled with His light. [See, for example, 1 Peter 1:15–16; 1 John 1:9.])

- T: *Triumphant* (God, through Jesus, has already triumphed over the enemy, so you can live according to *His* victory! [See, for example, Colossians 2:15; Revelation 5:9–10.])

As a light warrior, relying fully on God's Spirit, you are…

- W: *Willing* (You maintain a teachable posture of surrender before God; this is the opposite of being either apathetic or pridefully stubborn toward Him. [See, for example, Psalm 25:4–5; 51:12; Hebrews 5:7.])

- A: *Anointed* (God covers you, leads you, keeps you, and places His favor upon you to live in continuous victory. [See, for example, 2 Corinthians 2:14; 1 Thessalonians 5:23–24.])

- R: *Resilient* (Spiritual warfare is not for the faint of heart. You keep moving forward in God's purposes and do not grow weary in well-doing. [See, for example, Philippians 3:12–14; 2 Thessalonians 3:13.])

- R: *Radiant* (You have been clothed in the light. You continually shine with the brilliance of God's glory and constantly repel the works of darkness. [See, for example, 2 Corinthians 4:6; Philippians 2:14–15.])

- I: *Intense* (Whatever you do, you do it with all your heart. The zeal and passion of God consume you. [See, for example, Romans 12:11; Colossians 3:23.])

- O: *Overcoming* (There is a mountain in front of you; so, by faith, you can either rise above it or move it out of your way. Light warriors have options. [See, for example, Isaiah 40:30–31; Mark 11:22–24.])

- R: *Resistant* (You carry an unshakable faith that resists the enemy and all his deceptions. You choose to stand in the light and not back down from it. You were created for this realm. [See, for example, Psalm 118:5–14; Hebrews 6:13–20.])

PUTTING ON OUR ARMOR OF LIGHT

As light warriors, we've been instructed by God to put on our spiritual armor. You may have heard or read other teachings on the topic of the armor of God, but I want you to begin to think about this armor as armor of *light*. This armor of light cannot be penetrated by any forces of darkness. It provides complete protection and a supernatural source of strength. Think about that for a moment. It doesn't matter how evil the darkness may be; light always outshines the darkness. As we wear this supernatural armor, we begin operating in Christ's authority and in the Spirit's power to defeat every evil spirit and overcome every negative assignment that's sent our way from the kingdom of darkness.

Once you understand this truth, you will no longer need to suffer from spiritual warfare attacks. The Scriptures tell us that we are given supernatural strength for this battle:

> *In conclusion, be strong in the Lord [be empowered through your union with Him]; draw your strength from Him [that strength which His boundless might provides]. Put on God's whole armor [the armor of a heavy-armed soldier which God supplies], that you may be able successfully to stand up against [all] the strategies and the deceits of the devil.*
> (Ephesians 6:10–11)

We are encouraged to *"put on God's **whole** armor"* so that we can successfully withstand the dark strategies and deceits of the enemy.

The Scriptures speak in detail about this armor of light that God has provided for us as we march into spiritual battle. It has been given to equip us with the necessary tools to withstand enemy forces, sinful temptations, and difficult challenges in our endeavor to shine the light of the gospel into a darkened world. The apostle Paul, who was very familiar with the Roman army and its equipment, compared the Romans' stellar components of armor to each piece of God's armor and its divine purpose. However, I want to emphasize that this "light armor" isn't really like any type of natural armor because it shines supernaturally with the force of God's brilliance—a power that goes beyond anything that human beings could create in the natural. This is supernatural, radiating armor that encompasses God's people with His light. This armor is delegated for the use of *light warriors* alone. Let's take a look at Ephesians 6:13–17:

> *Therefore put on God's complete armor, that you may be able to resist and stand your ground on the evil day [of danger], and, having done all [the crisis demands], to stand [firmly in your place]. Stand therefore [hold your ground], having tightened the belt of truth around your loins and having put on the breastplate of integrity and of moral rectitude and right standing with God, and having shod your feet in preparation [to face the enemy with the firm-footed stability, the promptness, and the readiness produced by the good news] of the Gospel of peace. Lift up over all the [covering] shield of saving faith, upon which you can quench all the flaming missiles of the wicked [one]. And take the helmet of Salvation and the sword that the Spirit wields, which is the Word of God.* (Ephesians 6:13–17)

Our spiritual armor consists of six components, each one carrying its own prophetic significance. You'll discover that one of the greatest ways you can utilize this armor of light is by growing in your understanding of the revelation of its purpose and power. The apostle Paul gave us this list of the full armor with a certain order for its wear and use. Below, let's look at each piece of armor in more detail to examine how we can successfully use it as light warriors. I also share prayers that you can use daily as you put on each piece of the armor.

THE BELT OF TRUTH

"Stand therefore [hold your ground], having tightened the belt of truth around your loins…" (Ephesians 6:14). The belt of truth is the first piece of our armor of light. This is because the foundation of everything we do in the spiritual realm must be rooted in God's eternal truth. God's truth is light, and this truth functions as spiritual armor in our lives. (See Psalm 91:4.) Although it is often the case for many Christians, we should not be moved by temporary feelings or anxious thoughts. Our lives and actions must be secured in the ultimate truth of God's Word.

The belt of light represents spiritual truth, integrity, authenticity, honesty, and a strong commitment to living according to Jesus's teachings. When we make these practices our daily habit, we avoid falling into deception, and we cancel the enemy's lies that have tried to harm us.

Warriors of light fight for and defend the truth. There is a very real fight over truth in our society today. It's common to hear people saying things like, "Well, I'm going to live *my* truth," but genuine truth is not subjective according to our situation or the popular opinions of our culture. Real truth is not a thing; real truth is a Person, and that Person is Jesus Christ. He is Truth.

In the Scriptures, we are encouraged to wear truth like a belt that holds everything else together. If things begin to happen in our lives that appear to be contrary to what God has spoken, how will we respond? If we're wearing the belt of truth, we will remain firm to stand on God's promises, unmoved by circumstances or demonic intimidation, knowing that Jesus is the light of truth that is holding all things in place.

A belt is worn around the midsection of the body, and the concept of wearing the belt of truth in this way is prophetic. The truth of the gospel shines light from the very core of our being to all the other parts of our lives and beyond. We must let this light shine to influence every atmosphere into which we step.

It has become very common for Janet and me to be stopped by other people while we are going about our daily errands. If the people are Christians, they might say, "Are you believers? I can see you shining with the light of Jesus," while unbelievers might say, "Wow, you carry so much light! You have a really big aura around you!" In both cases, it becomes an opportunity for us to talk about Jesus and His goodness. The end result is that the believers are encouraged, and many of those who are lost get saved!

To put on this first piece of armor, you can pray in this way:

Father, in the name of Jesus, help me to live in Your truth today. Shine Your light of revelation into any place where lies or deception have tried to hide in the cracks of my life. I fully receive the light of Your truth, and I choose it as my core reality. Amen!

THE BREASTPLATE OF RIGHTEOUSNESS

"*...and having put on the breastplate of integrity* ["*righteousness,*" numerous translations] *and of moral rectitude and right standing with God*" (Ephesians 6:14). This next piece of spiritual light armor covers your chest and represents living a righteous and virtuous life through obedience to the Spirit. It signifies the protection of the heart and the importance of living in a way that is morally upright and in accordance with God's heart. The first place the enemy always aims to attack is the heart, and, for this reason, the Scriptures caution us, "*Guard your heart above all else, for it determines the course of your life*" (Proverbs 4:23 NLT). Spiritually speaking, your heart represents your soft and tender spirit. God desires to protect your heart with this breastplate of light that defends against any dark trauma, abuse, or other attack that would attempt to make you emotionally cold or hard-hearted. The childlike faith, innocence, and love that flow from your heart are important to Him. Love is such a powerful weapon against the forces of hatred that we must always protect our heart by wearing the breastplate of righteousness.

I have mentioned the importance of obedience to fortify this breastplate armor, but that may cause some people to reason that on our "off days" (you know, those times when we succumb to the temptations of the enemy and slip up), God no longer desires to protect us. Nothing could be further from the truth. The Scriptures teach us that we cannot earn holiness through our own human self-effort, based on our man-made works and earthly performance. (See Romans 3:21–22.) This is where God's ongoing grace comes in. This area is vital for us to understand, especially if we have previously lived in ignorance of, or in disobedience to, God or if we had a difficult childhood or young adulthood.

Jesus Christ's gift of righteousness assures us that we are always in right standing with God and covered by His grace. Romans 8:1 clearly states, "*So now there is no condemnation for those who belong to Christ Jesus*" (NLT). By faith, we can have this confidence in God's forgiveness and acceptance of us, and we can put on this breastplate of righteousness. This armor protects us from any feelings of unworthiness, guilt, or shame that would attempt to hinder our spiritual growth.

To put on the breastplate of righteousness, you can pray in this way:

Father, in the name of Jesus, help me to shine Your love everywhere I go. I'm thankful for Your grace, which covers me fully. I know that I am completely accepted by You. I choose to put on Your breastplate of righteousness, which guards my heart and protects my childlike faith and spiritual innocence. Amen!

THE SHOES OF THE GOSPEL OF PEACE

"*And having shod your feet in preparation [to face the enemy with the firm-footed stability, the promptness, and the readiness produced by the good news] of the Gospel of peace*" (Ephesians 6:15). Once you have secured your life in faith by wrapping the belt of truth around your waist (accepting God's Word as your core reality) and putting on the breastplate of righteousness (receiving the revelation of God's unfailing grace in Jesus), you will begin to sense God's everlasting peace illuminating you from the inside out. This is where "*righteousness and peace have kissed*" (Psalm 85:10)! Now you can put on the shoes of the gospel of peace. Prophetically, these shoes speak of your always being ready and prepared to be a peacemaker. In the light of God's glory, you are qualified for this daunting task.

The enemy spirit always attempts to bring divisive hatred among people, but remember these words of Jesus, which He spoke during His Sermon on the Mount: *"God blesses those who work for peace, for they will be called the children of God"* (Matthew 5:9 NLT). When you promote peace on earth, you reflect the light of heaven's glory for others to see Jesus in a very real way. After all, He is the *"Prince of Peace"* (Isaiah 9:6).

As mentioned previously, being a light warrior is all about releasing God's light—including the light of peace—everywhere you go. Only light can dispel darkness. You will often find yourself working to bring peace in your home and in family situations, as well as in relationships within your workplace and community. You will seek to bring unity among the people of God, searching for heavenly ways to unite the body of Christ—never to divide it.

Shoes of light are therefore provided as part of your armor to help you walk on the road less traveled, the higher path of peace. They represent your being firmly planted in the gospel and being ready to spread the love of Jesus to others. In this way, light warriors carry an evangelistic call. You can't keep quiet about the love of God because you know that your voice, speaking words inspired by the Holy Spirit, shifts the spiritual atmosphere, bringing both peace *with* God and the peace *of* God to the souls of weary travelers.

This strongly connects with your God-given call to help bring powerful change to the world around you. Wearing these shoes will help you walk into divine appointments with divine connections that produce divine outcomes. In order to wear these shoes daily, you must be willing to lay down your own will and walk in God's ways.

To put on the shoes of the gospel of peace, you can pray in this way:

Father, in the name of Jesus, I desire to work for peace. Thank You for providing me with Your shoes of light so that I might be firmly grounded in Your peace and help to share that peace everywhere I go as I bring Your good news to those who need to hear it. I want to walk on Your higher path. Amen.

THE SHIELD OF FAITH

"Lift up over all the [covering] shield of saving faith, upon which you can quench all the flaming missiles of the wicked [one]" (Ephesians 6:16). We must hold tightly to this next piece of spiritual light armor, the shield of faith. This

will require the supernatural strength that only the Spirit provides. The shield of faith symbolizes a firm trust and belief in God and His Word.

A Roman shield was oblong; it was about four feet tall and had curved sides; it was much larger than the round shields we typically imagine, and covered more of the soldier's body. Soldiers standing next to each other holding their shields closely together formed a wide protective barrier. Just as physical shields offered the soldiers protection from external threats, your supernatural light shield serves as a defense against negative thoughts, doubts, and fears that may come against you. It also helps to keep at a distance the demonic dark intruders and other distractions that would try to hinder your personal growth and spiritual progress.

This spiritual shield of faith has the ability to grow (see, for example, 2 Thessalonians 1:3), creating a force field of faith around you as it is utilized, protecting you from being weakened or spiritually extinguished. The shield of faith also helps you to advance in the Spirit, according to Hebrews 10:38–39: *"My righteous ones will live by faith.... We are not like those who turn away.... We are the faithful ones, whose souls will be saved"* (NLT).

Another benefit of this supernatural defense is that it provides you with a sense of security and assurance in the face of challenges and uncertainties. It instills confidence and courage because you know that you are protected and supported by God's often-unseen warrior angels and ministering spirits.

Let me explain what I mean about having this sense of security and assurance: I want you to think about a police officer who carries a badge. Another word for a police badge is a *shield*. This kind of shield is different from a soldier's shield. Instead of being a weapon of warfare, it is a highly recognizable symbol of authority. Although different police departments have variations in the shape, size, or style of their shields, they all mean the same thing: the shield is a symbol that the person who wears it has taken an oath to serve and protect their community and that they carry law enforcement authority.

Are there people in our society who would like to challenge that authority? Yes! Every day, we read news reports about people who have committed crimes of all kinds. Lawbreakers often resist the police when they are confronted. But, because a police officer wears a shield, he can call for backup, summoning more shield-wearing police officers to immediately respond to the scene. This is also how it is with us as believers. Jesus continually had access to the protection and assistance of God's angels (see, for example, Matthew 4:11; 26:53), and, as shield-bearers, we also have heaven's angelic warriors available to help us if and when we need backup. Because I carry this authority, I will not be troubled by any thoughts that the enemy may try to send my way. I have a large shield and far too many angels working with me to be disturbed by what the enemy does.

To take up the shield of faith, you can pray in this way:

Father, in the name of Jesus, thank You for causing my life to be encompassed by faith like a supernatural shield. Knowing what You have spoken changes everything; as I listen to and accept Your words, I receive spiritual enlargement. I fully receive this shield of faith and the authority that You have provided for me, and I choose to use it today for spiritual protection and defense. Amen!

THE HELMET OF SALVATION

"*And take the helmet of salvation…*" (Ephesians 6:17). The helmet of salvation is filled with light, and it is intended to radiate the mind of Christ. We must *choose* to put this helmet on our heads. The Scriptures remind us, "*Put on your new nature, created to be like God—truly righteous and holy*" (Ephesians 4:24 NLT). We begin to do this as we allow the Spirit to renew our thoughts and attitudes. This supernatural light helmet not only guards our minds and protects us from the lies, deceptions, doubts, and negative thoughts that can come from the enemy or from within ourselves, but it also provides us with a confident expectation of, and a positive outlook on, the future.

The helmet of salvation represents our assurance and confidence in our salvation through faith in Jesus Christ, and wearing it means that we understand our identity as children of God—as children of light. This helps us to reject any dark, negative thoughts and to replace them with the light of God's love and grace, and with an expectation that we will come into possession of every one of God's promises. We have a winning *attitude* and a winning *altitude*!

With this piece of armor in place, our minds are "*set on what is above,*" in the heavens, and all we can see is Jesus seated upon the throne of glory. (See

Colossians 3:1–2.) This light helmet of salvation reminds us that we are saved, forgiven, and filled with the Spirit and have an eternal hope.

To put on the helmet of salvation, you can place your hands on your head and pray in this way:

> Father, in the name of Jesus, I receive Your helmet of salvation. I invite Your light to minister to my mind and my thoughts. Even now, the light of Your truth is shining into every dark place within my mind and revealing Your glory. Guard my mind and protect it with Your saving power. Amen!

THE SWORD OF THE SPIRIT

"…and the sword that the Spirit wields, which is the Word of God" (Ephesians 6:17). As this verse indicates, this spiritual weapon represents the Word of God, which is referred to as a sword in other places in the Bible as well. (See, for example, Hebrews 4:12; Revelation 1:16; 2:12.) It signifies the power of Scripture, truth, and divine wisdom to wage spiritual battles, enable us to overcome temptation, and help us to discern right from wrong. This sword of light is such a powerful weapon! To effectively use the sword of the Spirit, we must familiarize ourselves with God's Word. We can do this by studying the Scriptures, meditating on their meaning, and memorizing key verses. I have found these practices to be very helpful because when I am dealing with difficult circumstances, this sword of light begins to arise directly from my spirit—the place where I have stored the Scriptures—and, as I speak these Scriptures aloud, they become a prophetic *rhema* word that powerfully shifts the atmosphere. (A *rhema* is a word, phrase, or passage from Scripture that God's Spirit quickens to you for application to your immediate circumstances and that fulfills God's will as you apply it by faith.)

We can use the sword of the Spirit as a weapon when we are faced with temptations, doubts, or spiritual attacks. We can wield this sword by speaking and declaring the light of Scriptures that affirm God's truth and power. Yet the sword of the Spirit is not merely a weapon for defense or attack; it is also a shining guide for living a godly life. (See, for example, Psalm 119:105.) If we apply the principles and teachings of this sword to our daily lives, it will shape our thoughts, attitudes, and actions.

The Spirit empowers believers to use the sword of light correctly and effectively. We must seek the Spirit's guidance and depend on His wisdom as we study, apply, and speak the Word.

One more thing: the sword of the Spirit helps us to pray with confidence, aligning our prayers with God's perfect will. When this sword arises from our spirit as a prayer, we find ourselves shifting gears into a deeper spiritual realm.

To take up the sword of the Spirit, you can pray in this way:

> Father, in the name of Jesus, I choose to use the sword of Your Spirit. I invite the light of Your Word to fill my spirit so that, from the depths of my being, I can release the light that cuts into darkness and causes it to flee. Thank You for giving me this powerful spiritual weapon. Amen!

The diagram on page 50 shows each piece of the armor of light with some corresponding Scriptures.

CALLED UP HIGHER

I want to remind you to use this spiritual armor by revelation. Ask the Spirit to give you His specific guidance and instructions for engaging in victorious spiritual warfare, and then step out in simple obedience once He speaks to you. You can trust that He will provide you with heavenly strategies for overcoming, regardless of what circumstance you're presently facing.

You've been provided with the full armor of light, and once you properly put it on and begin to use it, it becomes impossible for the enemy and his kingdom of darkness to win any battle against you. Yes, he might try to use some weapons against you, but he won't be able to ultimately prosper. Look at what the Bible says about this:

> *No weapon turned against you will succeed. You will silence every voice raised up to accuse you. These benefits are enjoyed by the servants of the Lord; their vindication will come from me. I, the Lord, have spoken!*
> (Isaiah 54:17 NLT)

PUT ON **THE FULL ARMOR** OF LIGHT

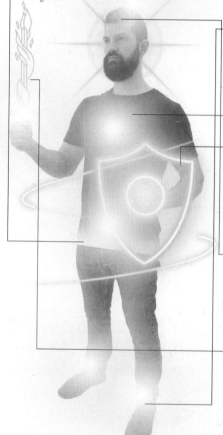

The Belt of Truth (Core Beliefs)

Ephesians 6:14: "Stand therefore, having fastened on the belt of truth...."

John 8:32: "And you will know the truth, and the truth will set you free."

John 14:6: "Jesus said to him, 'I am the way, and the truth, and the life. No one comes to the Father except through me.'"

The Breastplate of Righteousness

Ephesians 6:14: "...and having put on the breastplate of righteousness...."

2 Corinthians 5:21: "For our sake he made him to be sin who knew no sin, so that in him we might become the righteousness of God."

Isaiah 61:10: "I will greatly rejoice in the Lord; my soul shall exult in my God, for he has clothed me with the garments of salvation; he has covered me with the robe of righteousness."

The Shoes of the Gospel of Peace (Spiritual Walk)

Ephesians 6:15: "...and, as shoes for your feet, having put on the readiness given by the gospel of peace."

Romans 10:15: "And how are they to preach unless they are sent? As it is written, 'How beautiful are the feet of those who preach the good news!'"

Isaiah 52:7: "How beautiful upon the mountains are the feet of him who brings good news, who publishes peace, who brings good news of happiness, who publishes salvation, who says to Zion, 'Your God reigns.'"

The Shield of Faith

Ephesians 6:16: "In all circumstances take up the shield of faith, with which you can extinguish all the flaming darts of the evil one...."

Hebrews 11:1: "Now faith is the assurance of things hoped for, the conviction of things not seen."

1 John 5:4: "For everyone who has been born of God overcomes the world. And this is the victory that has overcome the world—our faith."

The Helmet of Salvation (Mind of Christ)

Ephesians 6:17: "...and take the helmet of salvation...."

1 Thessalonians 5:8: "But since we belong to the day, let us be sober, having put on the breastplate of faith and love, and for a helmet the hope of salvation."

Isaiah 12:2: "Behold, God is my salvation; I will trust, and will not be afraid; for the Lord God is my strength and my song, and he has become my salvation."

The Sword of the Spirit (Word of God)

Ephesians 6:17: "...and the sword of the Spirit, which is the word of God."

Hebrews 4:12: "For the word of God is living and active, sharper than any two-edged sword, piercing to the division of soul and of spirit, of joints and of marrow, and discerning the thoughts and intentions of the heart."

Matthew 4:4: "But he answered, 'It is written, "Man shall not live by bread alone, but by every word that comes from the mouth of God."'"

By focusing on these Scriptures corresponding to each piece of the light armor, you can meditate on the comprehensive protection and provision God has given to you as a *light warrior*.

All Scripture quotations are taken from *The Holy Bible, English Standard Version*.

It would be a good idea to make putting on this armor of light part of your morning prayer routine. This can become a very beneficial daily reminder of your call to be a light warrior. Of course, I'm not suggesting that you do this as a religious ritual, but rather as a way to connect to a deeper spiritual reality as the Spirit shines His revelation light on your spirit. The diagram on the opposite page includes Scripture references that you can personalize and incorporate into your prayers as the Spirit leads you.

You have been called up higher into this noble assignment of being a light warrior, and your heavenly mandate is for kingdom advancement. It's time for you, as a warrior of light, to march forward in your power and authority in Christ.

GREAT DAYS OF DIVINE ILLUMINATION

These are great days when God is bringing divine illumination to us, His light warriors. He is equipping us with His mind to do His work in the earth. When people see us and the way we conduct our lives, they should see the radiant brilliance of Jesus. When they meet us, they should feel something different—the warmth and loving-kindness of His light. When they come into our atmosphere, they should feel peaceful, healed, and filled with joy. They should feel at home. That's what carrying the light is all about.

As light warriors, we're looking for opportunities to provide solutions, not for places where we can create conflict. We are the problem-solvers, the peacemakers, the healers, the love-bringers, the growth-seekers, the encouragers. True spiritual warfare is all about occupying territory for the glory of God by advancing in His light. It's not so much about fighting as it is about resting. It is based on the finished work of Christ, which is already settled in heaven. As light warriors, we allow that truth to be settled in our hearts as well.

When a difficult situation arises in our lives, people watch how we react to it, how we handle it, how we cope with whatever happens. We may have failed to respond with faith, grace, and spiritual strength in the past, but we are moving forward to step into a place of secured victory.

You may feel defeated because of how you've handled situations in the past. You may feel like you've gone too far and "messed everything up," and you wonder how things can be turned right again. God is ready to work through you today. He's making a way for you. He's showing you what He can do through you. You are not defeated. You are victorious. You are an overcomer through Christ!

When confronted with life's difficulties, I have blown it many times, but the grace of God says, "Come on, let's do this again." It says, "There is a sufficiency for you." Similarly, the Spirit of glory is saying to us today, "I'm teaching you; listen and learn. Be willing to be taught by Me." True light warriors are teachable and ready for divine instruction.

Right now, let your mind be focused and established on the things of God. Don't allow the enemy's distractions to interfere with or bring a disturbance in this moment when God wants to teach you. Meditate on and pray about what you have learned in this chapter. Then, in the next chapter, we will talk further about how to live according to God's light.

YES, LET THERE BE LIGHT! CAN YOU FEEL THE SPIRIT'S POWER FLOWING THROUGH YOU AND CAUSING DARKNESS TO FLEE? YOU'RE WINNING THE SPIRITUAL WARFARE BATTLE BECAUSE YOU'RE A *LIGHT WARRIOR*.

CHAPTER 3

WORKING WITH THE LIGHT

"The Light shines on in the darkness, for the darkness has never overpowered it [put it out or absorbed it or appropriated it, and is unreceptive to it.]"
—John 1:5

Walking in your authority and power in Christ basically means walking in the will of God for your life.

Jesus Christ is the shining radiance of the Father's glory, and it's all about Him. It's all about having a personal relationship with Him, connecting with Him, allowing Him to speak to us, responding to Him in obedience, and allowing Him to work through our lives, saying, "God, I don't want to be anywhere else but with You. I don't want to do anything else except what You have for me." Such a prayer will change your life.

In Christ, walking in the glory isn't just a once-in-a-while event; it is a lifestyle, and it can be practiced every moment of every day. It's possible for us to walk each day in the power that destroys and defeats the works of the enemy. In accordance with this, God has given us power and authority to speak His truth over ourselves and over the situations of our lives. Because we are in this world, all sorts of challenging situations come at us all the time, but when we know our power and authority in Christ, we are able to exercise that power and authority over even the smallest affairs of life. This is what I call "working with the light."

We must remember that when we exercise God's authority, our speech is deeply involved in the process. We need to *think* authority, *talk* authority, and *walk* authority.

The Bible says,

> *A good person produces good things from the treasury of a good heart, and an evil person produces evil things from the treasury of an evil heart. What you say flows from what is in your heart.* (Luke 6:45 NLT)

What comes *into* us is important, but what comes *out of* us is equally important. In every way, we need to walk in the power and authority of Christ and speak in His authority and power.

To walk in the authority of Christ is to walk in the light. When we recognize who we are in Christ and the promises that God has made available to us, and when we know our rights as believers because Jesus lives in our hearts, we begin to speak differently. It can become very easy to focus on what's currently taking place around us in the natural rather than holding on, by faith, to what God has spoken. But the only way that things will change in the natural is for us to allow God to change them through us. As we glimpse His purposes in the supernatural realm, we can do this. What we have seen in the Spirit, we must begin to speak over our circumstances.

Far too often, good Christian people have prayed a prayer, and then the next thing that comes out of their mouths is doubt, unbelief, or even a curse. Sadly, many of them don't even realize what they're saying. Thankfully, God's Spirit is awakening many of us in the body of Christ to this reality. He is also illuminating our minds to better connect with His. I'll share more about this a little later in the book.

BOTH AUTHORITY AND POWER

In Luke 10:19, Jesus said,

Behold! I have given you authority and power to trample upon serpents and scorpions, and [physical and mental strength and ability] over all the power that the enemy [possesses]; and nothing shall in any way harm you.

Wow! "*Over all the power that the enemy [possesses]; and nothing shall in any way harm you.*" What a great promise! If we can capture the revelation in this Scripture and believe what Jesus was saying, it will be life-changing. He said we have the authority and power, and He should know: He gave them to us.

Authority and power are not the same. They are two different spiritual realities that we need to live in. And God has given them both to us. We will discuss each of these areas in more detail as the chapter progresses.

Jesus tells us what the authority and power are for—to overcome all the works of the enemy. This reality does not just have spiritual implications. *The Amplified Bible, Classic Edition* particularly names "*physical and mental strength and ability.*" What does this mean? It means that anything you can think of that has been negative in your life, any terrible situation, any abusive or traumatic experience through which the enemy has tried to come and wreak havoc, God can redeem. Praise God!

We know what the enemy does. He comes to steal, to kill, and to destroy everything he can. (See John 10:10.) Jesus said He has given us authority and power to overcome every situation. This means that whatever your circumstance looks like—a bad marriage, difficulties with your children, financial devastation, sickness that seems to ravage your body—God has it all covered. He has a better way for you, and His better way is through the power and authority He gives.

WHAT IS AUTHORITY?

What is authority, and what kind of spiritual authority do you already have? In the natural realm, there are different levels of authority for different positions, occupations, and responsibilities that people have been given. For example, in an emergency situation, when you call "the authorities" by dialing 911, they ask you, in essence, which authority you need—police officers, firefighters, or Emergency Medical Technicians (EMT). And this is important, because an ambulance paramedic doesn't have the same authority as a police officer, and a police officer doesn't have the same authority as a firefighter.

In recent years, wildfires have devastated various parts of our world, decimating whole communities. Would we send police officers to fight these wildfires? No, they don't carry the authority to deal with them. Instead, we send firefighters because they are trained and equipped to contend with such physical dangers, and they have taken an oath and been given the authority to fight against them. Again, different occupations require different authorizations.

As a believer in Jesus, what are you authorized to do? You are authorized to act in His name, and He has equipped you and trained you for this task. Your authority is Christ's authorization for you to work the wonderful works of God.

One definition of the word *authority* is "power or right to give orders, make decisions, and enforce obedience."[7] It is also defined as "a power or right delegated or given; authorization."[8] Walking in the authority of Christ means that you have received official permission for that authority—heaven's official permission. I love that. We are sanctioned to operate in heaven's authority as light warriors here on earth.

OUR SPIRITUAL AUTHORITY IN CHRIST

Christ's giving you His official authorization is like your receiving a blue check mark in the Spirit. You have received this authorization from Jesus so that you can walk in the light, live in the light, and enforce heaven's will here on earth, shining God's light into dark places.

In what Jesus spoke to His first-century disciples, particularly after His resurrection, we find the answer to the question "What does walking in the authority of Christ look like?"

> *Jesus came up and said to them,* **"All authority** *(all power of absolute rule) in heaven and on earth has been given to Me. Go therefore and make disciples of all the nations [help the people to learn of Me, believe in Me, and obey My words], baptizing them in the name of the Father and of the Son and of the Holy Spirit, teaching them to observe everything that I have commanded you; and lo, I am with you always [remaining with you*

---

7. Oxford English Dictionary, s.v. "authority," https://www.oed.com/search/dictionary/?scope=Entries&q=authority.
8. Dictionary.com, s.v. "authority," https://www.dictionary.com/browse/authority.

perpetually—regardless of circumstance, and on every occasion], even to the end of the age." (Matthew 28:18–20 AMP)

This passage outlines for us the authority in Christ in which we have been commissioned by Him to walk. Christ said that He has *"all authority"* (Matthew 28:18). My friend Joan Hunter often emphasizes that "all" means "inclusive of everything and exclusive of nothing." "All" means *all*. Jesus carries all authority in heaven and on earth. This includes authority even in the second-heaven realm, the realm of demonic warfare, where there is spiritual conflict, lots of intense pressure and battling, and much chaos and confusion. Yes, Jesus carries all authority in that second-heaven realm, and this means that our battles belong to the Lord. Why? So that the blessings can belong to the children of God. You and I are called to live in God's blessings. This is part of our authorization in Christ.

So, we must keep in mind that the authority we carry is the authority of Christ, and that is *"all authority."* Next, Jesus told us *where* we are to carry this *"all authority."* He said, *"Go therefore and make disciples of all the nations"* (Matthew 28:19 AMP). We are to use our authority in Christ to disciple nations, and we are to baptize those who believe *"in the name of the Father and of the Son and of the Holy Spirit"* (Matthew 28:19 AMP). If we have the authority to disciple nations, then surely we also have the authority to disciple our communities, our own territory, our dominion that God has given to us.

Does this include the realm of our families? Absolutely. God has given you authority to disciple your family, to raise your children in the glory. That's one of the things I love about the book *Childbirth in the Glory* that my wife, Janet, wrote.[9] Janet is teaching people how to believe for a child even before it's in the womb. Why? So that, as the child is conceived and begins to develop, parents can anoint that child, pray for them, and prophesy over them. When we do that consistently, from the beginning, we will raise glory children.

Our son, Lincoln, was born in the glory, with the shekinah presence appearing all over his head upon his arrival into the world (the doctors and nurses were amazed!), and we raised him in an atmosphere of glory. Our daughter Liberty was a miracle answer to our prayers, and she was born in the glory and raised in the glory also. Just when we thought we were finished

---

9. Janet Mills, *Childbirth in the Glory* (Shippensburg, PA: Destiny Image, 2023).

having children, the Spirit surprised us with His supernatural abundance, and our daughter Legacy was born in the glory; we've raised her in the glory as well. God wants us to disciple our family members—our children, our grandchildren, and our great-grandchildren—and He has given us the needed authorization through the words of Jesus to do this.

For example, Janet and I have the authority to decide who and what comes into our home. We have the authority to decide what kind of apps are on our children's phones (another way of authorizing who and what comes into our home). We have set up parental guidance through our phones to be able to manage this, even determining the times of day and the amount of time each day that our children can spend on their phones.

What else should we be doing in the authority Christ has given us? After we have made disciples in the nations, Jesus says we are to teach them *"to observe everything that I have commanded you"* (verse 20). You and I have been given authority to teach the Word and the ways of God to people, and, if we are parents, this especially applies to our children.

Why is this so important? Every single day, a child is learning. They can learn through observation, through habit, through practice, through the processes of living, or through instruction. The problem is this: for many people, their habits, practices, and processes have too often become entangled with the assignment of the enemy against us—which is to lie to us, to deceive us, and to destroy us. When parents believe the enemy's lies and deceptions, and when they express such things and live according to them, their children can quickly begin to believe—by way of their carnal, natural learning and observation—that everything about life is bad. They may think:

"Nothing goes right!"

"Everything's wrong!"

"The world is a very dark place!"

"I have no friends!"

"Nobody loves me!"

"I have no money!"

"I have nothing to live for!"

Where do they get these ideas? Again, it may be because their process of learning has been connected to the kingdom of darkness by what their parents and others have spoken or demonstrated after accepting the enemy's lies (likely without their even being aware of it). However, for believers and their families, this is not the way it should be—and such darkness can be counteracted. We can correct the negative thoughts we have been thinking and expressing in order to set ourselves and our children free.

I must admit that there have been many times when I have mistakenly said something that was not aligned with God's truth, but the Holy Spirit corrected me. Then I was able to reverse what I had just said. In that moment, I took authority, saying, "You know what? I cancel those words that just came out of my mouth." Then I spoke the truth over the situation.

Recently, I was at home, talking with our son, Lincoln, who is enrolled at a university, and I said to him what now seems like the strangest thing. I don't remember the exact phrase, but it was something concerning his money. I basically said, "Well, Lincoln, you need to be careful because you're a college student." When I said that, I realized I was implying that a college student doesn't have much money. A college student is impoverished. As soon as those words came out of my mouth, the Spirit corrected me, saying, "Do not speak that over your son."

Thank You, Holy Spirit. We are not to put poverty on our children. I'll never say that again. I will never again consider my son a "poor" college student. I took back what I had said, and I told Lincoln I was sorry and explained that the Holy Spirit had corrected me. Then I affirmed, "Lincoln, you can be blessed, and you can live in abundance. God can make your life flourish. You can have overflow even as a college student." I was so glad I corrected what I had said to him. Our words shape our thinking (as well as the other way around), and we need to speak God words. Within the following months, Lincoln became so blessed financially, with amazing employment and supernatural favor, and he was able to purchase a brand-new car! Our words matter, and they make a difference.

What we say and the way we say it is such a witness to other people. When we speak in a new way—based on the light of Scripture—in conversations with others, it impacts them, whether or not they are believers. It is also a witness to them about the power of words. God words and God statements can really change the atmosphere around us.

Janet and I have trained ourselves to say, "God morning" rather than, "Good morning" when we wake up. When we go out to church or wherever else we may be going, I say, "God morning" to the people we meet. At first, they wonder if I slipped up in speaking the word *good*. Then, after they have processed it a bit, they smile and respond, "Whoa! Yeah, God morning." It changes the whole atmosphere.

God can be the focus of your morning, He can be the focus of your day, and He can be the focus of your evening and night.

You may have said things you now realize were wrong. Own up to your mistake, get over your pride, get over yourself, repent, and apologize. Then make it right. Renounce what you said, change your vocabulary, and speak what God's Word says over every situation.

When we use our tongues wrongly, we can sabotage the blessings that God has prepared for us and our loved ones. But if we align our speech with God's truths, our very words become a source of life. Proverbs 15:4 declares,

A gentle tongue [with its healing power] is a tree of life.

I like that! Our words can become a tree of life to so many people in so many ways.

Normal human conversation can often be carnal and fleshly, without an uplifting element to it. But when we talk about what we have seen in the Spirit, what we have taken hold of in the Word, and how we can literally walk it out in our daily living through the authority we carry, it blesses those who hear it.

USE THE LIGHT SWORD OF THE SPIRIT

You are called to work with the light, and this is why every believer needs training in God's Word. When you're walking in the authority of Christ, you're walking according to the Word of God, and you're walking in the promises of God.

As expressed in the previous chapter, God's Word is light, and it becomes a supernatural sword in the hands of a light warrior. Derek Prince, an expert in spiritual warfare, said, "Somebody once told me, 'When you're reading your Bible, your Bible is also reading you.'"[10] We must first be receivers of the Word and practitioners of the Word, learning how to wield the power of this light sword. Then we can become releasers of the Word to those around us. Going through this process of receiving and then giving is vital.

When we are conditioned by the Word, our spirit enlarges. We are no longer confined by the natural realm, but we begin living in the supernatural realm. The Word of light brings us to a higher level. It lifts us up into realms of glory. That's why Janet and I love to teach the deeper things of God. It changes lives.

This passage in Matthew 28 ends gloriously:

Lo, I am with you always [remaining with you perpetually—regardless of circumstance, and on every occasion], even to the end of the age.

(verse 20 AMP)

This promise is so powerful that you need to write it down and put it somewhere you will see it frequently and be reminded of it! Your authority in Christ is not limited to when you're at church, when you're around your Christian friends, when you go to midweek Bible study, or when you're listening to a praise and worship album. The authority you have been given in Christ is with you all day, every day, *"perpetually."* This means continually, uniformly, and *"on every occasion,"* until the very close and consummation of the age—forever. It is Christ in you, and that is the hope of glory. (See Colossians 1:27.)

So, how can we know the fullness of our authority in Christ? We get into the Word, and we read the promises of God. There are many promises you need to hold on to in order to walk in your authority in Christ, things that you need to pray through, prophetically speak out, and then walk out practically. To sum up, then, to exercise your authority in Christ, you must know and act on your rights as expressed in God's Word. That's it.

AUTHORIZED TO STAND AGAINST THE ENEMY

Just because you have the authority, however, doesn't necessarily mean that everyone will follow the rules. There is a rule-breaker, and his names are Satan,

---

10. Derek Prince, "The Active and Powerful Word," Standing Strong (Part 6), Derek Prince Ministries, https://www.derekprince.com/teaching/03-5.

Lucifer, and the devil. I call him the enemy spirit of darkness, and he has many unruly cohorts called demons (or evil spirits). He is the "*father of lies*" (John 8:44), and, as we have seen, he comes to steal, to kill, and to destroy. He will try to break every rule and find every little loophole to distort God's truth and draw people away from their heavenly Father. If you don't know your authority in Christ, and you're not actively enforcing it, the enemy is very happy to illegally do something in your life that he is not permitted to do.

Let's read Luke 10:19 again:

Behold! I have given you authority and power to trample upon serpents and scorpions, and [physical and mental strength and ability] over all the power that the enemy [possesses]; and nothing shall in any way harm you.

Jesus has given us authority and power to "*trample upon serpents and scorpions*" and "*[physical and mental strength and ability] over all the power that the enemy [possesses].*" You carry the light that dispels all darkness. But have you been experiencing this reality in your life? Has the enemy ever tried to "mess you up"? I'm sure he has. Have you ever felt weak in the presence of the enemy? Again, I'm sure you have. Let's be truthful here. Have you ever felt sick in your body? Sure you have. Have you ever felt negative physical symptoms coming on? All of us have. Have you ever experienced the heaviness of the weight of depression or oppression? Have you ever been in a financial bind? Have you ever been in a place in your life where you felt unloved, or you felt like nobody understood you? Truth be told, many of us have had all of these experiences, and yet Jesus said, *"I have given you the authority and power…over all the power that the enemy [possesses]."*

All those negative things I just mentioned—they are the work of the enemy. Again, from time to time, we have all experienced them. Why? Because if we're not enforcing our authority, the enemy will try to illegally hijack our thinking, our emotions, and our lives. You must know your rights, understand who you are in Christ, and recognize what Christ has made available to you through the finished work of Calvary. Otherwise, the enemy will sneak in like the snake that he is, and he will try to make a mess of things.

NO MERCY FOR DEADLY SNAKES

Several years ago, my friend Tenley, who is the senior training manager at Louis Vuitton, brought to my attention a song she heard that has a similar theme to one of Aesop's fables. In Aesop's tale "The Farmer and the Viper," a man rescues a poisonous snake that is perishing from the cold of winter, keeping it close to his chest to warm up it up. As soon as the frozen snake thaws out, he fatally bites the man. Aesop's moral of the story is, "Kindness is thrown away on the evil."[11]

There's a lesson in this for all of us. Of course, we do not fight against flesh and blood, and when it comes to other people, Jesus teaches us to love our enemies and to do good to those who hate us. (See Luke 6:27.) However, we can't show any mercy to the enemy spirit or his demons because they have one goal—to destroy our lives. You might say, "Well, I would never show mercy to the enemy." However, sincere believers (although sincerely wrong) in effect do this all the time by not exercising their God-given authority. Any ground you are not taking for the kingdom of light is being ceded to the kingdom of darkness. Think about that!

THE DIFFERENCE BETWEEN AUTHORITY AND POWER

In Luke 10:19, Jesus said we would receive authority *and* power. We need both, and, according to this verse, Jesus has given us each of these aspects in order to combat the attacks of the enemy in every area of our lives. Remember, there is victory for every situation you might face.

What is the difference between authority and power? Suppose you own a number of acres of land in a wooded area. You have posted "No Trespassing" signs, and you have also put up some fencing because people have started to come and hunt on your property without permission, making it unsafe to walk the land. If people still climb over your fence to hunt, thinking that no one will see them, you have the right to confront them and enforce your rights of ownership. As a landowner, you have the authority to say, "Get off my land, or I will call the police." If people don't obey, you can take their picture and then bring it as evidence to the police, who will charge the people with trespassing, and you can also sue the trespassers in civil court. That's where the power comes in. We need both authority and power because the power is used to enforce our authority.

---

11. "157. The Farmer and the Viper," in *Aesop's Fables*, trans. V. S. Vernon Jones (New York: Barnes & Noble Books, 2003), 147. George Stade, consulting editorial director. With an introduction and notes by D. L. Ashliman and illustrations by Arthur Rackham.

With this in mind, let's talk in more depth about the power of God in relation to our authority in Christ.

RECEIVING THE POWER OF GOD

The power of God that backs up the authority He has given us comes through the work of His Holy Spirit in and through us. Therefore, to access God's power, you must first be willing to receive the baptism of the Holy Spirit. When you do, you will gain the power that enforces the authority Christ has given you. (See Acts 1:8.) Many believers read what the Word says, but because they have not yet received the baptism of the Holy Spirit and the infilling of God's power, they often struggle and begin to question God, doubting the truth and effectiveness of His Word. They wonder, "Is it truly real? Is it truly right?" because it doesn't seem to be working in their lives. It is real and true. Thankfully, through His Spirit, God provides the power that makes His Word active and effective in our lives.

If you have not yet been baptized in the Holy Spirit, Janet and I have developed resources that can help you. Our YouTube channel features a video entitled "Praying in the Spirit" that guides you through the Scriptures on how to receive the Holy Spirit's baptism. It also shows you how to minister the baptism of the Holy Spirit to others once you have received it yourself.[12] Additionally, we have videos detailing the benefits of praying in the Spirit, including the healing benefits of speaking in tongues, and more.[13] We pray that these videos will enrich your spiritual journey.

On some of those videos, there are activations that you can participate in. As you watch them with a hungry heart, I believe the baptism of the Spirit will happen for you too. God is faithful, and we have received many wonderful testimonies from people who have received their heavenly language through engaging with those videos. Some people who have waited years, even decades, to receive the baptism of the Holy Spirit have stepped into it in this way.

As you receive the baptism, you will see new results in your walk with God. In the past, you were hindered in many situations because you didn't

---

12. Joshua and Janet Mills, "The Power of Praying in the Spirit," Glory Bible Study, YouTube, https://www.youtube.com/live/25WxDxdfARU?feature=shared.
13. Joshua Mills—International Glory Ministries, https://www.youtube.com/channel/UCXHyZfWnncjKyHz-HZj8hCw.

understand your power and authority in the light. I believe that, now, many unusual miracles will take place in your life as you step into this revelation of who you are in Christ, what you carry, and what you have the ability to release. Christ has absolute authority, and the authority in Him under which you operate gives you certain rights, but you also have power, and that is the ability to enforce those rights. Again, that's the difference between the two: the authority gives you the rights; the power gives you the ability to enforce those rights.

THE POWER OF THE LIGHT

> *The light shines in the darkness, and the darkness can never extinguish it* ["*has not overcome it*" NIV, ESV]. (John 1:5 NLT)

> The darkness *has not* overcome the light and *never can* overcome it.

> *And having disarmed the powers and authorities, he made a public spectacle of them, triumphing over them by the cross.* (Colossians 2:15 NIV)

> *But the path of the just is like the shining sun, that shines ever brighter unto the perfect day.* (Proverbs 4:18 NKJV)

As light warriors, we are to be lights shining in the darkness. However, it's difficult to be an enforcer of the light if our focus is mainly on the darkness. As I mentioned earlier, you and I are not called to dabble with realms of darkness, constantly facing darker spiritual battles and being obsessed with dark beings. We are called to walk in the light. Some things that many of us have been taught to do in the past are not very spiritual at all. For example, some people spend most of their time cursing the darkness, saying things like, "I rebuke this." Although we need to stand against the enemy, constantly going around rebuking things is a negative focus when we should be focusing on the light and blessings of God.

The psalmist said,

> *You prepare a table before me in the presence of my enemies. You anoint my head with oil; my [brimming] cup runs over.* (Psalm 23:5)

Metaphorically speaking, a table of light has been prepared for you to feast on the goodness of God. Yes, enemies might surround you, but you have the power to choose what you focus on. Through this passage of Scripture, David gave us a key for living the overcoming life as an enforcer of light. He agreed with the light, which caused God's oil to overflow in his life and then flow out of his life. This, in turn, caused the light of God in David to grow brighter and brighter.

"You anoint my head with oil; my [brimming] cup runs over." These words might make it sound as if David had no enemies to contend with, but we know he did—many of them. Yet the anointing positioned him to sit and feast at the Lord's table even in the midst of his enemies. He found a spiritual feast and an abundance of God's goodness despite the enemy's intimidation. The key was his not focusing on the enemy but instead focusing on God. I encourage you to choose to agree with the light too. Then, watch and see what this supernatural agreement will do!

I've been accused of being naive in my approach to spiritual warfare, but I'm okay with that. It's all right if people think I'm foolish because I don't focus on the enemy and his work and choose to focus on God's light instead. I absolutely refuse to give the enemy spirit any glory. Unless we agree with the enemy, he is powerless. I am in complete agreement with the Word of God and the power of His Spirit. I am in alliance with the light.

One of the differences between a mature believer and an immature believer is where they place their attention: the mature believer is fully focused on the light, while the immature believer is often obsessed with the darkness. The chart on page 67 contrasts some of the signs of immature and mature believers.

As light warriors, we are being called to spiritual maturity. The Spirit desires for His people to grow up into the fullness of God's glory. I've noticed that one of the ways the enemy gets wonderful believers off track is by distracting them with frivolous activity. I've heard stories about ministries that run a "deliverance business," offering paid "deliverance sessions" to people week after week, and yet nothing seems to change in the people's daily lives. This is not a biblical practice. According to the Scriptures, we cast out demons. We don't play around with them, we don't counsel them, and we don't try to soothe them or negotiate a deal with them. We cast them out!

SIGNS OF AN **IMMATURE** BELIEVER:

- They are always talking about problems. (See Proverbs 18:6–7.)
- They are focused on demon spirits. (See Ephesians 5:8–11.)
- They constantly feel the pressure of demonic warfare. (See 2 Corinthians 10:3-6; John 1:5.)
- They carry a spiritual heaviness. (See Matthew 11:28–30.)
- They often talk about defeat. (See Proverbs 11:11.)
- They are conflicted with spiritual confusion. (See James 1:5; 1 Corinthians 14:33.)
- They are double-minded (they say they're an overcomer, but they live a defeated life). (See James 1:8.)

SIGNS OF A **MATURE** BELIEVER:

- They are always talking about victory. (See Romans 10:8–10.)
- They are focused on the Holy Spirit and glory. (See Isaiah 26:3.)
- They constantly feel the pleasure of God and His glory presence. (See Psalm 139:7–10.)
- They carry spiritual light and breakthrough. (See Micah 2:13.)
- They talk about overcoming. (See 2 Corinthians 4:13; Revelation 12:11.)
- They are convinced by spiritual truth. (See Romans 4:20–21; 2 Timothy 1:12.)
- They are single-eyed (they live what they speak). (See Matthew 6:22.)
- They rise above satanic warfare. (See James 4:7.)

The only way you can cast out demons of darkness is by releasing the light. You don't fight darkness with more darkness.

REJECTING DOCTRINES OF DEMONS

Now the Holy Spirit tells us clearly that in the last times some will turn away from the true faith; they will follow deceptive spirits and teachings that come from demons. (1 Timothy 4:1 NLT)

Once more, I am very concerned about the recent trend within charismatic circles that focuses all the attention on demon spirits. There are many books being written and seminars being offered to teach people about various demons and their evil assignments. At first glance, this might seem intriguing and, possibly, even very spiritual, but it is actually a slippery slope into idolatry because it appeals to the flesh. Anything that we elevate over the lordship of Christ is an idol.

Demonically inspired doctrine will sway your focus away from God and His will. It will attempt to move your attention from the light to the darkness. This leads to tragedy because whatever you focus on will increase in your life. Harboring continual suspicions or superstitions about the presence of demonic beings creates distraction, whereas standing on the Word of Truth creates clear focus. I heard one deliverance minister tell people that the presence of physical flies indicated the presence of demons, and that these demons were spying on our activity. That kind of teaching is false and only causes people to come under the bondage of fear. Every time they saw a fly, they would imagine a demon was chasing after them! Again, such teaching is pure deception, and it distracts believers from living holy lives focused on Christ and His truth.

Thus, one of the enemy's most seductive devices is to get your focused attention. Do not be deceived by the enemy's distractions. The more preoccupied we become with the enemy spirit, the more access he has into our lives. Be aware of what the people around you are saying because it's a great revealer of what's happening in their lives. As a general rule, people self-project. Those who continually focus on demons and demonic deliverance seem to be those who need deliverance the most. An inward struggle causes them to be obsessed with darkness, and, in turn, they talk about it more than anything else. Remember, the mouth can only speak what is in the heart.

Quite a few years ago, a well-known minister wrote a book about the Nephilim, *"heroes and famous warriors of ancient times"* (Genesis 6:4 NLT) who are mentioned in Genesis 6:1–4. This book's theme was that the Nephilim were the ungodly offspring of fallen angels who mated with human women. The book became very popular because it was a strange and unusual topic. It certainly caught the interest of many people. Unfortunately, for some of them, it created an ungodly obsession that made them feel the need to "discern" those around them who were supposedly "Nephilim" in disguise, and not human at all.

I remember sitting at a lunch table with several ministers who were convinced that one of the ladies at the conference was actually one of the Nephilim. This kind of activity is unhealthy and unproductive, and it becomes a terrible distraction, keeping people from doing what the Bible tells believers to do. Ironically, this is probably the biggest challenge for those who are involved in prophetic ministry—to stay focused, remain in scriptural alignment, and do what the Bible instructs (for example, share the good news, win souls for Christ, heal the sick, and cast out evil spirits). Anything that takes our focus away from these purposes is not from God. We need to become spiritually smart:

> …*Satan will not outsmart us. For we are familiar with his evil schemes.*
> (2 Corinthians 2:11 NLT)

SUBMIT TO THE LIGHT

The chart on page 70 outlines ten lies that people believe about themselves, as well as ten truths that release the light in our lives.

Jesus warned that if our eyes are dark, our whole body will be filled with darkness:

> *But when your eye is unhealthy, your whole body is filled with darkness. And if the light you think you have is actually darkness, how deep that darkness is!* (Matthew 6:23 NLT)

10 Lies PEOPLE BELIEVE ABOUT THEMSELVES & 10 Truths THAT RELEASE THE LIGHT

1. Lie: I am unlovable.

Truth: You are deeply loved.

"For God so loved the world, that he gave his only Son, that whoever believes in him should not perish but have eternal life." (John 3:16)

2. Lie: I am worthless.

Truth: You are valuable and precious.

"Are not five sparrows sold for two pennies? And not one of them is forgotten before God. Why, even the hairs of your head are all numbered. Fear not; you are of more value than many sparrows." (Luke 12:6–7)

3. Lie: I will never be able to change.

Truth: You can be transformed.

"Therefore, if anyone is in Christ, he is a new creation. The old has passed away; behold, the new has come." (2 Corinthians 5:17)

4. Lie: I am not good enough.

Truth: You are more than enough in Christ.

"But he said to me, 'My grace is sufficient for you, for my power is made perfect in weakness.' Therefore I will boast all the more gladly of my weaknesses, so that the power of Christ may rest upon me." (2 Corinthians 12:9)

5. Lie: I am defined by my past mistakes.

Truth: Your past does not define you.

"As far as the east is from the west, so far does he remove our transgressions from us." (Psalm 103:12)

6. Lie: I am all alone.

Truth: You are never alone.

"Be strong and courageous. Do not fear or be in dread of them, for it is the Lord your God who goes with you. He will not leave you or forsake you." (Deuteronomy 31:6)

7. Lie: My life has no purpose.

Truth: Your life has a purpose.

"For I know the plans I have for you, declares the Lord, plans for welfare and not for evil, to give you a future and a hope." (Jeremiah 29:11)

8. Lie: I don't have any talents or gifts.

Truth: You have unique talents and gifts.

"For we are his workmanship, created in Christ Jesus for good works, which God prepared beforehand, that we should walk in them." (Ephesians 2:10)

9. Lie: I can't be forgiven.

Truth: You can be forgiven.

"If we confess our sins, he is faithful and just to forgive us our sins and to cleanse us from all unrighteousness." (1 John 1:9)

10. Lie: I am not strong enough to handle life's challenges.

Truth: You have the strength to face life's challenges.

"I can do all things through him who strengthens me." (Philippians 4:13)

All Scripture quotations are taken from *The Holy Bible, English Standard Version.*

How can we lead in the light unless we have first been led by the light? If we desire to be enforcers of light, we must first allow the light to work in our lives.

I encourage you to begin to focus on God's Word instead of on the enemy's lies. Pay attention to God's prophetic voice that speaks within your spirit, acknowledge the finished work of Christ, and trust that this work truly is completed for you.

We must be renewed in the spirit of our mind. (See Ephesians 4:23.) This means undergoing a profound transformation in the way we think, perceive, and understand the world around us, with a focus on aligning our thoughts with God's will and truth. It involves shedding old, worldly patterns of thinking that are often influenced by sin, fear, doubt, and negativity, and embracing a new mindset that is characterized by love, faith, and hope. This mind-shift is not merely an intellectual exercise but rather a spiritual awakening in which we allow the Spirit to illuminate our understanding, cleanse our thought processes, and instill within us the mind of Christ. As we are renewed in the spirit of our mind, we become increasingly receptive to God's guidance, more discerning of spiritual truths, and better equipped to live a life that reflects His character and purposes.

ENFORCERS OF LIGHT

In practical terms, being an enforcer of God's light means actively living out and spreading God's truth. Here are some ways to embody this role:

Live with integrity. Ensure that your actions, words, and thoughts align with God's principles. This means being honest, kind, and just in your dealings with others, reflecting the character of Christ in your everyday behavior.

Speak truth with love. Be a beacon of God's truth by sharing His Word and principles in a loving and compassionate manner. This doesn't mean being confrontational but rather offering encouragement, guidance, and correction, when necessary, all rooted in the love and wisdom of God.

Practice forgiveness and grace. Extend forgiveness and grace to others as God has done for you. Doing this can transform relationships and create environments of healing and reconciliation.

Engage in spiritual disciplines. Regularly spend time in prayer, worship, personal reflection, and the reading of Scripture. These practices strengthen your connection to God's light and equip you to carry that light into the world.

Serve others selflessly. Look for opportunities to help those in need, whether through acts of kindness, generous charitable contributions, or simply being a supportive friend. Your heartfelt service can be a powerful testimony of God's love and light.

Maintain a positive attitude. In the face of adversity, maintain a spirit of hope and confidence rooted in your faith in God. Your resilience and positive outlook can inspire and uplift those around you.

Advocate for justice. Stand against injustice and advocate for those who are oppressed or marginalized. Use your voice and actions to bring light to situations where darkness prevails, promoting true freedom for all.

Cultivate a community of light. Surround yourself with other believers who are also committed to living in God's light. Encourage and build one another up in faith, creating a supportive and vibrant community.

Share your testimony. Don't be afraid to tell others about how God's light has transformed your life. Personal testimonies can be incredibly impactful and can inspire others to seek God's light for themselves.

Discern and expose darkness. Be vigilant in recognizing and addressing falsehoods, corruption, or sinful behaviors—in yourself and others—with the intention of bringing them into alignment with God's truth. This involves prayerful wisdom and a balanced approach to confrontation.

Ultimately, being an enforcer of God's light means spreading His goodness and transforming the atmosphere wherever you go. It's about letting your life shine brightly as a testimony of His glory.

EMPOWERED BY JESUS

In Luke 9, we see Jesus calling together the Twelve—His disciples, His apostles—and sending them out to minister and proclaim the gospel:

> *Then Jesus called together the Twelve [apostles] and gave them power and authority over all demons, and to cure diseases, and He sent them out to*

announce and preach the kingdom of God and to bring healing.
(Luke 9:1–2)

Let me ask you: are you a disciple of Christ today? If so, then this passage is for you. Just as Jesus gave the Twelve power and authority, He gives you power and authority today.

I want you to lift your hands to heaven and say, "Holy Spirit, baptize me afresh. I want a fresh baptism of Your power. I lift my hands to You, and I'm ready."

Some people say, "You can't do that. When you received the anointing through the baptism of the Spirit, you received everything there was all at once. There's nothing more of the Spirit to receive." However, I believe that most of us, when we first received the baptism of the Holy Spirit, were only able to receive it to a certain degree. At this point in our lives, we may be at a very different level. God is building a deeper foundation for us, and now we can bear much more. Therefore, we lift our hands to God and say, "God, I know there's more. Whatever You have for me is what I want." Yes, we have permission to ask Him for more.

God loves it when you're hungry and thirsty for more of Him. He absolutely does. And He is not running out of anything. He has an unlimited supply of anointing, power, and blessings. Therefore, every person on this earth has permission to ask Him for more. Hallelujah! Let's pray together:

God, I want more. I want more. I want more. Fill me with Your power. Help me to walk in and exercise and enforce Your authority in my life. Show me places where I have allowed the enemy to slip in and bring destruction, manipulation, chaos, and control. I break all agreement with the work of the enemy, and, in the name of Jesus Christ, I give the enemy an immediate eviction notice from every area of my life right now. I enforce the authority that You have given me through the power of the Holy Spirit. And, God, I thank You that this is a new day and that You are *"doing a new thing,"* as You say in Isaiah 43:19. A new glory is rising up inside me. Through You, I am walking in the authority and power of Your heavenly light.

Now, take your authority. Take your power. With it, you will have authority in your home, and you will have power to enforce that authority. The enemy tried to give you a mess and tried to make you settle in that mess, but that's not the home you were created to live in. You were created to live in the light of God's glory. The same applies to all areas of your life. Rise up now in your authority in Christ and demonstrate the power of the Holy Spirit.

It's time to serve some eviction notices:

- Deception, you are evicted.
- Sickness, you have to go.
- Poverty, I'm serving you notice to leave immediately.
- Family quarreling, your time is over. You must go.
- Pain, your rule has ended. Go, in Jesus's name.

You can evict every work of the enemy by using seven words: "Let there be light, in Jesus's name!"

I see new faith coming to you, new confidence to occupy territory that has belonged to you but, in the past, you were afraid to possess. In this day, you will not back down, you will not give in, and you will not give up. You are rising and standing in your rightful position in both authority and power.

YES, LET THERE BE LIGHT! CAN YOU FEEL THE SPIRIT'S POWER FLOWING THROUGH YOU AND CAUSING DARKNESS TO FLEE? YOU'RE WINNING THE SPIRITUAL WARFARE BATTLE BECAUSE YOU'RE A *LIGHT WARRIOR*.

CHAPTER 4

EMBRACING THE JOY-LIGHT

"You believe and trust in Him and you greatly rejoice and delight with inexpressible and glorious joy."
—1 Peter 1:8 (AMP)

When I was a sophomore in high school, I enrolled in a photography class. Unlike the digital cameras people effortlessly use today (and even unlike the instant cameras of my childhood), the cameras my classmates and I relied on to learn technical photography skills demanded expensive rolls of film and photo paper, as well as our having certain specialized knowledge, such as which aperture and shutter speed to use for the best results. And, unlike the instant gratification people get today from snapping an infinite number of photos and then viewing them on a smartphone screen the moment after taking them, we had to go through a series of intricate steps in a meticulous development process to produce and see the final images of the roll of pictures we had snapped in class. However, the process itself imparted a valuable lesson to me.

75

THE PROCESS OF BEING DEVELOPED

My school, H. B. Beal Secondary School in London, Ontario, Canada, was renowned for its emphasis on the arts. Right inside our photography classroom, there was a fully equipped photo-developing darkroom. There, surrounded by the scent of photographic chemicals and the dim red glow of the safety light, I learned not only how to bring to life the photos I had taken but also the importance of having patience, working with precision, and understanding the delicate balance between light and shadow—insights that transcended mere photography into broader training for life.

The photo-developing process in a darkroom involves carefully exposing photographic paper to light through a negative, then passing it through a series of chemical baths to reveal and fix the created image. This careful procedure transforms a seemingly obscure negative into a clear, beautiful photograph. Similarly, God shines His light through the negatives of our lives—our trials, brokenness, and flaws—illuminating and transforming them into outstanding results. As we soak in the light of His presence, He begins to reveal His grace and purpose in us. Just as the darkroom process requires time, accuracy, and light, God's transformative work in us requires time, truth, and light, ultimately bringing forth joy and clarity from what once seemed dark and irreparable.

TURNING NEGATIVES INTO POSITIVES

My friend Katie Souza, who wrote the foreword to this book, is an anointed prophetic minister. She carries a powerful revelation about the light, and, in the same vein as I've described above, I've heard her say, "Jesus takes every negative in your life—your attitude problems, the way you think, the way you react, your sickness and disease, the issue that's happening in your marriage, and anything else—and He shines His light through that negative and flips it to become a positive imprint."

When Jesus's light fills us, it has the power to transform our "negatives" into "positives." This encompasses all areas of our lives that may seem hopeless or damaged, such as sickness, fear, or personal flaws. Instead of succumbing to discouragement and aligning with the enemy's attempts to steal our hope, we have the choice to embrace God's joy. His joy brings light, and His light brings joy. That's how it works.

God's light conquers depression, anxiety, and hopelessness, shining brightly in the darkness. The Scriptures remind us, *"Consider it pure joy, my brothers and sisters, whenever you face trials of many kinds, because you know that the testing of your faith produces perseverance. Let perseverance finish its work so that you may be mature and complete, not lacking anything"* (James 1:2–4 NIV). This revelation teaches us to view trials from the proper perspective. We can and should always choose joy.

When the Scriptures state that God's joy is a supernatural source of strength (see Nehemiah 8:10), this is not a metaphor; it is a profound truth and reality. God's joy has the power to strengthen your spirit, soul, and body to fulfill whatever assignment He has given you. This is a key strategy for spiritual warfare. We must live and walk in the joy of the Lord.

LIVING FROM JOY

When we choose to live from a place of joy, we are synchronizing our hearts with God's heart. The psalmist David, writing about God, said, *"He who sits in the heavens laughs, the Lord scoffs at them"* (Psalm 2:4 NASB). Jesus is seated at the right hand of the Father in heaven, and together They laugh from Their place of authority. Continuing further in that Scripture, it becomes clear that God is laughing at the plans of the enemy because He knows they will come to nothing. This psalm reveals God's sovereignty over every earthly power and His divine plan of salvation through His Anointed One, Jesus Christ, His Son. God's power is above every other power. So, why should we worry? Instead, let's connect our faith to the truth that God rules victoriously. Will you let Him reign inside of you? If you say yes, then His joy should fill you even now. Despite what you may be facing in the natural, begin to sense the pleasure and goodness of God. Don't allow the demonic heaviness of the world to press you down. Release that heaviness. Shake it off. Recognize that Jesus has already overcome the world, and the enemy doesn't stand a chance because you are in agreement with Jesus. That brings immense joy.

One of my favorite depictions of Jesus is a vibrant sketch known as "Laughing Jesus" by the Canadian artist Willis Wheatley. It was initially entitled "Christ, Liberator."[14] For me, this portrayal captures Jesus's essence perfectly. He radiates joy! I also think it's interesting that the drawing was originally called "Christ, Liberator" because that's exactly what happens when we allow the joy of Jesus to overtake our lives. We become liberated. The things that once held us down have no more power to control us. Christ's joy sets us free!

Historically, religion has often depicted Jesus Christ as a solemn and stern figure, emphasizing His role as a judge, and frequently recounting the incident where He overturned the tables of the money changers and sellers in the temple. (See, for example, Mark 11:15–17; John 2:13–17.) However, religion seldom highlights Jesus's boundless love and goodness and the joy that shines from His countenance. (See, for example, Mark 6:30–31; 10:13–16; Luke 10:17–21.) The image of a joyful Jesus is a powerful reminder of His true nature, full of warmth and light. I believe that when we face our greatest difficulties, Jesus is standing with us. In fact, the Scriptures say that He is singing songs of joy over us: *"The Lord your God is in the midst of you, a Mighty One, a Savior [Who saves]! He will rejoice over you with joy;…He will exult over you with singing"* (Zephaniah 3:17). We need to open our spiritual ears to hear His songs of joy and open our hearts to fully embrace this reality. My friend Georgian Banov, cofounder of Global Celebration, who escaped the oppression of Communist-controlled Bulgaria, has said, "The world wants you to be happy but not holy, and religion wants you to be holy but not happy, but God wants you to be happy and holy."

A JOYFUL ENCOUNTER IN THE LIGHT

I grew up in the church as a fifth-generation Pentecostal, surrounded by family members deeply involved in Christian ministry. There were Sunday school teachers, worship leaders, evangelists, denominational leaders, and pastors on both sides of my family. Church was always a significant part of my life, and I am grateful for the rich spiritual legacy it provided. However, I have realized that to truly progress in one's relationship with God, it's essential to

---

14. Douglas Tod, "Meet the Creator of the 'Laughing Jesus' (Photo)," *Vancouver Sun*, January 19, 2014, https://vancouversun.com/news/staff-blogs/meet-the-creator-of-the-laughing-jesus-photo.

have a personal spiritual awakening. You can't rely on someone else's encounter with God; you need to experience Him for yourself.

At sixteen, I had such an encounter. Although I had accepted Jesus as my personal Lord and Savior at the age of seven and received the baptism of the Holy Spirit with the evidence of speaking in tongues shortly afterward, my mid-teen years were marked by doubt. I began questioning many practices and beliefs held by Spirit-filled believers. Reflecting on this period of my life now, I see how the enemy tried to sow seeds of doubt and unbelief into my heart, much like he did with Eve in the garden of Eden. Witnessing hypocrisy among some believers only added to my confusion, making it challenging for me to reconcile people's words with their actions. Troubled, I presented my questions to my father, who, despite his wisdom, was initially at a loss for answers. I didn't know it at the time, but he sought the Lord in prayer, asking the Holy Spirit to reveal Himself to me and provide me the clarity I needed.

Shortly afterward, I attended a revival meeting in my hometown with my parents. It was the first time I had attended that particular church, and I had no idea what to expect. As soon as we entered the meeting, I saw people manifesting the presence and power of God in ways I had never witnessed before—shaking, falling to the ground, and lifting their hands in worship, seemingly caught up in another realm. It was all very unfamiliar and quite shocking to me. I took my seat, feeling uneasy as I observed the expressive worship around me. It was far more intense than anything I had seen in our Spirit-filled church.

When the visiting evangelist took the pulpit and asked us to turn to the second chapter of Acts, I obediently opened my Bible. What happened next was beyond anything I could have anticipated. The moment I found the passage, it felt as if God's hand reached down from heaven and powerfully catapulted me out of my seat. Suddenly, I was on the floor, and I was laughing uncontrollably. I couldn't stop. At the same time, I rolled back and forth, twisting between the chairs. I was being filled with *"joy unspeakable and full of glory"* (1 Peter 1:8 KJV), experiencing an overwhelming divine joy I had never felt before. I laughed in that way for hours.

When the meeting ended, and the pastor needed to lock up the church, my parents had to lift me from the floor and carry me to our vehicle. Once we got home, since I was still laughing in the Spirit, they carried me to our finished basement, where I laughed myself to sleep on the couch. It was a profound encounter that marked the beginning of a new chapter in my spiritual journey.

TRANSFORMATION, DELIVERANCE, AND IMPARTATIONS THROUGH JOY

The morning after my encounter with the Holy Spirit, I woke up knowing that something within me had fundamentally changed. Previously, I had been plagued with questions and doubts about my faith. But now, in the light of God's glory, those questions seemed insignificant. It wasn't that I had received natural answers, but rather, through this powerful encounter, I realized that my questions had faded in the light of who Jesus is. The more I focused on Him, the more satisfied I felt. I no longer wanted anything or anyone else; all I desired was to spend time in the manifest presence of the Lord. God's joy had become a bridge that moved me from a place of doubt to a place of unwavering faith.

Another remarkable transformation occurred in my life. Throughout my childhood, I had often felt oppressed by the enemy. Although I was raised in a loving Christian home, the enemy spirit harassed me relentlessly. Many times, my dread at the thought of going to bed at night brought me great anxiety; although I wasn't able to express it at the time, I had an overwhelming feeling of anguish. I didn't really know how to deal with the demons that terrorized me night after night. Appearing like shadows, dancing on my bedroom walls and crawling up onto my bed, they tormented me with their sinister intimidation. I just lived with it, frightened by their evil presence and sometimes crying myself to sleep. I didn't know what else to do. But after I had that powerful encounter with the Holy Spirit, in which God filled me with His joy, everything changed. Despair creates darkness, but joy produces light. Once I received the joy of the Lord, I never encountered those demons again. Shadows cannot live in the light. One of the enemy spirit's strategies is to keep you locked captive in a world of darkness. The enemy traffics on misery, but Jesus has come to set you completely free from darkness and misery. Jesus came to give you true and lasting joy!

Thus, one of God's primary deliverance tools is joy. This tool is so simple that it's often overlooked. Some people may be surprised and perhaps even offended by this idea, but it's true.

The more you are filled with God's joy, the more His light begins to shine through you. Joy isn't just a feeling—it's a state of being. Actually, joy is a Person, the person of Jesus, and we read in Acts 17:28, "*For in Him we live and move and have our being.*" We can personalize this verse to declare, "*In* Him I live. *In* Him I move. *In* Him I have my being." We could rightfully even express it like this: "*In* Joy I live, *in* Joy I move, and *in* Joy I have my being." We come alive in the joy of the Lord, and His light powerfully shines through us! We become effective light warriors when we choose to live in His joy. The joy of the Lord becomes our supernatural strength.

Glory people are filled with joy and are therefore filled with light. Joy is not an afterthought—it is the first and constant thought that fills our entire being. We *choose* to live in the joy of the Lord. This brings us peace, ease, and a sense of complete contentment that overflows with gratitude.

My encounter with the Spirit at that revival meeting also left me with deep spiritual impartations. Some were immediately evident, while others unfolded over time. One such impartation was the gift of worshipping the Lord in Spirit and in truth. (See John 4:23–24.) As I spent time with Him, He filled me with songs to sing back to Him. In the privacy of my bedroom, my secret place, with my hands on a simple Yamaha keyboard, the Holy Spirit began to teach me how to play the piano to glorify Jesus. This marked the beginning of my journey in ministry. These gifts came through the joy, for God's joy releases the light.

THERE'S AN ENCOUNTER FOR YOU

If you are feeling dry or distant from God in your spiritual walk, take heart. Your very recognition of this distance and your longing for more of God are signs of His drawing you to Himself. They are indications that your heart is alive to the things of God, even if your emotions aren't aligned with that desire at the moment. Recognizing your desire for closeness with God is the first step toward a renewed experience of His glory. Open up now and invite His joy-light to fill you!

When Jesus's joy is turned on inside of you, it's like a spiritual vibration of light that changes everything. Suddenly, you see things differently, you feel things differently, and you begin to respond to things differently. When you give yourself to the light of His presence, the divine flow of the Spirit begins pulsating throughout your entire being, bringing goodness, peace, and even more joy—overflowing joy!

The encounter I had with the Holy Spirit during my teenage years led me to a significant realization, one that is firmly supported by Scripture: *"For the Kingdom of God is not a matter of what we eat or drink, but of living a life of goodness and peace and joy in the Holy Spirit"* (Romans 14:17 NLT). From the perspective of this verse, joy makes up one third of the kingdom of God, so we'd better embrace it! This revelation clarifies the stance we must adopt when aiming to engage in spiritual warfare from heaven's perspective.

EXPOSING SPIRITS OF RELIGIOSITY

Being filled with and experiencing God's joy in a tangible and profound way was the best thing that ever happened to me, and I was later surprised to discover that not everyone in the church embraced this joy. The religious spirit of darkness feels threatened by joy-light; it attempts to dismiss anything it can't control—and God's joy cannot be contained. Unfortunately, too many Christians are held captive by a spirit of religion.

Recently, after one of my services, I spoke with a pastor who expressed his concerns about my emphasis on joy. He said, "You should probably not do so much of the 'joy-thing' before a salvation altar call." He was referring to the Sunday morning meeting when I stepped back and allowed the Holy Spirit to take over. Joy began to bubble up within the congregation, leading to spontaneous bursts of laughter. It was not forced or manipulated; it was a glorious manifestation of God's joy, which I always welcome because it brings true and lasting change.

I've experienced this transformation in my own life in an ongoing way. The Bible says that it's the goodness or kindness of God that draws us to repentance. (See Romans 2:4.) However, we always have a choice: to receive what the Spirit is doing or to refuse His touch. When the joy-light shines upon people in a corporate gathering, it can powerfully set the stage for inviting the lost to find eternal salvation through Christ. The presence of joy can inspire some of the most meaningful altar calls. Rather than being offended by the joy, we should embrace it.

The Spirit's joy is a light-bringer, exposing spirits of religiosity and destruction that have tried to enslave people through fear and intimidation. There is no fear in the light! There is no restrictive captivity in the light! If Jesus has set us free, then we are *"free indeed"* (John 8:36, various translations)!

THE PURE FLOW OF GOD'S JOY

After that initial encounter with supernatural joy as a teenager, I earnestly sought the Lord with all my heart. As I mentioned earlier, I longed to be in His presence continuously, not just during occasional visits. I wanted to dwell with Him, and, night after night, I started writing love songs to God and worshipping Him in the privacy of my bedroom. I discovered that the more I opened my heart to God, the more I could receive all that He desired to pour into my life. It felt like I had tapped into a pure stream of joy, and the Spirit continually filled me—as long as I was willing to receive that filling.

And, with this flow came an abundance of light that dispelled the darkness. Being filled with God's joy left no room for the dark entanglements of alcohol (sometimes called "spirits"), drugs, or sexual perversion that can entrap both teenagers and adults. The fullness of His joy made me uninterested in those harmful distractions.

I can feel vibrations of glory-light moving in me even as I write these words. Can you feel something stirring inside you as you read them? In your innermost being, can you feel God awakening something new? His joy is beginning to arise within you, shining light into your life and dispersing the darkness. Can you sense it?

As I expressed earlier, sometimes, when God's spiritual light tangibly manifests, it feels like ripples or flowing waves moving throughout your body. It can even resemble a gentle electrical current—mild but distinct enough to be noticeable. Recently, Janet and I traveled to Europe for a ministry trip. Our first stop was Stuttgart, Germany. After checking into our hotel, we lay down for an hour-long nap to recover from our long overseas flight before our time of ministry in the evening. While resting, Janet felt those holy tremors, that glory "vibration," within her. Again, this is a common manifestation associated with the light. It's a sign that God is recalibrating you, bringing things into divine alignment through the power of His light. You can physically feel the shifts and stirrings within.

So, even as you read this, I'm prophesying over you: things that have been out of order in your life are coming back into divine order. A supernatural alignment is taking place within you. You are also receiving some clarification about things you've been sensing in the Spirit.

JOY IN SEEING GOD WORK

One of the most wonderful aspects of the glory realm is that, within this realm, God often does things for us we weren't even aware we needed. He is working both in the foreground and in the background of our lives. For example, we may readily perceive His workings, such as realizing, "I can tell that God is changing my mindset," or noticing, "God is transforming the way I speak." When we enter the glory, the Spirit transforms our thinking, altering our perspective so that we start to see things through the light of His glory. He also begins to refine our vocabulary. We can't talk in the manner that we used to. It's amazing to witness these immediate and noticeable changes. But, again, it's equally important to recognize that God is simultaneously working "behind the scenes" on our behalf, producing changes we may not initially realize. The Scriptures remind us that for those who love the Lord, He is working all things together for our good:

> And we know that in all things God works for the good of those who love him, who have been called according to his purpose. (Romans 8:28 NIV)

In the Old Testament, we see the same idea in Joseph's words to his brothers, who had sold him into slavery:

> As for you, you thought evil against me, but God meant it for good, to bring about that many people should be kept alive, as they are this day.
> (Genesis 50:20)

If we take time to think about this revelation, it brings so much joy! Joy is one of the primary manifestations of our being in the presence of Jesus, and of His presence dwelling within us. (See Psalm 16:11.) When we receive an impartation of God's joy, we can also release an impartation of the same! I think the children of God should be the most joyous people on the planet. When we really consider everything that Jesus has provided for us and the way the Spirit empowers us with His light, how can we not be joyous? I want you to lift your hands right now in the glory realm and receive an impartation of God's joy.

NO WEAPON CAN PROSPER IN THE GLORY

Because you are a light warrior, no weapon that is formed against you can prosper. (See Isaiah 54:17.) This is another amazing revelation. Isaiah didn't say the weapon would not be formed against you, but he did say that *if* the weapon is formed, it won't prosper. In other words, in the glory, we're not promised that we'll have a life without trouble or problems. Jesus Himself said, *"In the world you will have tribulation…"* (John 16:33 NKJV). However, He then added these words: " *…but be of good cheer, I have overcome the world"* (verse 33).

When we are *"of good cheer,"* our countenance will shine with supernatural joy. Our entire being should radiate the light-joy of the glory because we're not worried about the outcome of any given situation. We don't need to be anxious, worried, or terribly concerned because Jesus told us that He has already overcome whatever we're facing. We are simply responsible for carrying the joy of Jesus everywhere we go.

If we don't carry the joy, who will? The world doesn't have any real joy. Why? Because there's no true joy without Jesus. Just knowing that the Overcomer lives inside us brings us much joy!

If trouble comes your way, you need to remember that the weapons that have been formed against you cannot prosper as long as you choose to remain in the joy-light. Darkness can never overtake the light. This is both a scientific and spiritual impossibility. It is true that, in the natural, there are degrees of light and degrees of darkness. For example, we use incandescent light bulbs to light indoor spaces, and although they bring illumination, there can still be room for some shadows to remain. The rays of the sun are a much more powerful source of light, yet even the sun's rays can be blocked by objects, producing dark shadows. However, the glory-light of Jesus is the most powerful light in the universe. Wherever God's light shines, all shadows must instantly vanish. His light causes all darkness to flee.

Yes, living in the light of God's glory provides so much joy! There is freedom from every demonic bondage when we embrace the truth that we are the children of light. If we choose to live in this truth, we choose to live in joy. If we choose to live in joy, we choose to live in the light of God's glory. The Scriptures declare that this is the path of life:

> *You will show me the path of life; in Your presence is fullness of joy, at Your right hand there are pleasures forevermore.* (Psalm 16:11)

Living in the light is the highest form of living because every other realm in the universe is subject to the glory realm. When we are in God's manifest presence, He reveals His goodness to us, and this leads us to live a life of contentment and overflowing supernatural joy. Living in God's joy releases His light, and His light then releases even greater joy.

IS IT A MESS OR A MIRACLE IN THE MAKING?

A light warrior understands that the joy of Jesus is one of the greatest spiritual warfare weapons against the works of darkness. The promise you have in the glory is that whatever the enemy attempts against you cannot prosper, but you must view your life through this heavenly perspective from the glory realm. Many sincere believers have been taught that when things don't go as planned, they should start cursing the devil and binding his attacks. As previously mentioned, this mindset has led people to see the devil in everything, which is a fundamentally misguided approach. Continually focusing on the enemy only empowers him to act in our lives. Why should we give the enemy such power? As a born-again believer, I am a light warrior. The enemy and the dark forces of his kingdom stand no chance against the light of God that dwells within me. When things don't go as expected, I need to ask the Spirit for a higher perspective. Instead of fixating on the devil in the details, my spiritual eyes should be trained to embrace the light of God's goodness and purposes.

Many times, when things go differently than what I've planned, it's because God has something better in mind for me, but I must be discerning enough to see it. Sometimes we're so focused on the mess that we don't realize that it's simply material for a miracle or another form of blessing. God is willing and ready to sort it out for us, but we must be willing to cooperate with Him.

For example, recently, I was getting ready to travel to Asia with my whole family. As I was preparing to load all our suitcases into my vehicle to drive us to the Los Angeles airport for the trip, my remote key wouldn't open the trunk of the car. This was perplexing because I hadn't previously experienced any problems like this with my vehicle. I pushed the button on my remote a number of times, to no avail.

I then opened the car door and pushed the button inside the car that opens the trunk, but that device, too, wasn't working. Eventually, I attempted to manually open the trunk from outside the car, but that wouldn't work either. I was forced to call an auto mechanic to come and examine my car, and it turned out that the car battery was completely dead. Although we were on a tight schedule, needing to drive two hours to LAX, I trusted that the Spirit was working something to my advantage. I choose to live in the joy-light, and nothing can be allowed to steal my joy.

Since my car wasn't working, I had to rent a vehicle from a local car rental agency so I could drive my family to the airport. The amazing thing is that after everything was said and done, I realized that I had actually saved money. By having my car sit at home in the carport, I avoided paying for three weeks of parking at the airport! I could have looked at this situation as the enemy trying to retaliate against me because of our ministry assignment in Asia, but I refused to pay attention to the enemy. I was too busy living in the light to do that! Once we returned from our trip, it was a simple fix to get a new battery for my vehicle, and I was very thankful that the issue had occurred at home instead of while I was out traveling on the road somewhere.

I can testify that trusting God to work all things for my good releases me from tension, anger, and fear in the midst of inconvenient and difficult circumstances so I can continually live in the joy of God's light. Some people have a habit of giving the enemy way too much credit for things that happen in their lives. I encourage you to stop talking about the enemy and start bragging about Jesus, and see how quickly your life changes.

LET HEAVENLY WISDOM GUIDE YOUR SPIRITUAL WARFARE

Spiritually speaking, there's a significant difference between facts and truth. In James 3:13–18, we read about two types of wisdom: earthly wisdom and heavenly wisdom. It's interesting to note that the Bible tells us King Solomon was the wisest man on earth. (See 1 Kings 3:12; 4:29–31.) This was, of course, the case until the time of Jesus. Eventually, Jesus's wisdom far surpassed Solomon's. The reason for this is that Solomon started well by embracing heavenly wisdom, but, later in life, he became entangled in worldly wisdom—human wisdom. If you read Solomon's story in 1 Kings 1–11, you'll find that his end was not very good. You can walk in worldly wisdom and believe you know everything, but worldly wisdom leads only to destruction. For example, worldly wisdom says, "Only think about yourself. Do whatever it takes to get ahead." This is fleshly, carnal thinking and is based on worldly "facts" (information or apparent causes and effects apart from the wisdom of God), assumptions, and perspectives. In contrast, Jesus says, "*If anyone desires to be first, he must be last of all, and servant of all*" (Mark 9:35). Some believers (often unknowingly) are trying to use natural tactics to wage spiritual warfare, but the results of such an approach are devastating, and it's obvious that they're not winning the war.

Heavenly wisdom is grounded in the eternal truth of God's Word and on spiritual laws. To use another example, heavenly wisdom says, "*A generous person will prosper…*" (Proverbs 11:25 NIV). This is entirely contrary to the worldly wisdom that would say people should use their money to indulge themselves because they "deserve" it. The verse continues, "*…whoever refresh others will be refreshed.*" This verse paints a beautiful picture of offering water to the thirsty, giving bread to the hungry, and witnessing someone being refreshed and restored to health. When we nurture others with abundant blessings, those blessings are poured back over us. (See also Luke 6:38.)

The Scriptures encourage us with heavenly wisdom to "*do to others what you would have them do to you*" (Matthew 7:12 NIV). When we do this, it activates the spiritual law of sowing and reaping: "*Whatever a man sows, that he will also reap*" (Galatians 6:7 NKJV). In the glory, the Spirit teaches us to trust in God's higher ways. I believe that you're reading this book because you desire to operate in a more effective way to win the war against evil.

As I indicated earlier, when it comes to spiritual warfare, some people have taught that we must become extremely worked up and aggressively confront the enemy in the same manner in which he operates. However, I have found that such perspectives align more with the agenda of darkness than with the truth of God's light. Make no mistake: this does not mean making peace with the enemy. On the contrary, we are to forcefully push back against his evil agendas, but we must do so by operating in the opposite spirit. This is what gives us the upper hand. We operate on a higher level, following the way of love and letting peace be our guide.

James, the brother of Jesus, provided us with divine revelation about the posture believers should adopt in spiritual warfare: *"Peacemakers who sow in peace reap a harvest of righteousness"* (James 3:18 NIV). In other words, when the enemy attacks us with hatred, accusations, and outright derision, we remain seated in heavenly places, ruling from a position of righteousness, peace, and joy in God's presence, and not allowing the enemy to dislodge us from our position. As light warriors, during such times, we're being recalibrated to live victoriously by trusting in and relying on God's truth.

Heavenly wisdom reminds us that the joy of the Lord is our supernatural strength. (See Nehemiah 8:10.) If we walk in anger, depression, and heaviness, or if we take everything too seriously, we will always feel under attack by the enemy. But if we walk in the joy-light of Jesus, following His heavenly wisdom, we will receive supernatural strength to overcome every situation we face. Picture this joyous light brilliantly radiating from your life, surrounding you, defending you, and protecting you from all harm.

I remember a time when I was holding weekend meetings in Bismarck, North Dakota. After the first service, I returned to my hotel to find music blaring loudly from the room next to mine. Hoping the occupants would turn down the music, I sat there and gradually became more and more irritated as the music continued. Alone in my room, my thoughts started racing, and I felt these neighbors were being exceptionally rude. Finally, I called the front desk to report the noise. They assured me that they'd handle it, but, after five, then ten, then thirty, minutes, the loud music continued. Frustrated, I banged on the wall with my shoe, hoping the people would get the hint, but nothing changed.

Exasperated, I called the front desk again, only to be told that no one was registered in the room next to mine. Perplexed, I insisted on a solution. The hotel staff came up, and when they opened the door, they found the room empty. It was the radio alarm that was blasting music. There were no rude guests, just a runaway clock radio! My mind had concocted an entire scenario out of unfounded assumptions.

This experience showed me the importance of letting the Spirit shine His light on our situations so that we can avoid falling for the enemy's deceptions. Some Christians, when faced with a form of darkness, quickly conclude they're under heavy demonic attack, and this allows their minds to spiral out of control. Instead of believing the enemy's lies (or our own imaginations), we must choose to turn on the light by living in the joy of the Lord. His joy illuminates the truth and dispels deception.

OUR SOURCE OF JOY-POWER

As light warriors, we must always keep in mind that our source of joy-power comes from the light of God's glory, the most powerful force in the universe. When we enter the glory realm, God begins to teach us through His Spirit. This divine teaching often requires us to unlearn certain things from our past. God is faithful to guide us through this process, but we must give Him permission by being teachable, by yielding to Him, and by surrendering to His light. I've discovered that revelation often unfolds progressively. God shows us a step of faith to take, and, once we take that step, He reveals the next step. In this way, He continually leads us by His Spirit of light.

Have you ever been afraid of the dark? My daughter Legacy absolutely dislikes dark rooms and refuses to enter them. A fear of the dark is common among children, possibly due to a fear of the unknown or the possibility of stumbling into something unseen. Physical darkness often evokes a sense of fear that many people prefer to avoid altogether.

Similarly, I think there are a lot of believers who, when they walk into a spiritually dark place, are overwhelmed with anxiety or overcome by feelings of fear, insecurity, and worry—there are often a variety of uncomfortable feelings that come. And then, because of bad teaching, people may say, "Well, if it's really dark, there must be a lot of demons in here, too many for me to face." They feel an uneasiness about waging warfare against the hordes of hell. Let me tell you, as soon as you give your mind and imagination to the enemy, he will take advantage of that. The enemy will play on the template of your mind and try to ingrain all types of deception into your thinking.

Even if you find that a satanic attack is not just your imagination and that you are being confronted by demonic forces, remember, all you need to do is turn on the lights. A demon is like a cockroach. As soon as you turn on the light, that thing will be exposed and run for its life. It cannot stay in the light. The Bible says that we are to walk in the light, even as God is in the light. (See 1 John 1:7.) God's Word is light. *"Your word is a lamp to my feet and a light to my path"* (Psalm 119:105).

Do you realize that when truth comes to you in the glory, you're given all power over every work of the enemy? It doesn't matter what type of curse somebody has tried to put on you; what evil spell they've spoken over you, your relationships, your finances, or your body. It doesn't matter how long the generational curse runs back in your family line. When the truth comes, it comes to turn on the light within you. (See Psalm 119:130.) Immediately, the darkness must leave. Again, I'm giving you a spiritual warfare key from heaven that is so simple, most people will attempt to disregard it. To make it plain, the key is this: if you choose God's Word, you'll choose His joy, and if you walk in His joy, you'll walk in His light.

Therefore, before you start getting scared thinking about the enemy and his agenda, I want to reaffirm the best and easiest solution for changing the spiritual atmosphere. The greatest way to deal with darkness is by simply turning on the light. If you don't want it to be dark anymore, just flip the switch.

You might say, "But I don't know where the switch is." You *are* the switch! You are an atmosphere. Wherever you go, you must carry the joy-light! I can't emphasize enough that joy is a choice. I encourage you to choose joy, and, as we conclude this chapter, I want to share with you a three-part method for doing that.

HOW TO CHOOSE JOY

All around the globe, I've had the privilege of teaching three spiritual steps for receiving the joy of the Lord. These are practical steps you need to choose to follow. These steps are effective as you think about who the Lord is and what He has done for you. The first step is to say, "Ha ha!" You can start using it right now. Just say it: "Ha ha!" Keep repeating it until you begin to feel it. When facing any difficult situation, release a hearty "Ha ha" over it. How can you say "Ha ha" in the midst of your situation? Because the joy of the Lord is your strength, and in His presence is fullness of joy. Receive God in your life as your joy and strength.

The second step is to say, "Hee hee!" This will take your joy a bit further. Combine the first expression of joy with the second and say them out loud: "Ha ha! Hee hee!" Repeat that several times. Again, continue until you feel joy start to bubble up from deep within you.

Now, here's the final step: say, "Ho ho!" As you can see, we are progressing deeper into joy. Although it may not seem like it, choosing to be joy-filled is a conscious decision. You can sit there as you're reading this and dismiss these expressions as foolishness, or you can put into practice the Bible's instruction in Philippians 4:4 to *"rejoice in the Lord always."* Jesus is joy manifested. When you choose joy, you are choosing to manifest the light of Jesus in your life.

Now, let's put all three expressions together: "Ha ha! Hee hee! Ho ho!" Repeat these words over and over until you align your thoughts and your speech with God's Word and are truly immersed in the joy of the Lord.

When I taught these three "joy steps" at Glory Life Center in Stuttgart, Germany, Brother Yun, known worldwide as "The Heavenly Man," was present in the meetings because he was also speaking at the conference. Brother Yun is renowned for his years of imprisonment in China due to his efforts to spread the gospel. During his imprisonment, the Spirit granted him miraculous supernatural encounters, including an escape from jail reminiscent of God's rescues of His people in biblical times.

Brother Yun was so excited to learn these steps to choosing joy that he shared them with many leaders in the underground church in China. He told me that the results were phenomenal! Numerous leaders who had been feeling discouraged experienced an immediate shift in their mindset. As they intentionally said, "Ha ha! Hee hee! Ho ho!" and chose to laugh over their problems, their spirits were lifted. The Chinese church was discovering a new form of spiritual warfare—one that brought them immense joy!

Later, while I was ministering at a large conference at Victory Christian Center in Houston, Texas, I shared the story of Brother Yun and the joy-filled experiences of believers in Germany and China. Pastor Tony Krishack, the senior leader at Victory Christian Center, listened intently, absorbing these spiritual steps to add to his ministry toolkit. Later that year, while I was ministering in Australia, I received a text message and video from Pastor Tony, who was on a mission trip to India. He wrote something to this effect: "Just thought I would let you know that 'Ha ha! Hee hee! Ho ho!' worked in India! Thank you for this new message. I'm in the Northeast India, Darjeeling area, and we're having a spiritual joy drinking party! Many miracles are happening."

I was thrilled to hear how these spiritual warfare steps to choosing joy were transforming the atmosphere in India and releasing the new wine of the Spirit over the people. But that wasn't the end of it. A short while later, Janet and I took a ministry team with us to Japan. While teaching at Church of Praise in Osaka, I encouraged the believers there to open up to the joy of the Lord, teaching them to use the three joy expressions, "Ha ha! Hee hee! Ho ho!" It wasn't long before many of these believers began transitioning from the feelings of the natural realm to the supernatural joy of heaven. Laughter started breaking out in the meeting, and many people were set free. You see, laughter can be a catalyst that God uses to alleviate emotional pain while supernaturally addressing deep-seated issues of abuse, trauma, and past hurts. In that glorious atmosphere, we released our team to minister to the beautiful Japanese people.

One team member, Doug, later told me that he discovered he could choose to laugh, and by consciously making that choice, he released an anointing for joy into the atmosphere. This is exactly what I'm talking about. Joy is a choice. When we choose to enter into joy, God takes those seeds, anoints them, and multiplies them with an even greater outpouring of joy! Doug shared, "As I chose to release the joy, supernatural joy began to bubble up inside me, and it was the most powerful experience I have ever had in the Spirit."

LAUGHTER IS LIGHT MEDICINE

I want to highlight one more crucial aspect of joy in spiritual warfare: its power to break the chains of sickness, disease, and pain. The light of God, released through joy, has the extraordinary ability to destroy all infirmities! Proverbs 17:22 (NIV, NLT) tells us, "*A cheerful heart is good medicine.*" There are profound spiritual, emotional, and physical benefits to joy and laughter, and science has confirmed what the Bible has always taught: joy is genuinely good for our health! "Laughter enhances your intake of oxygen-rich air, stimulates your heart, lungs, and muscles, and increases the endorphins that are released by your brain," ultimately reducing stress. Laughter can also help combat depression and sorrow, helping people to have a more positive outlook on life and elevating their overall mood.[15] Additionally, "'heightened stress magnifies the risk of cardiovascular events, including heart attacks and strokes'.... Laughter releases nitric oxide, a chemical that relaxes blood vessels, reduces blood pressure and decreases clotting.... There also appear to be cognitive benefits."[16] We'll delve more deeply into healing light in the next chapter, but, right now, I prophesy Job 8:21 (NLT) over you: *"He will once again fill your mouth with laughter and your lips with shouts of joy."*

YES, LET THERE BE LIGHT! CAN YOU FEEL THE SPIRIT'S POWER FLOWING THROUGH YOU AND CAUSING DARKNESS TO FLEE? YOU'RE WINNING THE SPIRITUAL WARFARE BATTLE BECAUSE YOU'RE A *LIGHT WARRIOR.*

---

15. Dana Sparks, "Mayo Mindfulness: Laughter for Stress Relief Is No Joke," Mayo Clinic News Network, June 26, 2019, https://newsnetwork.mayoclinic.org/discussion/mayo-mindfulness-stress-relief-with-laughter-is-no-joke/.
16. Richard Schiffman, "Laughter May Be Effective Medicine for These Trying Times," *The New York Times*, October 2, 2020, https://www.coursehero.com/file/128980816/Laughter-May-Be-Effective-Medicine-for-These-Trying-Times-The-New-York-Timespdf/.

CHAPTER 5

RELEASING HEALING LIGHT

*"Then shall your light break forth like the morning,
and your healing (your restoration and the power of a new life) shall
spring forth speedily; your righteousness (your rightness, your justice,
and your right relationship with God) shall go before you
[conducting you to peace and prosperity], and the glory of the Lord
shall be your rear guard."*
—Isaiah 58:8

Light, in different forms, is used in modern medical science for such purposes as laser surgery, the treatment of skin ailments, and the destruction of viruses causing infectious diseases. Recognizing this led me to believe that if medical science can harness natural light for healing, then logically I could also speak God's spiritual light into my body and command the darkness to leave. This just makes sense. It's a simple idea, but that's often how God operates—through a spark of revelation, which I like to call a "creative spark." It's our responsibility to nurture that spark and recognize the potential it holds. Light warriors recognize that the dark curses of sickness and disease must flee when we choose to release God's healing light!

When I first received this revelation, I decided to act in faith on these thoughts. Janet had been suffering from a severe migraine for several days, so I told her that I was going to try this new approach of releasing God's healing light. She was excited and in agreement for me to apply my faith in this way. I said something like, "Headache, you must leave! Right now, I release the light of God! God is light, and in Him there is no darkness, there is no sickness, there are no migraines. So, let there be light!"

In an instant, Janet looked at me, her eyes wide with surprise, and exclaimed, "It worked!" Her migraine was completely gone. This was so exciting because I witnessed the revelation becoming a manifestation as I stepped out in bold activation! As light warriors, we must be willing to act upon the instructions that the Spirit brings us in His light.

THE SUN OF RIGHTEOUSNESS WITH HEALING

Janet and I knew that, in the natural, light had numerous healing benefits for both the mind and the body, but now we discovered that a supernatural healing light from the Spirit was available to us. I think it's interesting that Malachi's messianic prophecy about Christ foretells of His being the "Sun of righteousness" who arises with healing in His wings and beams of light. (See Malachi 4:2.) In a very real way, His light covers His children with glory like a mother bird covers her young ones with her protective feathers.

The latter part of this verse is extremely important because it alludes to the truth that this healing light will strengthen the body and allow those who are touched by it to *"go out and frolic like well-fed calves"* (verse 2 NIV). The *New Living Translation* describes it as *"leaping with joy like calves let out to pasture."* The idea is that the calves are energized, made strong, and released according to the light. I can see the radiant rays of God's brilliant healing light filling you completely and, in turn, being released through you.

Shortly after receiving this exciting revelation, we traveled to a conference in Montélimar, France, where I shared my newly discovered insights about the healing light. After my message, a woman approached the altar seeking healing for an irregular heartbeat. Doctors had recently warned her that the condition was serious, and that, if left untreated, it could potentially lead to heart failure or other dire conditions. Inspired by what I had shared, she felt that God's light could provide the healing she was looking for. I was reminded of a defibrillator, which delivers a jolt to restore a person's heart rhythm. I firmly believed that God's light could achieve a similar effect! I instructed her to place her hands on her heart, while I covered them with my own. I then proclaimed, "Let there be light," repeating it several times. Almost immediately, she exclaimed, "I just felt the power of God!" This was a sign that the Spirit was at work. Later, she joyfully testified in the meetings that she had been healed and now had a regular heartbeat. *Let there be healing light!*

After I began moving in this revelation about God's healing light, one of the next places Janet and I went to minister was at revival meetings with Edgar and Holly Ann Baillie in Rockford, Illinois. Several people with arthritis attended our meeting. I called them out by a word of knowledge, and, at the end of my message, they came to receive prayer. A woman who was suffering from diabetes and a businessman who had just been diagnosed with prostate cancer also came up for healing. As I ministered to each one, in my spirit, I could see sparkles of the visible shekinah glory filling the room. It seemed to be gently raining in the atmosphere all around us. It was a sign that God's healing light was being released over us in such a precious way. One of the women who had arthritis was slain in the Spirit as we prayed for her. She came up to me afterward and told me that she had seen a vision while lying on the floor and receiving her healing. She said, "I saw the most beautiful, pure heavenly light! It was swirling around and around like a portal of glory." This was very similar to a vision that my pastor's wife, Joan, had seen and shared with me at about the same time. Both of these visions were confirmation of this new and exciting revelation God was giving us. He was teaching us about His light and showing us that it carries healing power for anyone who is willing to receive it.

Another woman who attended that meeting was persistently coughing with severe pain in her chest. She had gone to see her doctor that week, and he had discovered a black spot on her lungs. She was desperate for a miracle.

Janet placed her hands on this woman's chest and spoke healing light to her: "Let there be light!" She simply commanded the darkness to go. When Janet finished her prayer, the lady looked down at her chest and noticed tiny sparkles of shekinah glory glistening with heavenly light across her blouse. It was a sign that God was at work. Later that week, she went back to the doctor and returned home with a wonderful praise report. She sent us her testimony in an email, saying, "When Janet prayed for me, the pain instantly left my body. When I went back for my doctor's visit, he took another X-ray, and he couldn't find the spot. Praise God!" *Let there be healing light!*

I continued asking the Spirit for further revelation, and I also pursued research into medical studies related to the topic of light. I knew there were additional connections for us to make. Seeing how light worked in the natural was giving us faith to see God's light working in the supernatural. In this pursuit, I came across a health article stating that light could be used for various health benefits, including weight loss. This seemed revolutionary in the natural, but now we would begin to test it *supernaturally* in our meetings. My faith was boosted to another level!

Not long after that, I was scheduled to minister as one of the keynote speakers at a Christian conference near Vancouver, Canada, with more than 2,500 people in attendance. At the conference, I shared this revelation about God's light, and, this time, I read aloud the article I had recently discovered. As I read it, I encouraged the people to press in to hear it with ears attuned to the Spirit. I knew that if they could make this connection, they would receive the healing benefits of God's light! Sure enough, miracles began to happen. As I declared, "Let there be light!" over the crowd of spiritual seekers, mass healing began to take place without my placing my hands on anybody. In that atmosphere, I spoke the following by a word of knowledge: "Several people are receiving supernatural weight loss in God's light. You need to check your pants, skirt, or dress." No sooner had I said this than shouts of joy began to fill the room! People were checking their clothing and finding that it was very loose. God's light was at work! At least thirty women rushed to the stage to testify about this supernatural weight-loss miracle. *Let there be healing light!*

In the same meeting, other people testified that their hips, joints, and bones had been healed. An elderly gentleman reported that a golf-ball-sized growth had instantly disappeared from the side of his neck. A woman got up out of her wheelchair (to which she had been confined for more than a decade) and ran around the front of the stage. One man said that all of his clinically diagnosed depression had instantly left him, and although we didn't have the capacity to capture all of their testimonies, so many other people lifted their hands to testify that they had been healed in some way. Miracles were on full display. *Let there be healing light!*

After I returned home, the miracle reports continued to come in. The host ministry contacted me later to say that, in that meeting, people had been healed of cancer, diabetes, and liver disease. Yes, God had been at work, releasing *His* light. In these examples, I want you to recognize that through the power of the Spirit, light warriors are healers. Let us remember that it is not our own power, but rather the power of God, that flows through us for healing.

WAYS TO RECEIVE AND RELEASE DIVINE LIGHT FOR HEALING

THE SPOKEN WORD

One of the greatest ways in which we can receive divine healing through God's light and direct it to others is through the spoken word. In the beginning, God declared, *"Let there be light"* (Genesis 1:3), and it was so. There was no struggle or striving. God didn't have to wrestle with spiritual forces to make it happen. As He spoke, the creative power of His words instantly released light into the atmosphere and birthed all of creation. Whenever our omnipotent God speaks, the universe must obey. Whatever God speaks happens. It's as simple as that.

The psalmist sang about this process when he composed these words:

He sent out his word and healed them, snatching them from the door of death. (Psalm 107:20 NLT)

Death does not have the final say; God does. God's voice is filled with creative light, and when He speaks, it releases healing light that brings health and wholeness. Remember what Proverbs 4:20–22 says:

My son, attend to my words; consent and submit to my sayings. Let them not depart from your sight; keep them in the center of your heart. For they are life to those who find them, healing and health to all their flesh.

In Genesis 1:3, when God said, *"Let there be light,"* and the light shone, He separated the light from the darkness, and said that it was *"good"* (verse 18). That should be a profound personal revelation to all of us. Sickness, disease, pain, and suffering are not part of God's heavenly kingdom of light. They come from the kingdom of darkness. So, just as God took authority and separated the light from the darkness, you, too, can take authority over these areas and command the light to come. Command all darkness to be separated from your life and from your physical body.

When Jesus ministered on earth through the power of the Holy Spirit, many people recognized His supernatural ability to heal the sick in uncommon ways. A centurion who desperately desired healing for his paralyzed and pain-stricken servant pleaded with Jesus, *"Only speak the word, and my servant boy will be cured"* (Matthew 8:8). Clearly, this man understood that the healing light of Christ could be released through the spoken words of Jesus. In response to the centurion's faith, Jesus replied, *"Go; it shall be done for you as you have believed"* (verse 13). The verse continues, *"And the servant boy was restored to health at that very moment."* Again, whatever God speaks happens, and, because Christ now lives in you, as you are led by the Spirit, you can do the same.

DECREEING THE LIGHT

One of the most profound revelations a person can discover is that humanity was created in the image of God. You and I are both made in God's image. The darkness of sin threatened to sever this divine connection, but that is precisely why Jesus Christ was sent to earth as the Light of the World: to reconcile us to God and restore us to our rightful place as those who bear His image and carry His light. Understanding this reality should give us the confidence to speak His words and expect them to come to pass. When we speak God's words in faith and by His leading, it is as if God Himself is speaking through us.

While I was ministering in Belfast, Northern Ireland, I witnessed an extraordinary sight: a shaft of divine light beaming down upon a woman standing in the congregation. This radiant light rested on her head and then supernaturally flowed throughout her entire body, cascading down her back and reaching all the way to her feet. In that moment, I intuitively understood that God was bringing divine alignment and healing to her back and neck, and that this heavenly touch would extend to other areas of her body as well. Acting on this revelation, I spoke out what I was seeing prophetically. Instantly, the physical manifestation of that word became evident—it was as if she had been touched by divine electricity! The woman felt the undeniable power of God coursing through her, and she received complete healing in her neck and back, and throughout her entire body. That night, she stood before the congregation and testified to the miraculous work God had performed as the healing light was released upon her!

Some time ago, a ministry friend reached out to me in confidence after receiving a dire diagnosis by his doctors, who reported that multiple cancers were spreading rapidly throughout his body. He had been given a grim prognosis that, from a natural standpoint, seemed like a death sentence. This friend, who had a powerful healing and miracle ministry and had witnessed countless lives being healed of cancer and various other diseases, now found himself facing a bleak medical report.

It's important to remember that the enemy doesn't play fair; he doesn't care about your past successes in healing the sick. I've said it before, and I'll say it again: the enemy always attempts to attack you in the area of your greatest anointing. The anointing you carry is a threat to his kingdom of darkness. Because you carry the light, he will attempt to do anything in his power to diminish the effectiveness of that light. Don't let him do it. Stand in your anointing and let the light within you shine brightly.

Despite the severity of my friend's medical diagnosis, he reached out to me because he understood the supernatural power of faith agreement. Recognizing that we could harness our collective faith to confront this challenge, we joined together in prayer. Following our initial prayer, I sought direct guidance from the Spirit. With His assistance, I carefully wrote a decree to speak on behalf of my friend. This decree was designed to align with God's promises and declare healing and restoration over his body.

A HEALING DECREE TO SPEAK OVER OTHERS

In essence, this is the decree I wrote under the direction of the Spirit:

From the top of your head to the bottom of your feet, let there be light!

No shadow of sickness or disease can remain.
All darkness flees as the glory light invades your body.
I speak light to your body.
I speak light to your bones.
I speak light to your heart.
I speak light to every organ, muscle, nerve, blood cell, and blood vessel.
I speak light to your lungs.
I speak light to your liver and kidneys.
I speak light to your reproductive system.
Let there be light!
I speak light to your skin.
I speak light to your digestive tract.
I speak light to your soul.
Light fills your mind, will, and emotions.
Let there be light!
God's healing, miracle-working light prevails in you.

As I wrote down these words and began to speak them aloud over my friend, I could actually visualize him being filled with God's healing light. I saw an all-consuming light flooding his entire body. It started with small flashes of light around his head. Then, with a sudden surge of power, these flashes shot all the way down to his feet. Finally, like a burst of sunshine exploding, the light completely filled his entire body.

It was so powerful. As I spoke this decree, I could see the light shining in and through every area of his body. This experience reminded me of the following verse:

You shall also decide and decree a thing, and it shall be established for you; and the light [of God's favor] shall shine upon your ways.

(Job 22:28)

The light had immediately begun shining when I spoke the decree. When you speak according to God's will, He actively watches over His Word to fulfill it in a divinely supernatural manner. (See Jeremiah 1:12.) In this situation, the light began to shine in accordance with the words I had written and spoken under the Spirit's guidance. Recognizing the importance of this decree, I knew I needed to send it to my friend and encourage him to recite it over himself daily, so I made a few minor adjustments to personalize it for him. He began speaking this decree three times a day, declaring life and health into his situation with spiritual authority and power, and, as he did so, he started to experience the touch of God's healing light.

A HEALING DECREE TO SPEAK OVER YOURSELF

You might feel inspired to use this decree for yourself or to write a similar one that resonates and feels right for you. The important thing is to be guided by the Spirit, because when we align with Him, it truly works:

From the top of my head to the bottom of my feet, let there be light!
No shadow of sickness or disease can remain in me.
All darkness flees as the glory light invades my body.
I speak light to my body.
I speak light to my bones.
I speak light to my heart.
I speak light to every organ, muscle, nerve, blood cell, and blood vessel.
I speak light to my lungs.
I speak light to my liver and kidneys.
I speak light to my reproductive system.
Let there be light!
I speak light to my skin.
I speak light to my digestive tract.
I speak light to my soul.
Light fills my mind, will, and emotions.
Let there be light!
God's healing, miracle-working light prevails in me.

How do you feel as you speak these words and deeply receive them as a spiritual reality? Can you sense a healing heat on your forehead or on another specific part of your body? Again, sometimes God's light manifests as a slight electrical sensation moving across your fingertips or tingling down your spine. Maybe you're experiencing feelings of peace and comfort, like gentle waves. There can be many different expressions and manifestations of healing light.

Just take a moment before reading further and allow yourself to fully connect with both the decree and the effects of it.

You might consider reading this decree over yourself (or a loved one) again, focusing on God's light filling you completely. I've found it particularly powerful to place your hands on your heart and mind while speaking the decree. Alternatively, you may feel led to place your hand on a specific body part that needs healing. This practice allows God's healing light to flow through both the decrees that you speak and your hands as you yield them to Him. *Let there be healing light!*

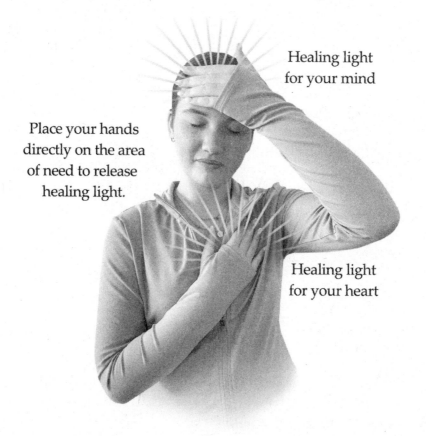

Healing light for your mind

Place your hands directly on the area of need to release healing light.

Healing light for your heart

It is crucial to take the time to recognize and become fully aware of how the Spirit is working in and through you, enabling you to benefit more effectively from His presence and power.

After I wrote the healing light decree and sent it to my friend, I did some further research on the Internet pertaining to disease. I discovered that many different cancers present themselves as dark shadows on a CT scan. One source said:

- Lung cancer may appear as a shadow, with or without a well-defined nodule or mass.
- Benign tumors may similarly appear as a shadow or a spot.
- Tuberculosis is a bacterial infection of the lungs that often has no discernible features on X-rays in early disease but can cause the appearance of a shadow.[17]

I thought this information was interesting because the Spirit had instructed me to speak light over my friend's body. I had been given supernatural insight on how to deal with the dark shadows of disease.

As has been famously stated, "Darkness cannot drive out darkness, only light can do that."[18] Through the light of God's glory, we are given a powerful spiritual warfare strategy to defeat the dark forces of sickness, disease, and infirmity. The key lies in the healing light. I continually envisioned my friend in the Spirit and persistently spoke light over his spirit, soul, and body.

This friend is still a miracle-in-the-making, as it has now been a two-year journey for him. He recently sent me this update:

The scans taken this time last year that showed active cancer in my bones from my skull to my legs now only shows four small spots of detectable cancer activity in the bones and none in my prostate, liver, bladder, or any soft tissue. The doctor's words were, "This is spectacular." Although I'm not as strong as I once was, I am gaining strength each week. Most people would not even know what I've been dealing with; I look and move strong. I literally soak in the declaration of light three times at night. It means so much to me.

---

17. Lynne Eldridge, M.D., "What Does It Mean to Have a Shadow on the Lung?" Verywell Health, December 4, 2023, https://www.verywellhealth.com/shadow-on-the-lung-meaning-and-causes-2248903.
18. "Quotations," Martin Luther King, Jr. Memorial, National Park Service, https://www.nps.gov/mlkm/learn/quotations.htm.

THE TOUCHPOINT OF OUR HANDS

In addition to spoken declarations and decrees, another way that we can transmit healing light is through the touchpoint of our hands. Above, I talked about how we can place our hands on our heart and mind while speaking the healing decree. The laying on of hands is one of the foundational practices of the Christian faith. (See, for example, Matthew 8:14–15; 9:18–19, 23–25; Acts 13:1–3; 2 Timothy 1:6; Hebrews 6:1–2.) The laying on of hands for healing is a powerful act that releases God's light to transfer from one individual to another.

HEALING HANDS OF LIGHT

Many times, while ministering to the sick, I've envisioned what this transfer looks like in a spiritual sense. When we lay our hands on sick people, it's as if divine light and power begin to flow, imparting God's healing grace. I want you to picture your hands becoming conduits of heavenly power, glowing with a radiant light that signifies the presence of the Holy Spirit. As you touch the afflicted areas, this light permeates the sick person's body, bathing their cells, tissues, and organs in a warm, restorative radiance.

Spiritually, a connection forms, linking our faith and the anointing of the Spirit to the individual's need for healing. The divine light flows from our hands, carrying with it the essence of God's love, mercy, and healing power. We can see this demonstrated in New Testament examples of the early believers, as shown through the Scriptures in the diagram below:

Mark 6:5
Mark 16:18
Luke 4:40
Acts 9:17–18
Acts 28:8

This powerful healing light not only targets the physical ailment but also often serves to heal emotional and spiritual wounds hidden beneath the surface.

Several years ago, I had the extraordinary privilege of being invited to minister in Reykjavik, Iceland. It was my first visit to this beautiful nation, and I was filled with anticipation, eager to see how the power of the Spirit would move among the people there. During one of our glory meetings, the atmosphere was charged with expectancy, and the Spirit began to impart very specific words of knowledge to me. One particular word stood out with compelling clarity: "Someone here has been committing self-harm. You've been cutting yourself because you hate yourself, but God wants you to know that He loves you, and you are deeply loved."

No sooner had I spoken these words than a young girl, visibly moved, stood up. With trembling hands, she lifted the sleeves of her long-sleeved shirt, exposing her arms, which bore the tragic evidence of her pain—cut marks and scars etched deeply into her skin. The congregation fell silent, absorbing the weight of the moment. It was clear that she had endured immense emotional pain, leading her to physically harm herself as a misguided attempt to numb the trauma. The Spirit's presence was palpable, a gentle yet powerful light shining on the darkness that had plagued her heart.

Feeling the Spirit's leading, I approached her gently and asked if I could pray for her. She nodded, her eyes filled with a mixture of hope and vulnerability. As I laid my hands on her, I commanded the light of healing and miracles to envelop her entire being. What transpired next was nothing short of miraculous. Before our very eyes, the scars and cuts on the young girl's arms began to vanish, as if a divine eraser were removing every trace of her suffering. The room was filled with awe and reverence as God's healing light manifested tangibly upon her body.

It was a powerful sign to everyone present. While we witnessed the physical healing with our eyes, we knew that God was also performing a profound and unseen work in her heart and soul. It was a divine supernatural moment that demonstrated the power of God's love, healing not just the surface wounds but mending the deepest parts of the young girl's being.

DIVINE RESTORATION

Psalm 147:3 reassures us that *"He heals the brokenhearted and binds up their wounds,"* highlighting God's compassion and tender care in addressing our deepest hurts. The Spirit's healing light penetrates the darkest pains, offering a balm for the soul and a remedy for the body. By inviting His light into our lives, we open ourselves to the divine healing that mends brokenness and restores damaged lives. This radiant healing not only alleviates immediate suffering but also brings a transformative peace, encouraging us to walk forward in wholeness and renewed strength.

You might visualize healing light as beams or waves, gently yet powerfully sweeping through the body, mending what is broken and restoring what has been lost. This holy light continually flows, sustained by our prayers and faith, until the healing is complete. There are times when we will lay our hands upon someone for only a few moments, and the power is released to work quickly. At other times, as we lay our hands upon the sick, the Spirit will lead us to linger for a while, gently allowing the recipient to receive wave after wave of healing light as they soak in this power that is changing them gradually. Discerning the flow of light for each individual situation is key. We become vessels of God's miraculous power, channels through which His grace and light can effectuate healing, enabling His light to accomplish what medical interventions alone cannot—but this only happens as we cooperate with Him.

When the Bible says of believers that *"they will lay hands on the sick, and they will recover"* (Mark 16:18 NKJV), that's because our hands are the hands of God on the earth. God's hands are healing hands, and yours are, too. The Scriptures give us a picture of an explosion of powerful light shooting from God's hands, at His command:

> *He covers His hands with the lightning and commands it to strike the mark.* (Job 36:32)

I can prophetically feel the power of the Spirit swirling within my core (what the Scriptures call our innermost being) as bright, warm, golden light. And from that place deep within, I give permission for the power of the Spirit—His healing anointing—to flow up to my shoulders and down through my arms, with His brilliant beams of light finally being released through the palms of my hands. Sometimes it feels like gentle heat or pulsating electricity flowing through my palms, while, at other times, it feels like lightning bolts are being released. At times it is so powerful that it shocks me!

At God's direction, we should command healing and expect the light to flow out of our hands like a lightning bolt that strikes the mark and causes all sickness, disease, and pain to leave! Again, the hands of believers are healing hands because they are filled with healing light. When laying hands on the sick, it is necessary to do so with faith, trusting in the Holy Spirit's ability to work through you. This act releases His healing light, flowing through your hands into the recipient.

AGREEMENT WITH OTHER LIGHT WARRIORS

A third way of bringing healing is to join with other light warriors in prayer and agreement. Again, if your hands are God's hands on the earth, then you can be assured that, through the Spirit who lives inside you, an explosion of powerful light flows from your hands too! And, spiritually speaking, you can raise the degree of light and power by being around other light warriors who know they carry the light, too.

Have you ever paused to consider the function of a simple light bulb? It's a common device, yet it illuminates our world in profound ways. In the United States, most incandescent light bulbs have now been phased out. The brightness of an incandescent bulb was generally determined by its wattage—the higher the wattage, the more radiant the light. Today's version of the light bulb is often an energy-efficient LED light that uses less wattage to create luminosity, so the unit of measurement we use to indicate the degree of brightness is the lumen. Yet, whether in an incandescent or LED form, the light bulb holds a powerful spiritual lesson for us as believers, one that can transform our understanding of healing prayer and the power of joining together with others in faith.

In the Bible, we find this fascinating instruction in the book of James: *"Is anyone among you sick? He should call in the church elders (the spiritual guides). And they should pray over him, anointing him with oil in the Lord's name"* (James 5:14). At first glance, this might seem like a very straightforward practice, but there's a deeper spiritual principle at work here—one that mirrors the concept of wattage (power) or brightness (lumens) in light bulbs.

Each believer carries within them a measure of the Spirit's anointing, a spiritual "wattage," if you will. When we pray individually, we shine with the light of our personal faith. But something extraordinary happens when we come together in prayer with others, uniting our hearts and extending our hands for healing.

Imagine a room filled with light bulbs. Each bulb contributes its individual light, but, together, they create a brilliance that far surpasses what any single bulb could achieve. In the same way, when we come together as anointed Spirit-filled believers, our individual "wattages" or "lumens" combine to produce a spiritual luminescence that can drive back darkness, bring healing, and manifest God's glory in remarkable ways.

As each believer lays their hands upon a sick individual, they add their "spiritual energy" to the equation. It's as if we're combining our individual wattages, creating a brighter, more powerful spiritual light. The collective prayer isn't just *additive* in its impact—it's *exponential*.

This supernatural principle of spiritual amplification is beautifully illustrated in another biblical verse: *"How could one man chase a thousand, or two put ten thousand to flight...?"* (Deuteronomy 32:30 NIV). Notice the math here—it's not just a doubling from one to two but an increase of tenfold! This illustrates again the miraculous multiplication that occurs when believers unite in faith and purpose.

The laying on of hands for healing is more than a symbolic gesture—it's a natural application of this supernatural principle. I believe that as more hands are laid on a person in need of healing, there's a greater flow of spiritual power. It's like creating a spiritual circuit, where the energy of the anointing flows more freely and powerfully.

An understanding of this should challenge us to rethink our approach to ministry. Sometimes we might feel that our individual prayers are insufficient, that our faith is too small to make a difference. But when we recognize the power of unity, we realize that every prayer, every act of faith, contributes to a greater flow. We need each other!

Many seasoned believers laying their hands together on the sick... so that healing power can flow.

James 5:14

This concept can also be likened to the concentrated power of a laser beam used in surgeries. Just as a laser focuses scattered light into a single, potent stream capable of cutting through tissue with precision and power, the act of multiple believers laying their hands on a sick individual focuses their collective faith and anointing into a unified, powerful force for healing.

I've discovered that this intense, concentrated spiritual energy brings about more effective and profound healing. Many times, as I'm ministering from the platform, the Spirit will give me a specific word of knowledge for releasing healing to an individual in the meeting. From the platform, I will speak the word, and this releases light from my voice, but I will also often call upon other believers in that meeting to gather around the individual to lay their hands on them, releasing healing light, and this is often the key to unlocking greater miracles. The principle is this: as you increase the anointing, you increase the healing light!

A TUNNEL OF LIGHT

Another way that I've enjoyed ministering healing light over the years is through what Janet and I have termed a "fire tunnel" or "glory tunnel"—but we may even want to consider calling it a "tunnel of light." It's an easy concept: I'll ask several ministers to form two lines in which they are facing each other by a distance of a few feet, in order to create a prayer tunnel through which people in need can walk and receive an impartation for healing and other spiritual blessings. This practice is deeply powerful.

Each minister, standing as a pillar of light, brings their unique miracle anointing to this healing tunnel. As a sick individual walks through the tunnel, they aren't just passing through a physical space but are enveloped in a profound spiritual experience. This journey through the tunnel of light is a form of "light therapy" in a prophetic sense. The combined prayer of faith and anointing of these ministers releases an intense concentration of divine healing spiritual power. As the person moves through the tunnel, they receive a continuous infusion of this spiritual light, which, as we have seen, can bring about significant healing, restoration, and renewal.

Many people have shared testimonies with me about the healing of cancers; the resolution of infertility issues; and the curing of necks, backs, hips, knees, and digestive problems after passing through a tunnel of light. Anything is possible in the realm of God, and, as light warriors, we're called to release that realm as we release the light!

This understanding of healing light should revolutionize how we view our corporate prayer gatherings and times of ministry. Again, each person who joins in cooperation isn't just adding another voice or another hand; they're actually amplifying the spiritual power present by becoming a conduit for the healing light to flow in greater capacity. It's a reminder of the importance of our showing up, of being present, of surrendering to the Spirit and being willing to be part of the *"greater works"* (John 14:12, various translations) that Jesus said those who believe in Him would do. I really love team ministry because it powerfully increases the impact of the anointing.

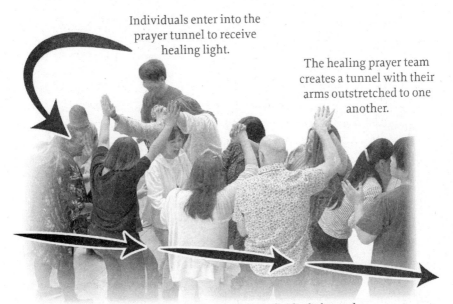

Individuals enter into the prayer tunnel to receive healing light.

The healing prayer team creates a tunnel with their arms outstretched to one another.

It is not necessary to lay hands on individuals, but rather to create an atmosphere for healing light to flow.

HEALING FROM A DISTANCE

One of the remarkable aspects of Jesus's ministry example for us was His ability to heal from a distance, demonstrating the divine reach of His healing light. In the account found in Matthew 8:5–13, the Roman centurion approached Jesus and asked Him to heal his servant, who was suffering terribly. The centurion expressed his faith in Jesus's authority by saying, *"Just say the word, and my servant will be healed"* (verse 8 NASB, NIV). Jesus marveled at this faith and responded with words of healing light, stating, *"Go; it shall be done for you as you have believed"* (verse 13 NASB). At that very moment, the servant was healed, even though Jesus did not physically touch him or visit his location. This incident illustrates the profound power carried in Jesus's words, which transcended physical boundaries to bring about miraculous healing.

Janet and I have witnessed the same type of thing happen many times as we have ministered through our weekly online Glory Bible Study. As we've sat in front of the camera praying for and declaring healing, the power of God's light has reached viewers all over the world, bringing them a healing touch.

A DIVINE CONNECTOR

Thus, the light of God's glory becomes a divine connector. In the light, an unbroken flow of healing can be transmitted across great distances. Just like television or telephone frequencies that are sent from one tower to another through the airwaves, we connect with others who need healing by transmitting "healing frequencies" from the glory realm. As I was in prayer concerning these things, the Spirit reminded me of the following Scripture, which speaks of the spiritual connection we can achieve (regardless of distance) when we walk together with other believers in the light:

> *But if we [really] are living and walking in the Light, as He [Himself] is in the Light, we have [true, unbroken] fellowship with one another, and the blood of Jesus Christ His Son cleanses (removes) us from all sin and guilt [keeps us cleansed from sin in all its forms and manifestations].*
> (1 John 1:7)

When God's Word is in our mouths, we become powerful instruments of His will, able to speak life, truth, and healing light into situations that are beyond our natural reach. Scripture affirms this idea in Isaiah 55:11 (NIV), where God declares, "*So is my word that goes out from my mouth: It will not return to me empty, but will accomplish what I desire and achieve the purpose for which I sent it.*" By internalizing and speaking God's Word, we echo His divine intentions, ensuring that His promises and purposes are brought to fruition. When we carry God's Word in our mouth—a light sword in the Spirit—we wield a divine authority capable of transforming realities and bringing about God's kingdom on earth.

Jesus's longest (and possibly greatest) prayer recorded in the Scriptures is found in John 17. To sum it up in a few short words, this was His prayer: "*That they may be one [even] as We are one*" (verse 22). We often think about this statement in terms of unity: brothers and sisters in Christ walking together for the common good of our ministries, communities, regions, and nations. But I want you to think about it also in terms of long-distance healing. If we recognize that we are first connected to the Source of all life (through a personal relationship with Jesus Christ), and that we are also spiritually connected to one another as believers, why wouldn't it be reasonable to think that we would be able to minister to each other beyond space and distance?

As I've already mentioned, many times, when I'm preparing to pray for someone in altar ministry after a preaching session or in another one-on-one capacity, I visualize the power of the Spirit rising up from within me. In my spirit, to build my faith in God's ability to heal in that moment, I've learned to capture a vision of a golden shining power flooding my innermost being and flowing up into my shoulders and down my arms and then emerging from the palms of my hands as impartation power. I believe that you, too, have this holy light flowing through you by the power of the Spirit. This light carries the ability to release healing and change the world.

When I see this holy light in my spirit, it looks like a brilliant golden color. But, as I have taught these principles to students all over the world, some students have shared with me that sometimes they see it as a bright white light or a purplish-blue light, or even as a burning fire. The important thing is for you to capture a vision of this power in your mind. I want you to not only see it but to feel it too.

I know—we don't walk by feelings; we're people of faith. But there are times when God will have us stretch our faith by trusting Him to reveal Himself to us in a physical way. That's what I'm talking about right now. I want you to trust the Spirit to reveal Himself to you in such a way that you would *feel* the light flowing through you and out of you. This is not something that can be manufactured, and that is why I say we need to trust the Spirit to reveal it to us. Yet whether we feel anything or not, we can have faith that His power will work through us.

HOW TO RELEASE HEALING LIGHT FROM A DISTANCE

To prepare yourself to release healing light from a distance, it is important to have a recognizable destination. This might seem like an obvious step, but you wouldn't want to spend time praying and releasing the light while not knowing exactly what you were doing it for. That would be pointless. So, follow these simple steps as you practice this spiritual exercise:

1. Pray and seek the Spirit regarding the person (and their situation) to whom you will minister this healing light.

2. Take time to set an atmosphere for the light to fill you and your surroundings. You will know this has been accomplished when you sense God's peace and His loving presence.

3. Shut your eyes and, by faith, begin to visualize (in your mind and spirit) the healing light flooding your innermost being and then exploding throughout your whole body, especially flowing up into your shoulders, down your arms, and out of the palms of your hands.

4. Position your hands outward to release the light to your ministry subject. You will be releasing this light from a distance, which means that you may or may not see the person in a vision, but you may feel the healing light flowing from your hands toward your subject. Let the light flow, and don't rush this experience.

5. You may want to speak into the light as you release it, using decrees from this book or ones that you have personally received from the Spirit.

6. Once you feel that your time of ministry has concluded, offer a prayer of gratitude to the Lord.

7. The final step will be contacting your ministry subject (using discretion, depending on the nature of the prayer and your relationship with the person) and asking them what they may have felt, seen, or experienced, or what miracle they may have received from this time of healing at a distance. Don't be surprised if some of the first manifestations are spiritual or emotional in nature. Many times, the Spirit needs to remove these blockages before He is able to release the fullness of healing on a physical level.

One day, when Janet and I were at our home in Palm Springs, California, our friends Joe and Bella Garcia, pastors from Canada, contacted us. They had taken their son, Joel, to see a doctor because he hadn't been feeling well, and he had then been rushed to the emergency room because he was found to be suffering from pericarditis, which is a swelling and irritation of the thin, saclike tissue around the heart. This condition can be dangerous and even life-threatening if left untreated. Doctors ordered blood tests, an EKG, X-rays, and an ultrasound for Joel.

When we received this message, we immediately began directing God's healing light to Joel's heart through prayer. As I prayed, I felt led to send him one of our soaking music tracks entitled "Healing Is Here." I sent it by text, and when Joel received it, he immediately put his headphones on, shut his eyes, and focused on the words and music being conveyed through the audio. He later told us that when he began listening to the track, he was instantly caught up into a vision.

In this vision, at first, everything was completely dark. Then, Joel suddenly noticed a doorway opening in front of him and a light shining into the darkness. He walked toward the door and was able to step through it. When he did this, the light was so bright that it completely consumed him. At that very moment, all pain instantly left his body, and he began to feel much better.

Joel still underwent the tests at the hospital, and when the results came back, everything was clear, with no sign of pericarditis. He had received his healing in the light of God's glory that he had seen in that vision. Something powerful begins to happen when we give ourselves permission to soak in the healing light of God's presence.

GOD'S LIGHT BRINGS WHOLENESS

This chapter is entitled "Releasing Healing Light," yet healing light applies not only to physical and emotional healing but also to our overall wellness and to what we might call "preventative healthcare" to help us achieve wholeness in body, mind, and spirit. I would like to share one area in this regard that Janet and I have discovered. We know that exposure to natural light helps regulate the body's internal clock, known as the circadian rhythm. A properly regulated circadian rhythm promotes better rest, increased energy levels, and overall well-being. Similarly, the light of God's presence helps to establish a rhythm of restfulness that aligns with our natural circadian rhythms. This alignment can lead to an overall balance in our lives. Just as physical light influences our sleep-wake cycles, spiritual light helps align our inner being with God's divine order. Exposure to the light of God's Word and His presence has a powerful impact on both our emotional and spiritual well-being.

Our physical circadian rhythm can be affected by various factors, including a lack of exposure to light, not enough sleep—and jet lag. With our many travels, particularly internationally, we have had to deal with jet lag, and, in our personal journey to overcoming this condition, we have discovered a powerful practice: speaking and "commanding" light over our bodies to combat the disorientation that comes with crossing multiple time zones. As believers, we understand the significance of aligning our spirit with our physical being, and this practice harmoniously ties both of these areas together. We can speak light over the seven "body clocks" (circadian rhythms) that regulate various aspects of our physiology and behavior:

- Sleep
- Physical activity
- Eating
- Hormonal release
- Body temperature
- Digestion
- Immune system

These seven body clocks are controlled by a master clock in the brain—the hypothalamus—and many local clocks in the organs, tissues, and cells (see diagram on the next page). In speaking light to these areas, we address, in practical ways, the root cause of jet lag, which is often the misalignment of these internal rhythms. Many times, the reason people experience severe jet lag is that their various clocks are not synchronized, but through the power of speaking light, we can keep these clocks in balance, minimizing the adverse effects of travel.

When we travel by plane across time zones, one of the crucial first steps we have learned to take is to immediately adjust to the new time zone. It's essential to set our watches to the local time of our destination and to mentally commit to living in that time zone from the moment we land. We avoid looking at our "home" time zone, which helps us to psychologically and physically adapt to the new environment. This initial act of alignment sets the tone for the effectiveness of our spiritual practice. (You can apply the same principle to everyday life by working to maintain a consistent schedule and a regular pattern of sleep.)

Releasing Healing Light 119

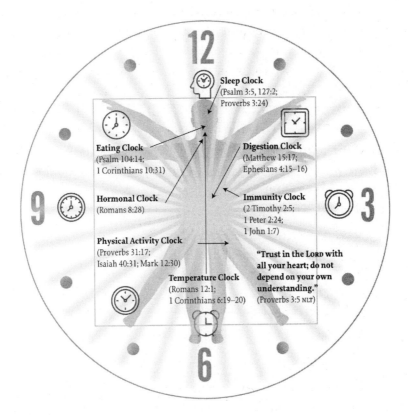

In conjunction with this, Janet and I partner with the Holy Spirit, commanding His light to permeate our body clocks. Again, when our internal systems operate on different schedules, our entire system becomes out of sync, causing discomfort such as fatigue. By speaking light and life to these clocks, we bring them into perfect alignment. We declare that each clock stays in harmony with the others and also with the new time zone, ensuring our overall well-being. This practice not only enhances physical health but also reinforces our spiritual connection and reliance on divine guidance for our complete well-being. Whether you are anticipating a trip through one or more time zones, or you generally feel that your internal rhythms may be out of sync, pray for God's light to bring your seven "body clocks" into alignment.

Healing light is for our body, mind, and spirit so that we may live in wholeness and vitality:

Beloved, I pray that you may prosper in every way and [that your body] may keep well, even as [I know] your soul keeps well and prospers.

(3 John 2)

YES, LET THERE BE LIGHT! CAN YOU FEEL THE SPIRIT'S POWER FLOWING THROUGH YOU AND CAUSING DARKNESS TO FLEE? YOU'RE WINNING THE SPIRITUAL WARFARE BATTLE BECAUSE YOU'RE A *LIGHT WARRIOR*.

CHAPTER 6

ACTIVATING ANGELS AND DISARMING DEMONS

"Are they [God's angels] not all ministering spirits sent forth to minister for those who will inherit salvation?"
—Hebrews 1:14 (NKJV)

"And these signs will follow those who believe: In My name they will cast out demons...."
—Mark 16:17 (NKJV)

In the spring of 2009, Janet and I traveled to Hong Kong. We had been invited to minister at the Grace and Glory Conference with our friends Pastors Rob and Glenda Rufus. We were there to join with hundreds of other spiritually hungry believers from all over Asia and other parts of the world. It was an honor to be invited, and I was extremely excited about teaching on the glory realm.

As our plane was preparing to land on Lantau Island, I looked out the window to view the lush green scenery and water that surrounded the area. In my spirit, I could feel God's pleasure toward Hong Kong and His desire to bless His people there. Deep within my heart, I knew that *He* ruled as King of Kings over this region of the earth and that He would have His way if we gave Him permission to move.

As I stood to speak at my first session of the conference, I felt compelled to share what had been revealed to my heart while I was landing in Hong Kong. When I told those in attendance that the Spirit had shown me the name of the ruling Spirit over Asia, I could see the intrigue on many people's faces; they were ready to receive this deeper revelation. In the past, some of them had been told that a red dragon ruled over the land and that a Leviathan-type serpent ruled in the sea, and many sincere intercessors had struggled greatly trying to combat these invisible forces by cursing their power.

I asked everyone to take out their notebooks and pens and to get ready to write down this profound revelation that had been disclosed to me while on the plane. With bated breath, almost everyone in the room was ready to hear what I was about to announce. Then I proceeded to reveal that the name of the ruling Spirit over Hong Kong and over the whole of Asia was none other than the Holy Spirit Himself.

This concept was an astonishment to many of those in attendance, but, following my proclamation, there came an eruption of excitement and spontaneous shouts of joy. Praise and celebration filled that room, for the truth had been revealed, and this light instantly exposed the deception of the enemy that he was supposedly in control there. The same truth about God being the Ruler over all can be said regarding every nation on earth. We can join with the angels in heaven, who declare:

> *To Him Who is seated on the throne and to the Lamb be ascribed the blessing and the honor and the majesty (glory, splendor) and the power (might and dominion) forever and ever (through the eternities of the eternities)!* (Revelation 5:13)

It is in only the context of God as Ruler and Christ's full victory through His death and resurrection that we can truly understand spiritual warfare and our participation in it, as well as the role of angels and the limitations of demons in spiritual warfare.

ARE ANGELS OF LIGHT GOOD OR BAD?

When addressing the topic of angels and demons, especially in a book dealing with the light, one of the first Scriptures that comes to my mind is 2 Corinthians 11:14:

Satan himself masquerades as an angel of light.

I'm positive that many people reading this book will wonder what we're supposed to do with this Scripture. Does it mean that all "angels of light" are possibly Satan in disguise? What is the implication and present-day warning for us? In writing to the Corinthian church, the apostle Paul was discussing the topic of false teachers. He was conveying to the early believers the foolishness of relying on outward images and natural appearances. The emphasis of this Scripture passage is on the importance of guarding ourselves against what is counterfeit. We can do this by using the God-given gift of the discerning of spirits. (See, for example, 1 Corinthians 12:10.)

It was with this background that Paul addressed the issue of Satan himself masquerading as an angel of light. The Scriptures wisely caution us to test the spirits. (See 1 John 4:1–3.) Some well-meaning believers have become so troubled by the possibility of evil spirits presenting themselves as angels that they have discarded the present-day ministry of angels altogether. This is tragic. Why? Because their rejection of angelic ministry comes from a spirit of fear (which is ultimately aligned with the enemy's deceptive intentions), and it directly contradicts the teachings of the Bible. God's Word teaches us that angels are so active in this present day that we may even entertain one of them without realizing it. (See Hebrews 13:2.)

We do not need to be afraid of operating in the Spirit realm and of working with angels. We can enter into this realm with confidence in the ability of Jesus's blood to protect us, His Word to guide us, and His light to open our eyes to see clearly. Yes, keen discernment is needed among the children of God now more than ever before. We can already see how the enemy has tried to capture this present-day culture with enticing entrapments that on the surface appear to be "virtuous" and filled with light, when, at their core, they are dark, self-serving deceptions. The gift of the discerning of spirits will help protect you, as a light warrior, from partnering with the work of the enemy. God's angels of light are active and ready to help you. Welcome them!

One sun-soaked afternoon in Palm Springs, I found myself at home for a brief one-day retreat between ministry trips. The warmth of the desert sun filled our house, so I decided that it was the perfect time to take my daughter Legacy for a refreshing swim in our pool. We had been discussing some of the recent life transitions that our family was going through and praying for God's help with all the changes. Legacy had been dealing with some feelings of sadness about moving from one city back to another and having to leave her friends and familiar surroundings. I thought some time in the pool would provide us with more opportunity to talk, while also giving us some exercise, and she was excited to spend this time with me.

Legacy ran ahead of me out the door and down the steps, and suddenly I heard her yell, "There's an angel outside of our house! I just saw an angel." It all happened quickly and without warning. In a heartbeat, Legacy rushed back up the steps toward me, and I immediately pulled out my phone and asked her to share what she had just seen while I recorded it. Legacy described her brief yet powerful encounter by saying that the angel was standing at the bottom of the steps and appeared to be the size of an average person. This angel was wearing a luminescent white robe, and, although transparent, they radiated light, and they had sparkles in their shoulder-length hair.

Legacy had quickly turned toward the house to see if I was coming outside, but when she turned back to see the angel again, it had vanished. That is when she shouted out to me. We continued walking down toward the pool, and Legacy looked at me and said, "Dad, I think God sent that angel so we could know that He's answering the prayers for those things we just talked about." That moment was so precious and powerful. An angel of light was delivering a message of encouragement to us.

HOW TO PROPERLY DISCERN ANGELS OF LIGHT

When it comes to interacting with angels of light, it is especially important to begin with a biblical perspective for operating in the spiritual realm. As

I wrote in my book *Power Portals*, people who follow false spiritual teachings attempt to gain access into the supernatural realm by their own merit and through mystical means that have nothing to do with Jesus. This practice is spiritually illegal and always results in tragedy. Jesus said that there is only one way into the divine supernatural, and that is through the portal of God's glory. So, as we test the spirits, we must also examine our own hearts, motivations, and methods.

In learning to discern all things in the Spirit realm, I've developed a test that I call "The 3-R's Test," which highlights these questions: (1) What is the revelation? (2) What is being recognized? (3) What are the results? This is a scripturally safe way to discern whether an angelic encounter is true or false. I would encourage you to use this simple yet profound guide when spiritually navigating this realm.

1. WHAT IS THE REVELATION?

If an encounter contradicts the revelation of the Word of God, stay clear of it. God will never go against His Word. Everything that holy angels of light communicate will fall perfectly in line and be totally consistent with God's Word. All of our spiritual experiences must be grounded in the Scriptures. (See Isaiah 55:11; Matthew 24:35; John 17:17.) What this means is that although we may have new and wonderful encounters with angels, they are always God's messengers who bring words in accordance with Scripture.

2. WHAT IS BEING RECOGNIZED?

Next, ask yourself this question: "What is being recognized through this spiritual encounter?" Are your eyes being directed toward the angel? Or is the angel directing your attention toward Jesus and the fulfillment of His plans for your life? Jesus Christ must be glorified through every authentic spiritual experience. (See, for example, 1 Corinthians 1:3.) I've noticed that true angels of light reflect the glory of God's presence, and this brings honor to Him. They carry His light. They emanate His glory, not a glory of their own. When I see the angels of heaven, it draws me to worship Jesus and to posture myself at His feet. If the encounter serves to elevate Jesus Christ as Lord over all, pay attention. However, if the experience lowers Jesus Christ from His position in the

Godhead—or puffs up you or the angel—stay clear of it. (See, for example, John 1:1; Romans 16:27.)

3. WHAT ARE THE RESULTS?

What is the resulting fruit from an angelic interaction? The Bible clearly tells us that good trees produce good fruit. This imagery represents anything that is spiritually grown in our lives. The "fruit" of your encounter will reveal the "tree" from which it came. (See Matthew 7:17–20; 12:33.) True angels of light produce good fruit because they do not speak for themselves. Once again, they are heavenly messengers that carry God's words to His people. In turn, this produces the good fruit of the Spirit that we read about in Galatians 5:22–23.

Let's pray for an increased awareness that will enable us to connect with these ministering spirits. As light warriors, we can welcome heaven's host of angels to be stationed around us and to move ahead of us as they battle for us against the realm of darkness. We can pray in this way:

> Heavenly Father, I thank You for the mighty angelic warriors You have stationed in my home, in my place of business, and everywhere I go. I thank You for surrounding my life with Your powerful angels of protection, deliverance, and comfort. Open my spiritual eyes to discern the movements of Your angelic hosts as they execute their assignments in my life. I trust that their vigilant presence is encamped around me. I declare that Your angels of healing and abundant provision are actively engaged in fierce battles to bring forth a greater harvest in every area of my life where there has been lack and despair. I trust in Your divine strategy to dispatch angels of divine love to fortify and protect my relationships. Heighten my awareness of angels on extraordinary assignments in my life. I am grateful for their unwavering support. Thank You also for encompassing me with Your vigilant angels who watch over my church, city, and nation.
>
> With Your Word firmly hidden in my heart, as it says in Psalm 119:11, I speak Your truth boldly, knowing that the angels will respond and minister at Your command. I will forever praise You and give You all the glory. May Jesus be magnified in my life forevermore. Amen!

SUPERNATURAL LIGHT BEINGS

All around the world, people are having encounters with angels of light. Several years ago, I was ministering at a conference in Keuruu, Finland, and I shared some of my testimonies about seeing angels. One of my hosts became very excited about this topic because he had recently seen an unusual photo that had been taken in one of the old wooden cathedrals in Helsinki. It was obvious that he had been personally impacted by it, and he wanted to know what I thought about it.

He pulled out his phone and showed me the photo. In it, you could clearly see at least six, possibly seven, glowing white pillars of light gathered around the altar area. They were approximately seven feet in height, and although they resembled human forms and were wearing bright robes, they were clearly materializing in a supernatural way. Behind them hung a beautiful painting of Jesus Christ, who was positioned in the center of their appearance. The scene was very holy and reminded me of these words of John: *"I saw the seven angels who stand before God"* (Revelation 8:2).

The photo greatly intrigued me, and it seemed to impact others who saw it with a godly sense of awe. Things like this seem to be happening more and more as people are awakening to the light of God's glory. I wonder: is the Spirit allowing us to see these things so that we will understand the access we have to the angelic realm as light warriors?

God's angels are light beings because they are filled with His brilliance, and they are light bearers because they carry His truth, His honor, and His glory. The angels do not move at their own discretion. Instead, they patiently wait for divine instructions from the voice of God. (See Psalm 103:20.) As light warriors, we carry God's voice, and we have been given authority to command angels and activate them on divine assignment, according to heavenly instruction. The amazing thing about it is this: I believe that once angels receive their assignments, they move at the speed of light! Do you know how fast that is? According to scientists at NASA, "light travels at a constant, finite speed of 186,000 mi/sec." That means that an angel traveling at the speed of light could "circumnavigate the equator approximately 7.5 times in one second."[19] That's

---

19. "How 'Fast' Is The Speed of Light?" NASA Glenn Research Center, https://www.grc.nasa.gov/www/k-12/Numbers/Math/Mathematical_Thinking/how_fast_is_the_speed.

really fast! Angels are able to deliver the answers to our prayers in an accelerated way, and this is one of the benefits of moving in God's light.

ANGELS HELP TO BRING PROTECTION

Angels also help to protect us from danger. One winter, while Janet and I were living in Birmingham, Alabama, we met our son, Lincoln, in Nashville, Tennessee, to celebrate his birthday. Lincoln had driven up to Nashville from Birmingham earlier that day with his friend Jonathan because they wanted to watch a Tennessee Titans football game before meeting us at a steakhouse for dinner. When we connected that evening, we all had a wonderful celebration. Although Janet and I planned to stay the night at a hotel in Nashville, Lincoln had to drive Jonathan back to Birmingham that evening so that his friend could catch an early flight the next morning. So, we said goodbye to them, and they drove off.

Once they got on I-65 to head south, they began noticing that it was snowing quite a bit; the further they drove, the more snow seemed to be coming down. By the time they approached the Alabama state line, the visibility on the road was extremely low. The few cars that were still driving on the interstate had their flashers on. All of a sudden, Lincoln hit a patch of ice, and the car started spinning! It looked like they were going to hit the center median, but then the car went flying across the road to the other side, and it seemed like they would end up in a ditch. In a moment of desperation, Lincoln's heart released a prayer to God, and the car suddenly came to a halting stop—perfectly placed on the off-ramp exit. It was unexplainable! Lincoln called me on the phone and said, "Dad, this could only be God! My angels protected us. We almost got into a terrible accident; my car could've been wrecked, but we were saved."

I believe that God sent His angels to watch over our son, and He has angels to watch over your loved ones, too. We must be willing to learn about this and to teach our family members, including our children, how to engage with the angels that God has assigned to our lives. Our son, Lincoln, has grown up being taught these principles, and he has learned how to lean into the divine supernatural realm and call on God's angels when necessary.

Recently, I was leading a ministry team in Japan and had an unforgettable experience that really underscored the power of divine intervention.

We had traveled to Osaka and decided to visit the Osaka Castle on a prayer pilgrimage, anointing the gates around the property and releasing prophetic words that the Spirit had given us for the nation. However, an unexpected emergency arose (which was resolved by that evening), and I had to leave the group while they climbed to the top of the castle for a breathtaking scenic view. I entrusted my wife, Janet, with leading the group that day, even though, despite her multiple visits to Japan, this was her first time in Osaka.

The next stop on their itinerary was the Dotonbori area, a bustling and scenic part of the city, but Janet was unsure of how to navigate the subway system to get there. Undaunted, she decided to ask a bystander for directions as she walked down the path toward the main road. Fortunately, she found someone who not only spoke English but was also exceptionally kind and helpful. This stranger didn't just provide directions; he graciously walked the entire group all the way to the subway station, about a mile and a half, ensuring that they got there without any trouble. His kindness and patience were extraordinary, and he went above and beyond to assist them.

Later that evening, back at the hotel, the team shared this story with me. One of the team members posed an intriguing question: "Do you think he may have been an angel?" Reflecting on their account, I couldn't say for certain, but the thought was compelling. According to Scripture, we know that angels, appearing as everyday people, are sent on divine assignments to help us in times of need. This experience reminded me that angels of light can look just like you and me, and they often show up in the most unexpected ways to guide and comfort us on our journeys. They help us to move forward as they shine light into whatever situations we may face.

ANGELS HELP BRING ABUNDANCE

A few years ago, Lincoln moved out of our home to study at Oral Roberts University in Tulsa, Oklahoma, and, one day, he told me that he needed some money. I asked him how much he needed, and he said, "Dad, I need ten thousand dollars." I said, "Okay, it's no problem. I'm going to teach you something that I learned from Kenneth E. Hagin's teachings, and it works. If you really need that money, God really has it available for you, but you'll need to put your angels on the job. You must direct them to do it." So, I taught Lincoln this decree by asking him to repeat it after me:

In the name of Jesus, I claim ten thousand dollars. Satan, take your hands off my money. Ministering spirits, go and get it and bring it to me.

Lincoln said that decree out loud, and he really believed it in his heart. Over the next few weeks, I spoke with him a few times, and, each time, I asked him, "Did you get the money yet?" Each time, he responded, "Not yet." I encouraged him by telling him to keep directing the angels to do their job. Often, they'll respond in such an unusual way that you could never have seen it coming—and that's exactly the way it happened for my son. Within two months' time, the money came to him supernaturally, and he rejoiced in the faithfulness of God! I got excited, too. It's wonderful to see your children walking in the light of revelation. Again, I am comforted by knowing that Lincoln's angels travel with him wherever he goes, and that he knows how to properly discern them and utilize their assistance.

BECOMING SENSITIVE TO ANGELIC PRESENCE

As light warriors, we need to learn to become sensitive to angelic presences in our lives. God's holy angels, filled with spiritual light, require spiritual alertness to discern and perceive them. Marsha, from Irondale, Alabama, shared a story with me about how, as a Southern Baptist, she used to see flickers of light flashing around her living room. At the time, she hadn't received any biblical guidance regarding angels, although she believed they existed. Without any understanding of the ways in which angels might appear, she was dumbfounded by this "light activity" that was often taking place in her home. She somehow sensed that it was spiritual in a positive sense, but, otherwise, she was unsure of what to make of it.

Later on, as this woman ventured into deeper spiritual truth and received the baptism of the Holy Spirit, she was in a position to receive further revelation concerning God's angels. She was elated to realize that angels had been moving in her life long before she even knew what to do with them! Now, she's aware of these angels and is ready to work with them for God's kingdom purposes.

When Janet and I first lived in Palm Springs, California, we had a very friendly next-door neighbor named Phyllis who loved to bring her little dog,

Fluffy, to our home for visits. Phyllis was a kind-hearted woman with a desire for genuine connection, and her visits always brightened our day. One interesting aspect of these visits was Fluffy's unusual sensitivity to the spiritual atmosphere in our house. Phyllis, who was not a believer at the time, noticed that Fluffy could discern something very different in our home. Whenever we would begin to testify about Jesus, angels, and other spiritual matters, the atmosphere intensified, and Fluffy's behavior would change from excitable and energetic to calm and attentive. Initially, this behavior puzzled Phyllis, but it didn't take long for her to accept that the supernatural realm was very real, witnessed through her own beloved pet.

Whenever Fluffy wasn't feeling well, Phyllis would knock on our door and earnestly ask us to perform "hands-on healing" to release healing light over Fluffy. Miraculously, it always worked. Fluffy's obvious relief after each prayer was a testimony to God's boundless love for all of His creation, including animals. After all, He created them and gave them unique sensitivities to His presence.

Many years later, our family decided to adopt a little puppy of our own, and our daughter Liberty lovingly named her Buttercup. This sweet dog has been a tremendous blessing to our family in countless ways. Much like Fluffy, Buttercup has demonstrated a heightened sensitivity to the spiritual realm that permeates our home. At various moments, her behavior has alerted us to the presence of angels or other spiritual movements, prompting us to become more spiritually attuned ourselves. While this might seem strange to some people, these phenomena are scripturally grounded.

Consider the biblical story of Balaam and the speaking donkey. If Balaam had been more aware of the spiritual realm, he might have directly recognized the angel positioned in front of him with a drawn sword rather than learning about it through his donkey. The donkey saw the angel when Balaam could not, highlighting how God's creatures can perceive spiritual realities that we sometimes miss. (See Numbers 22:22–31.)

I've found such spiritual sensitivity in animals to be the case not only in my own experience, but also in the experience of many others who have reported similar instances with their pets. In his book *Angels on Assignment,*

Pastor Roland Buck shared several stories about how his dog, Queenie, would interact with angels during their visits to his home.[20]

These occurrences challenge us to become more fully aware of the spiritual realm around us.

SEEING ANGELS OF LIGHT

Many believers have seen angels that appear to carry the light and fire of God. I often see angels in silhouette form—light beings without initial detailed definition. Despite this incomplete vision, I have learned to act based on what I can discern. When I do so, more details are usually revealed, steadily enhancing my spiritual perception.

There are other ways in which angels might appear. They may be seen as beams or orbs of light, dancing in our peripheral vision, moving with an ethereal grace that signals their divine origin. In some cases, angels might appear as intense, blinding flashes that momentarily bathe our surroundings in heavenly light, leaving an unmistakable imprint of holiness. Or, they may manifest as shimmering figures, where their entire being seems to be made up of pure, glistening light that fluctuates like a gentle, heavenly breeze.

These varied manifestations can occur during moments in which we are in deep prayer or meditation or during intense spiritual experiences, often accompanied by a profound sense of peace, awe, and divine connection. I firmly believe that everyone has the capacity to develop this kind of spiritual sensitivity through active faith and practice.

ACTIVATING ANGELS

With this background on angels, we will now look more closely at their role in spiritual warfare and how to participate with them. God has angels surrounding your life right now, and you need only to open your spiritual eyes to perceive this manifestation of the Lord's presence.

The very first step toward dispatching angels in spiritual warfare is knowing that these warrior angels are ready, willing, and well able to fight any

---

20. Roland Buck, *Angels on Assignment* (New Kensington, PA: Whitaker House, 2019), 19–20, 44, 73.

battle against the forces of darkness that are attempting to obstruct you from living in the full blessing that Christ has paid for by His victorious blood. The Scriptures make it very clear that God's angels are *"ministering spirits sent forth to minister for ["accompany, protect"* AMP)] *those who will inherit salvation"* (Hebrews 1:14 NKJV). Knowing that these angels have been assigned to you as an heir of salvation should push back any fear that the enemy may try to bring against you. In the biblical account where the king of ancient Syria was attacking the Israelites and surrounded the city where the prophet Elisha was living, Elisha said to his servant, *"Do not be afraid, for those who are with us are more than those who are with them"* (2 Kings 6:16 AMP).

WORKING WITH WARRIOR ANGELS OF LIGHT

Recently, while I was ministering at a church in Los Angeles, I looked out toward the left-hand side of the congregation and saw a large angel, about fifteen feet tall, standing halfway down the aisle. At first, all I could see was a fine outline of his figure, but, as I continued to look (and speak about it at the same time), the details became much clearer. By all appearances, he was a warrior angel. In his left hand, he was holding a shield that looked about five feet in height, and, in his right hand, he was holding a large sword.

As I began to pray in the Spirit to receive further revelation about the angelic vision I was seeing, I heard in my spirit, "The Lord is your Defender, the Lord is your Defender, the Lord is your Defender." Through this prophetic encounter, additional understanding began to unfold. I saw that this angel was just a symbol of a battalion of warrior angels that had been assigned to that church to battle in spiritual warfare, and I therefore publicly gave him permission to move. In that meeting, God was calling us out of the stress of battle and into the rest of abiding in the victory.

You, too, have been called out of darkness into the glorious light of God's kingdom. (See 1 Peter 2:9.) There are many angels of light moving on warfare assignments so that you can live in the blessings of God. One way in which we can work with the holy angels on assignment is by following the instructions below. Take note of the specific details:

1. *Recognize the presence of angels in your midst.* What do you see, hear, feel, or sense? Where are they specifically located? (Sometimes you will have spiritual discernment about their position or movement.) What are they currently

doing; what is the spiritual activity that's taking place (for example, delivering a specific message, ministering healing, bringing protection)?

2. *Begin to audibly describe what you are seeing in the spiritual realm.* For instance, if you're with a group of people, you can say, "I see an angel standing right there. He's reaching his hand out toward you." Just describe exactly what you see. Don't feel any pressure to exaggerate or add extra details. As you speak, more details may come. If they do, continue sharing what you see. If you're alone and see an angel, it's still important to speak out and describe what you're seeing. Why? Because this will help you capture and remember the moment. If you're alone, you could say something like, "I can see you. I can see the outline of your head, neck, and shoulders. I'm glad that you're here. Is there anything else that I should know about you?"

3. *Ask the angel why they have been sent.* This will help you to understand how you should interact with them. If you don't hear an audible or inward response to your question, you may want to continue to look in the Spirit to see if you notice any particular details that could be a clue as to their intended ministry assignment. For example, if they are holding a sword, that's a good indication that they are a warrior angel ready to fight on your behalf. If they are holding a shield, they have possibly come to defend you from an enemy attack. You may also want to consider the colors of light that fill or surround them. These can also be indicators of the supernatural duties they have been sent to accomplish.

4. *Use your authority in Christ to speak to and dispatch your angels to perform their ministry.* This is an often-forgotten aspect of working with angels. Remember, according to the Scriptures, angels move according to the spoken words of God. (See Psalm 103:20.) As a believer, you carry God's voice and have been granted spiritual permission to activate angels on divine assignment.

TRUSTING IN THE LORD OF HOSTS

It's important to remember that Jesus Christ is the Commander of the Lord's Army. We must open our spiritual eyes to see this reality! During the conflict with the king of Syria, Elisha prayed concerning his frightened servant, *"'Lord, please, open his eyes that he may see.' And the Lord opened the servant's eyes and he saw; and behold, the mountain was full of horses and chariots of fire surrounding Elisha"* (2 Kings 6:17 AMP).

One of God's names is Jehovah-Tsaba, which means "Lord of Hosts." The Hebrew word *tsaba* can be translated into English as *hosts*; other meanings include "that which goes forth, army, war, warfare."[21] Jesus, as the Lord of Hosts, reigns and rules over the angel armies that fight in the Spirit realm. When we focus on Jesus, we gain a vision of His glorious victory. From this position of clarity, we can confidently begin praying and thanking God for dispatching His armies of angels to fight our battles. We can also trust that God will give us the right words to speak to activate this angelic assistance.

It's also important for us to pay close attention to the movement of angels around us. Sometimes this movement might be overt, while, at other times, it might be subtle. Spiritually tune in and allow your spirit to connect with the Spirit of God. Be watchful everywhere you go. There is no doubt in my mind that, as you do this, you will begin to recognize God's angels around you. Once you become aware of them, it's your God-given responsibility to activate them into service. This is part of what it means to release the light.

Additionally, many times, I have become spiritually aware of angels after spending time in prayer. Angels of light are attracted to the prayers of God's people. (See, for example, Acts 12:5–7.)

Are you willing and ready to direct angels using the name of Jesus? Exercise discernment, as outlined in this chapter, and then just do it, watching for the signs and atmospheric shifts that follow. I believe that God is telling us today the very same thing that He told Moses so long ago: *"Now then go, and I, even I, will be with your mouth, and will teach you what you shall say"* (Exodus 4:12 AMP). Sometimes we think we know how God should give us a miraculous victory, but, at times, our ideas of how God will work are very different from the ways in which He actually accomplishes the triumph for us. Let Him have His way.

In 2 Kings 6, we discover that the warrior angels didn't directly engage in battle with Israel's enemy. Instead, it seems they enabled Elisha to blind and confuse the Syrian army. (See verses 18–19.) This caused the enemy to be led in another direction, thereby accomplishing the task of supernaturally winning the battle before it even began. This outcome resulted in God's victory as He foiled the plans of the enemy army, which gave up without a fight.

---

21. Larry Pierce, "Outline of Biblical Usage," in "Lexicon: Strong's H6635 – ṣāḇā'," Blue Letter Bible, https://www.blueletterbible.org/lexicon/h6635/kjv/wlc/0-1/.

Again, God's ways are usually not man's ways. (See Isaiah 55:8.) We must let God be God and remember that His victories are the best victories. Don't become worried or unsettled during the process. Warrior angels are able to minister in many different ways. Let's look at some examples:

- The *"Commander of the army of the LORD"* appeared to Joshua before his battle in Jericho. (See Joshua 5:13–15 NKJV.)
- Warrior angels went into battle before David with the sound of marching in the mulberry trees. (See 1 Chronicles 14:13–17.)
- An angel of the Lord opened the doors of the jail holding the apostles, setting them free. (See Acts 5:17–25.)

There are many other examples.

You can trust that God and His angels are ministering on your behalf. God always has your best interests in mind, He knows what is good for you, He knows what will help you grow, and He understands the end from the beginning. It's like my friend Desiree Ayers has said: "The enemy had a plot, but God has a plan!" Yes, you can trust Him.

> *Trust in and rely confidently on the LORD with all your heart and do not rely on your own insight or understanding. In all your ways know and acknowledge and recognize Him, and He will make your paths straight and smooth [removing obstacles that block your way].*
>
> (Proverbs 3:5–6 AMP)

RECEIVING STRENGTH AND COMFORT AFTER SPIRITUAL ATTACKS

Not only does God release His angelic armies into the midst of our difficult situations in order to orchestrate divine turnarounds and supernatural victories, but He also sends angels to minister personally to us, bringing refreshing, comfort, and encouragement after a spiritual attack has occurred.

When Elijah was running for his life from Queen Jezebel, he was emotionally drained and physically exhausted. In his time of need, an angel came and ministered to him, providing heavenly food and supernatural strength. (See 1 Kings 19:1–8.) We also know that angels came to minister to Jesus after He was tempted by the enemy in the wilderness. These angels brought Jesus nourishing food and served Him during this time of need. (See Matthew 4:11

AMPC, AMP.) An angel also strengthened Jesus in the garden of Gethsemane when He experienced great mental and emotional stress before His arrest and crucifixion. (See Luke 22:39–43.) So, again, welcome the angels of light that God sends to your life and know that they are being released to minister wholeness to your spirit, soul, and body.

God wants you well, and knowing this should cause you to give Him praise. Our confidence is in God, and we give Him all the glory!

> *Not to us, O Lord, not to us, but to Your name give glory because of Your lovingkindness, because of Your truth and faithfulness.*
> (Psalm 115:1 AMP)

DISARMING DEMONS

As we learn to activate angels, we also need to learn more about how to discern and counteract demonic attacks as we recognize the limitations of their power and influence. There are sixty-six verses in the Bible that deal with demons and evil spirits. To some people, that number might seem great. However, I want to bring to your attention the fact that there are at least 394 Scripture references about angels. The spiritual scale is much heavier on the side of heavenly light and glory.

Remember, when Satan rebelled against God and fell from heaven, he took only one-third of the angels with him. (See Revelation 12:4, 9.) This means that two-thirds of the angelic forces are still holy, active, and ready to serve the purposes of God and His people—and that includes you.

NO FELLOWSHIP WITH FRUITLESS DEEDS

As I wrote earlier, true spiritual warfare is not about playing endless games of naming evil territorial spirits, looking for new weapons to bind them, and seeking out their hidden agendas. The Scriptures clearly give us this word of caution:

> *Take no part in and have no fellowship with the fruitless deeds and enterprises of darkness, but instead [let your lives be so in contrast as to] expose and reprove and convict them.*
> (Ephesians 5:11)

Unfortunately, in recent years, an ungodly obsession with evil spirits has been a major stumbling block within the charismatic and Spirit-filled churches at large. It's almost as bad as some false religions. There are other religions that firmly believe in the existence of millions of different deities. (In reality, these "deities" are evil spirits posing as helpful spiritual entities.) If you were to ask the followers of those religions all the names of their "gods," they would be unable to name them all. Why? Because there are so many. Sadly, I've seen this same type of confusion attempting to capture the minds and attention of some devout Christian believers. In a pursuit to "get to the bottom of the truth about demons," they have fallen off the deep end into a bottomless pit of demonic slime. They're constantly searching for a deeper understanding of the demons "Jezebel," "Haman," "Python," "Mammon," and others, when all they really need is to get a vision of Jesus and the light of His glory!

Remember that Jesus said,

Seek the Kingdom of God above all else, and live righteously, and he will give you everything you need. (Matthew 6:33 NLT)

Whatever you focus on will increase in your life.

Several years ago, it seemed like everyone was talking about weird animal spirits. A couple of ladies came to me in California, telling me that they were possessed by octopus and squid spirits. A man in Canada told me that he had a spiritual snake wrapped around his waist. In addition, while I was preaching at an outdoor camp meeting in Virginia, an Indian family desperately approached me saying that their twelve-year-old son was demon possessed, and they were looking for answers. They proceeded to tell me that they had previously gone to a deliverance ministry, and the minister had "discerned" that their son had a "monkey spirit." He gave them a long list of things to do in order to deliver their son. This list included prayer and fasting, giving specific offerings, and attending certain deliverance sessions. However, in all their "doing," this "monkey spirit" still seemed to stay caged within their son's body.

I could feel this family's desperation. They were spiritually, emotionally, and physically exhausted. If what you're doing is not casting out a demon, then you're just playing games. Although, one time, Jesus did seem to ask a demon its name (see, for example, Mark 5:1–17), and prayer and fasting may be necessary before driving out a demon (see Mark 9:14–29), the pattern of

Jesus—who was always spiritually prepared through prayer and fasting—was simply to rebuke demons, ordering them to leave. We must stop being so concerned with naming demons and just start casting them out!

I asked the boy if he truly wanted to be free, and, with his body shaking, he said, "Yes, yes, yes!" I knew he desperately wanted his freedom, and his family desperately desired to see a lasting change in his life, but they had been so badly hurt by people posing as deliverance ministers that they were not sure if the next prescribed remedy would actually work. In times like these, you must use your authority in Christ on people's behalf.

Even though the boy was making noises and flailing his arms like a monkey, I told him to look me in the eyes and repeat a prayer after me. It took boldness and patience to work with him, but if you're firm in the Spirit, the evil spirits must obey you! I said to him, "Repeat these words," and then I led him in this prayer:

> In the name of Jesus, I take authority over every evil spirit that has intruded upon my mind and body. I command these spirits to be silenced, and I command them to leave me right now! I am filled with God's light. Therefore, all darkness, leave my spirit, soul, and body. I am free, in Jesus's name!

As soon as the boy finished saying that prayer, he collapsed to the ground, and an ungodly energy force instantly left his body. This was obvious to all who were observing the supernatural deliverance. The boy looked up at me and at his parents, and, with a very new, peaceful, glowing countenance upon his face, he said, "I'm free!"

There's no need to "monkey around" when it comes to dealing with evil spirits. Searching for demons will only result in your falling into the enemy's seductive trap of temptation, intimidation, and lies. Do you remember the serpent's words to Eve in the garden of Eden? *"Can it really be that God has said…?"* (Genesis 3:1). The enemy spirit will always attempt to twist your mind so that you don't believe the truth. He knows that the carnal human nature is drawn toward drama, conflict, and chaos. However, those of us who believe in Jesus have been given a new nature in Christ, and that new nature should propel us toward the truth of living as children of light.

So, don't try talking to a demon. If you were to receive a response, it would be a lie anyway. Once more, you cannot defeat demons if you enjoy playing around with them. Jesus always used His authority to silence demons. (See, for example, Luke 4:35, 41; Mark 1:25, 34.) I expressed previously that those who have an ungodly obsession with constantly talking about and engaging with demons are generally the ones who need real deliverance from their torment. Although such people call themselves Christians, their family life and marriages are torn, and they walk around with defeat in their bodies and confusion in their minds. All this is due to the influence of the enemy in their lives, which they have permitted largely through a wrong understanding of their spiritual authority.

In my personal observation, I've noticed that the souls of those who have this obsession have been fractured, and they are in need of God's light to shine His truth on their outlook and on their situation. That light heals and restores shattered minds, wills, and emotions. The enemy has tried to wreak havoc with these believers, maybe even more so than with those to whom these individuals have tried to minister. It shouldn't be this way, and that's why I'm attempting to shine light on this matter through this book.

It is possible for people like this to find true and lasting freedom, but that will come only with their willingness to live in contrast to the kingdom of darkness. We must focus on and fully receive the gospel truth. We're told in the Gospels that we have been given real and authentic power to cast out evil spirits, but, to do this, we have to use our authority in Christ, believing His Word, and His Word alone. True spiritual warfare is all about the gospel—not just in word, but also in power!

It comes down to believing and proclaiming the gospel truth, which enables us to live a gospel life filled with gospel light. This is how we make genuine advances and actively move forward in our spiritual life and calling as *light warriors*.

TAKE AUTHORITY OVER EVERY EVIL SPIRIT

However, many Christians I've met are afraid to cast out demons. They're "spooked out" at the thought of being involved with this kind of activity. Maybe it's because of the way movies and television shows have theatrically presented exorcisms. But the Scriptures tell us, "*These signs will follow those who believe: In My name they will cast out demons*" (Mark 16:17 NKJV).

As a light warrior, you've been given the responsibility to take authority over darkness. Casting out demons doesn't need to be difficult. After all, in the Gospels, we find twelve instances where Jesus cast out demons (we will review those instances below), and, before leaving the earth, He told us that we would do the same things He did, and even greater things. (See John 14:12.) Noting that instruction should give us a bold determination to bring the light of freedom to those who have been bound by the chains of darkness.

The following are types of evil spirits that we may encounter, and over which we must take authority. I have generally described such spirits based on Scripture so that you can be cognizant of them; they are not for "naming" purposes or for dwelling on them and their nature, as I cautioned about earlier.

- A spirit of infirmity or affliction (See, for example, Luke 13:11–13; Acts 10:38; 1 John 3:8.)
- A spirit of depression (See, for example, Nehemiah 8:9–10; Psalm 30:11–12, 42:5; Proverbs 17:22; Isaiah 61:3; Luke 4:18.)
- A spirit of fear (See, for example, Psalm 23:4, 27:1; Isaiah 43:1; Mark 5:34–36; 2 Timothy 1:7; 1 John 4:18.)
- An unclean spirit (See, for example, Matthew 10:1; John 15:3; Romans 6:19; 1 Corinthians 6:19–20; Ephesians 5:3; 1 Thessalonians 4:7.)
- A spirit of violence (See, for example, Genesis 4:6–7; Proverbs 14:29–30; Matthew 5:21–26; Ephesians 4:26, 31; James 1:19–22.)

We must take authority over the enemy and his demonic legions as we arise in this hour and let our light shine.

FOLLOWING JESUS'S EXAMPLE

Let's now consider these cases where Jesus cast out a demon or demons, so that we can follow in His footsteps as light warriors:

- Many people who were afflicted with sickness and disease were cured and received deliverance from evil spirits as Jesus released the light of healing and freedom through His absolute authority. The Scriptures tell us that He *"would not allow the demons to talk because they knew Him"* (Mark 1:34). We must know who we are in Christ; when we do, even evil spirits will recognize Jesus's light of authority upon our lives and submit to the light of His glory that we carry.

- Jesus traveled throughout Galilee *"preaching in their synagogues and driving out demons"* (Mark 1:39). Anointed preaching has the ability to drive out evil spirits. When you preach the truth of God's Word, it shines light and carries the power to dislodge the lies and entrapments of the enemy.

- While Jesus was teaching in a synagogue, a man possessed by a demon began to speak up. This manifestation of darkness required that Jesus combat it by speaking and releasing the light. The Scriptures reveal that *"Jesus rebuked him, saying, Hush up (be muzzled, gagged), and come out of him!"* (Mark 1:25). Once Jesus released light through that firm command, *"the unclean spirit, throwing the man into convulsions and screeching with a loud voice, came out of him"* (verse 26). The onlookers were amazed by this supernatural feat, saying, *"With authority He gives orders even to the unclean spirits and they obey Him!"* (verse 27). When you command evil spirits to come out—when you release the light in this way—they will come out. In another recorded deliverance, this time of a young boy, we're told that *"Jesus rebuked the demon, and it came out of him, and the boy was cured instantly"* (Matthew 17:18). Afterward, Jesus reprimanded His disciples for not having enough faith to take authority over the evil spirit themselves. (See verses 19–21.) Anything done without faith is powerless. It takes faith to please God (see Hebrews 11:6), and it takes faith to drive out darkness.

- Jesus ministered healing deliverance to the people in Capernaum by simply radiating the light of God's glory and allowing those who were *"disturbed and troubled with unclean spirits"* (Luke 6:18) and otherwise ill to touch Him (see verse 19). The Scriptures record that, as they did, *"healing power was all the while going forth from Him and curing them all [saving them from severe illnesses or calamities]"* (verse 19). We see the same type of deliverance on another occasion in Mark 3:10–11. We must be approachable enough to others to allow the radiance of God's light on our lives to impact those who need it the most. As we extend ourselves to touch lives with the light of deliverance, we should expect supernatural turnarounds.

- Jesus performed additional deliverances for people that released the light of freedom and drove away the darkness: a mute man (see

Matthew 9:32–33; Luke 11:14), a blind and mute man (see Matthew 12:22), the demon-possessed daughter of a Canaanite woman (see Matthew 15:21–28), and a crippled woman (see Luke 13:10–13). We will look at a final example from Matthew 8 below.

After reading through these biblical examples, you will have noticed that each time Jesus cast out a demon or demons, it was not a difficult process. It doesn't seem as if the process took hours or days to accomplish, even though the demons sometimes tried to put up a fight. For example, when Jesus cast out evil spirits from two fierce and savage demoniac men of the Gadarenes, all He had to do was say, "Go!" and the demons came out of them and went into a herd of pigs that were grazing on the hillside nearby. *"And [Jesus] said to them, Begone! So they came out and went into the hogs, and behold, the whole drove rushed down the steep bank into the sea and died in the water"* (Matthew 8:32). Jesus knew how to release the light, and, when you do the same, it will bring people immediate deliverance from darkness. There is an ease in the glory.

Yes, there will be instances in deliverance when you will need to do something different from what you've done before, and it may take some time in prayer to discover the proper spiritual method. Each scenario is unique. But I want to encourage you to use the light. You are a light warrior, and the light of God is the greatest weapon you carry against every work of the enemy!

Take some time to further study the words and ways of Jesus concerning how to release the light for deliverance. Allow Him to be your "how-to" example for casting out demons in a biblical way as a light warrior. If we walk in His ways, we will obtain His results.

YES, LET THERE BE LIGHT! CAN YOU FEEL THE SPIRIT'S POWER FLOWING THROUGH YOU AND CAUSING DARKNESS TO FLEE? YOU'RE WINNING THE SPIRITUAL WARFARE BATTLE BECAUSE YOU'RE A *LIGHT WARRIOR*.

CHAPTER 7

MOVING AS CHARIOTS OF LIGHT

*"Show love to the LORD your God by walking in his ways
and holding tightly to him."*
—Deuteronomy 11:22 (NLT)

As a light warrior, you can begin moving as a "supernatural chariot of light," and I want to show you how! We'll begin by looking at the word of the Lord that was given to the Israelites, His chosen ones, in Deuteronomy 11:22, to enable them to enter into and enjoy the promised land. Here is a summary of His instructions: (1) love the Lord your God, (2) walk in His ways, and (3) hold tightly to Him. The same instructions apply to us today. As those who believe in God's Son, Jesus—those who are *"chosen…to be his own people"* (1 Thessalonians 1:4 NLT)—we must pay attention to what God is saying to us. As we love the Lord and obey His Spirit's prophetic instructions, and as we live our lives according to His Word, victory is ours.

A JEWISH REVELATION: BEING CHARIOTS FOR GOD

In Deuteronomy 11:22, the phrase that the *New Living Translation* renders as *"holding tightly to him"* is translated as *"hold fast to Him"* in the

New King James Version and as *"cleave to Him"* in the *Amplified Bible, Classic Version*. This phrase was understood by the Jewish people to mean not just keeping the Lord in your heart or paying attention to Him once in a great while, as we might think of it today. Instead, it is the idea of attaching yourself fully to Him, clinging to Him, holding on to Him—and not letting go. This is the way of life we must cultivate to be filled with God's light and convey that light to others as light warriors.

According to the Hasidic Jewish mindset, the following is one of the ways to understand this concept:

> ...to remember God and your love for Him always and at all times, so that you never remove your mind from Him, when you are walking on the way or lying down or rising up—until even when you are conversing with other people, in your innermost heart you are not with them but are in the presence of God. And it can be said about those who are on this exalted level of spiritual attainment, that their souls are bound up in the bond of life, and that they share in eternal life even in this world, for they are themselves a dwelling place for the *Shechinah*."[22]

The revelation we can glean from Deuteronomy 11 is this: it is when you give yourself fully to the Glory that you will recognize that the Glory has given Himself fully to you. As you cling to Him, you will become aware that He is pouring out *on* you, *in* you, *through* you, and *around* you. Suddenly, there will be blazing glory everywhere.

We talked earlier about how the shekinah glory is the visible or manifest glory of God. This is the glory of His presence that brings transformative change to the atmosphere. When you begin to cling to God, you will be a dwelling place for the shekinah, carrying the very presence of heaven. Everywhere you go, you will become a powerful atmosphere that enhances whatever atmosphere was there before you arrived—whether that atmosphere carries an equal or a lesser amount of God's manifest presence or completely lacks any sense of His presence. (Remember that believers coming together with one heart and purpose will create an atmosphere of exponential spiritual power.)

---

22. The Ramban (Nachmanides), "Commentary on *Chumash*," quoted in Yitzhak Buxbaum, *Jewish Spiritual Practices* (Lanham, MD: Rowman & Littlefield, 1977), 6.

It is through cleaving or holding on to God and receiving the shekinah glory that "the Divine Presence comes to dwell within you, and you become a chariot for God."[23] I want you to think about that statement for a moment. What does a chariot look like? What comes to your mind when you think of a chariot? Many of us have seen replicas of ancient chariots in old Hollywood movies like *The Ten Commandments*. There were some very nice-looking chariots in that movie. They were adorned with gold and held weapons of warfare. Another example is the chariots in the film *Ben-Hur*. Other than in movies or in museums, or through pictures searched on the Internet or in reference books, it's hard to see a chariot these days. They are no longer in use in the natural, but God is still using chariots in the Spirit realm.

A chariot is defined as "a two-wheeled horse-drawn battle car of ancient times used also in processions and races."[24] This was not an object you placed in a corner. It was a fast-moving vehicle used primarily for battle. It was made for motion and was used in situations that required speed.

I want to declare today that you are a chariot for God, and He is bringing an acceleration to your movement. What would take ten years in the natural, God can do in an instant. We need that immediacy because the time is now short as the days of Christ's return draw near, and we cannot afford to delay. God is calling us to move with the light speed of His Spirit, to move with the shekinah glory of His presence, to move in an accelerated way.

God's desire is to manifest heaven here on earth—in Los Angeles, New York, Mexico City, Vancouver, Frankfurt, Paris, Helsinki, Moscow, Buenos Aires, Hong Kong, Bangkok, Tokyo, Dubai, Cairo, Lagos, Johannesburg, Sydney, Bombay, Jerusalem—all over the world. His desire is to manifest heaven where you live and work. No more delay! Let the acceleration come!

TRANSLATED FROM THE EARTHLY TO THE HEAVENLY

When we think about a chariot of light, we might think about the testimony of Elijah in 2 Kings:

---

23. Buxbaum, *Jewish Spiritual Practices*, 6.
24. *Merriam-Webster.com Dictionary*, s.v. "chariot," accessed October 1, 2024, https://www.merriam-webster.com/dictionary/chariot.

> *And it came to pass, when the* Lord *was about to take up Elijah into heaven by a whirlwind, that Elijah went with Elisha from Gilgal.*
>
> (2 Kings 2:1 nkjv)

This passage speaks about what we might call a mentorship relationship or partnership. God always has a connection for you and for those around you, and when you make the right connections, supernatural things happen. There is a lot that I could expound upon within this text and the verses that follow, but I want to jump all the way down to verse 11:

> *Then it happened, as they continued on and talked, that suddenly a chariot of fire appeared with horses of fire, and separated the two of them; and Elijah went up by a whirlwind into heaven.* (2 Kings 2:11 nkjv)

The reason I want you to take note of this verse is that, as we talk about being chariots of light, I hope you understand what I'm trying to say. I'm presenting the idea of your being a carrier of the divine presence to such a degree that you are a fiery manifestation of the shekinah glory of God in the earth. I want you to see what happened with Elijah because a chariot of fire came to pick him up and carry him from the natural to the supernatural. It carried him from the realm of darkness into the realm of heavenly light. It carried him from this earthly realm into the glory realm. He who has eyes to see, let him see. He who has ears to hear, let him hear. He who has a spirit to perceive, let him begin to perceive what happens when a chariot of light manifests on the earth. When you become a chariot, you carry God's power for translation and transportation from one realm to another.

The first chapter of Colossians talks about what happens when Christ comes into our lives, and I want you to note this passage as well:

> *Giving thanks to the Father who has qualified us to be partakers of the inheritance of the saints in the light. He has delivered us from the power of darkness and conveyed us into the kingdom of the Son of His love, in whom we have redemption through His blood, the forgiveness of sins.*
>
> (Colossians 1:12–14 nkjv)

Whereas the *New King James Version* says that God has "*conveyed us,*" some translations, such as the King James Version, say He "*translated us.*" This again expresses the concept of moving from one realm to another realm. We have been translated into the kingdom of the Son of God's love.

Yes, God created you to be a chariot, to be a carrier of the *dunamis* fire, so that wherever you go, not only will you change the atmosphere around you, but you will also transform the people you meet. It will be nothing short of a miracle! God has given you the responsibility of spreading the gospel, preaching the good news, reaching out and ministering to those whom He puts in your path, sharing His light. Why? Because, as a chariot, you carry the ability to convey others out of darkness, out of the depths of the sadness, sickness, and misery they've been in. God has given you the responsibility of moving them in the Spirit from the place of sin, darkness, and wickedness into the place of knowing Jesus as their personal Lord and Savior. In order that He might be their all in all, He has chosen us to help move them, or translate them, into His kingdom of light.

People who don't even know it yet are waiting to encounter you as God's chariot of light. You are the answer to someone's prayers. You are the solution that God has placed on the earth. You carry the good news of the gospel. You carry the same Spirit that raised Christ from the dead. You are a chariot of light. You can't back down; you must release the light!

THOSE WHO CARRY HIS PRESENCE

Light warriors are chariots for God who carry His presence everywhere they go. This means that we can no longer afford to live outside of His presence. We must cultivate an atmosphere for the glory every single day for the sake of our families, our friends, and our coworkers. We must do this in our homes and in our workplaces, wherever we are.

I know that, in some workplaces, people are not permitted to speak about their faith. That's okay. Just shine your light. There is more than one way to usher in the glory. You carry the presence of Jesus, and when you walk into a room, it's as if Jesus Himself has just walked in.

You can sing in the glory, you can whistle in the glory, and you can hum under your breath in the glory. You can even dance in the glory by simply wiggling your toes in your shoes while lifting your heart toward heaven. Do whatever you have to do to usher in the atmosphere of the glory wherever you happen to be.

The Scriptures say that when David returned the ark of the covenant—representing the glory of God's presence—to Jerusalem, *"they set the ark of God upon a new cart"* (2 Samuel 6:3). In a prophetic way, as a chariot of light, you are becoming a "new cart" that will usher the manifestation of glory light into new places as the Lord directs. The prophet Ezekiel saw a "portable" throne of God that moved on heavenly wheels. (See Ezekiel 1:15–28.) Will you carry God's manifest presence? Are you willing to carry Him everywhere you go?

The wheels on your chariot are turning. This speaks prophetically of the turnaround that God is bringing as you, a chariot of God, move about in the earth. As you move, that turnaround is coming with you. God goes before you, preparing the way. He is *around* you and *in* you, and He wants to minister *through* you as you show up in the places where He directs you.

You're carrying the shekinah that brings transformative change. We must move as God guides us. This means we need to stop saying, "I don't like going to [fill in the applicable place in your life] because it's so spiritually dark; it has such a heavy atmosphere." Spiritual warfare is not difficult, no matter where you are, once you recognize that you are a light warrior who carries the glory! The glory brings the breakthrough.

LOVE IS OUR MOTIVATOR

God wants you to be a chariot of fiery love. He desires for His bride to be glorious, radiant, and powerful in this hour, and if we are to rise in this way—filled with His *dunamis*—we can withhold no part of ourselves from Him or from our service for Him. Fear is often the root of our withholding, but love will be our motivator. Love provides a way forward. It brings motion to the wheels on our chariots. Know today how very much loved you are by God in every area of your being and of your life, and that there is no lack in His love.

There is no lack in what God wants to pour out to you and through you to others. There is no lack in His kingdom. When we come into a place where we understand the lavish love of God, something is unlocked in us, because faith works by love. (See Galatians 5:6.) In the past, we've been controlled by fear, but no more! As expressed in the drama series *When Calls the Heart*, based on the book by Jeanette Oke, "The light of love restores every lost voice."[25] Faith is rising, and we're moving out of fear as we begin operating in greater levels of God's great love. The wheels on our chariots are turning.

Remember, we're not talking about any old chariot here. Your chariot is not like the chariots of the *Ten Commandments* or the chariots of *Ben-Hur*. Yours is supernatural and so much more glorious. It is set ablaze with the fire of the Spirit, and that fire accompanies you everywhere you go. Receive what God is doing in you and through you, and act on it.

Sometimes God's fire comes to burn up that which is not pleasing in His sight, to purify you and cause you to come forth as pure gold. (See Job 23:10.) Let it burn. Then dedicate yourself as His chariot to carry His fiery light wherever you go.

Thus, when God's presence is in us, we become His chariot. When we invite the presence of God's Holy Spirit, He comes with His fire, and He comes with His power. And when His power comes, miracles begin to flow. When His power comes, healings begin to flow. When His power comes, we become a conduit for deliverance to bring breakthrough.

FIRE, POWER, AND MIRACLES

When Janet and I were living in Birmingham, Alabama, we would frequently teach at the Bible college there, and it was a wonderful experience. We had the honor of instructing students who came from many different places, nationally and internationally. One of the classes we most enjoyed teaching was on the supernatural basics of living a Christian life. When we taught "Supernatural Soulwinning," we would place an emphasis on *the work of the Spirit*. Again, there is an ease that comes in the glory. In fact, when the glory comes on the scene, you don't have to do much at all. You just flow with the Spirit, and God does the rest. He draws men and women to Himself by His Spirit.

One day, we announced to the students that, the next day, we would be teaching on the baptism of the Holy Spirit. Our mentors, Charles and Frances Hunter, had taught us that without the baptism, you *pray for* the sick, but with

---

25. *When Calls the Heart*, episode 3, "A Telling Silence," directed by Michael Landon Jr., written by Ken Lazebnik (Nashville, TN: Word Entertainment LLC, 2014), DVD.

the baptism, you *heal* the sick. There's a difference, and it's the baptism of the Holy Spirit that makes that difference.

This reality was prophesied by Jesus Himself:

I assure you, most solemnly I tell you, if anyone steadfastly believes in Me, he will himself be able to do the things that I do; and he will do even greater things than these, because I go to the Father. (John 14:12)

But you shall receive power (ability, efficiency, and might) when the Holy Spirit has come upon you, and you shall be My witnesses in Jerusalem and all Judea and Samaria and to the ends (the very bounds) of the earth. (Acts 1:8)

As mentioned earlier, the power Jesus spoke of in Acts 1:8 is *dunamis*, or miracle-working power, and you receive it when the Holy Spirit comes upon you. It is from this Greek word *dunamis* that the English words *dynamite* and *dynamic* are derived. The *dunamis* of God is explosive. It's dynamite. It's dynamic power that releases the reality of God into our everyday circumstances.

I like the fact that Jesus Himself promised us this power. We can count on His Word. So many believers are looking to God for miracles, looking to Him for power. Jesus said we received power when we were filled with the Holy Spirit. When the Holy Spirit comes, the power comes with Him. And when we are filled with the Spirit of God, the power should begin to operate in us and through us. We *have* God's light, and we should start releasing that light.

Perhaps we should change the way we look at this matter. Instead of seeking more miracles and more power, we should be seeking more of God's Spirit. Let's invite the Holy Spirit to come and fill us on a daily, hourly, and minute-by-minute basis. Let's allow Him to continually fill us with who He is. Why? Because when God comes with His Spirit, we get that explosive *dunamis* power operating in our life. When that power is operating, we can be effective witnesses everywhere, for we are now power portals, miracle workers, light warriors—chariots of light.

At the time when Jesus prophesied the outpouring of the Holy Spirit on believers, we don't know exactly how many people were listening, but we do know that at least a hundred and twenty of those who heard obeyed His instruction to wait in Jerusalem to receive this power. Those one hundred and twenty who obeyed and waited were the ones who received the Spirit on the day of Pentecost. If you follow the divine instruction, you will receive the divine result.

Many people seem to complain about what God is *not* doing in their lives. Why? Maybe it's because they're not obeying His clear instructions. We must align ourselves with the Lord, then hold on to Him, cleaving to Him and His glory, so that we become fiery chariots for His powerful presence. We cannot depart from His presence and expect the same results. We cannot depart from His presence for business reasons or for the sake of raising our families—and it is not necessary to do so. Remember, we can be in His presence no matter what we are doing or where we are. Everywhere we go and in everything we do, we must remain in His powerful presence.

CREATE A POINT OF CONTACT

As we move about as chariots of light, one of the ways in which we bring transformative change is by creating a point of contact. Jake Secor, one of the students we taught at the Bible school, told us, "When you announced that you were going to be teaching on the baptism of the Holy Spirit, it was something I had been desiring for a long time. I immediately knew that I was going to receive the baptism of the Holy Spirit in that next class."

Hearing him say this excited me because I realized that Jake had created a point of spiritual contact by taking the words I had spoken and making them his own. Our words can become a point of contact, and what we say matters. What we speak into the atmosphere contains and carries power. That's why we need to speak God's words. That's why we need to speak about Him, what He is doing, and how He is moving. Your words release light, and that becomes a point of contact for people around you to connect with and say, "Okay, they just said it, and so I'm going to receive it."

Do you have friends who are very sick, dealing with some kind of illness or pain that their doctors have given up on as incurable? As a chariot of light, you can be a voice of light that speaks into that atmosphere. You can bring the healing light of God to them as you begin to speak what God has said. Declare to them the good news: "By His stripes you were healed. It's a done deal." (See Isaiah 53:5.)

When you open your mouth, it's as if flames of fire are coming off of your tongue, flames of the Holy Spirit, fire that is burning away sickness, burning away infirmity, burning away disease, burning away pain, and releasing healing glory. Hallelujah!

Today, God wants you to create some points of contact for *dunamis* power to flow into your life and also to flow from your life. Whether it is words, an offering, a Scripture, or a prophetic action, create a point of contact for the *dunamis* light to be transmitted in a tangible way. The glory is very interactive. You must be willing to participate with what the Spirit is doing. You can't delay in the glory. Discern the movement of the Spirit and give yourself fully to it, cleave to it, and hold on to it.

If we think about our lives in an abstract way, we'll never really get anywhere or do anything. But if we can focus on something tangible, if we can receive the vision God has for us and for the situations we encounter, and if we can create a point of contact for them, it's in those places where *dunamis* power shows up.

Remember that Jesus said, "*You shall receive power (ability, efficiency, and might [*dunamis*, miracle-working power]) when the Holy Spirit has come upon you*" (Acts 1:8). If you believe these words, you create an opportunity for that power to explode within you! Create a point of contact, just as Jake decided to do. Embrace what God is doing and let Him know that you will be a carrier, a fiery chariot, of His glory.

AN ERUPTION OF POWER!

On the day when Janet and I taught our Bible students about the baptism of the Holy Spirit, we presented them with the corresponding Scriptures, starting with the promise of Acts 1:8 and moving on to the description of the coming of the Spirit at Pentecost in Acts 2. On Pentecost, the Spirit came with wind and fire. The wind was to blow away the old and bring forth the new. That wind filled the believers and brought them new hope.

The wind of the Spirit is still blowing today—bringing healing, deliverance, and miracles. Let that wind move you. Some answers are coming to you right now in the wind of God's Spirit: solutions to problems that have existed for a very long time. Because of the acceleration of the Spirit, you will soon have your answer. No more delay! Receive your healing. Receive your financial deliverance. Receive the miracle for your home. Receive the miracle for your business. When God breathes His breath of life, it brings newness, freshness, and restored hope.

When we gave our Bible students the invitation to receive the baptism of the Holy Spirit, there were four students who had not yet received the baptism, and they all came forward. Jake was one of them. We prayed for all four, but when I laid my hands on Jake, it was like an explosion, a bomb going off. He was so ready to receive that all we had to do was just touch his forehead, and the connection was made. Suddenly, heavenly languages began to flow out of him. He released the flow of the Spirit and went on in that way for an hour, then two hours. He couldn't seem to stop.

This was on a Thursday, the last day of the school week, and when we gathered for our next class the following Tuesday, Jake was still speaking in tongues. Someone asked him about it, and he said, "I can't stop." If he wasn't answering someone's immediate question, he was speaking in tongues. He had been overflowing like this for the whole weekend and on into that next week.

The only issue was that he came from a good Baptist family. The church his family initially attended had told him that tongues were not for today. Yet, Jake had gone home the previous Thursday, and he had shared with his younger brother what had happened to him, showed him the related Scriptures, and laid his hands on him, and his brother, too, had received the Holy Spirit and begun to speak in tongues. That family now had two tongues-speakers, and their home was being filled with the fire of God.

When Jake came back to school on Tuesday, as he continued to speak in tongues, he was prophesying into the atmosphere. The head of the school, Pastor Tim Beck, approached Janet while I was ministering in music at the keyboard and said, "I think we should change our plans today because we have to make room for the move of God." He invited all the students in all three classes—the first-, second-, and third-year students—to come forward if they wanted to receive a new touch from God. Then we released Jake to go lay his hands on the other students. Before long, one by one, they were all being filled with the fire of God, and the power of God flowing through them was awesome. Most of the school was down on the floor under the power of the Spirit, having a wonderful time in the glory.

DISCERN WHERE THE SPIRIT IS MOVING

After this, we simply couldn't go back and conduct school "as usual." God was calling us to do something different. We couldn't just stay in that building and keep what God was giving us for ourselves. Everything that God brings into your life comes in seed form with the responsibility to sow it into the right people, places, and atmospheres. We must be keen enough in the Spirit to discern the fertile soil for the seed so that a harvest might come forth, and then that harvest will bring more seed.

Yes, God was speaking to us, and we had to take what was happening *in* the school *outside* of the school. Not far away was a huge Buc-ee's gas station. It isn't really right to call it a gas station; it's the Disneyland of travel centers. It has everything, and it's a very busy place. We sent half the students to Buc-ee's and the other half to the outlet mall on the other side of the interstate. Soon, the students were releasing the light in Buc-ee's and at the outlet mall, and it was changing the atmosphere with power and glory. Talk about chariots of light! Some people were getting saved, others were getting healed, and still others were being delivered.

Jake was at Buc-ee's, partnered with another student. That student was sharing the gospel with people, and he met some who were already believers yet had never received the baptism of the Holy Spirit but were open to it. When Jake and his fellow student came across such believers, Jake would lay his hands on them, while continuing to speak in tongues, and release God's power, and these believers would be filled with the Spirit! Before long, they would be speaking in tongues for the first time.

I was excited to see what God was doing among these students, and, in the following days, I began testifying about it in the places where I went to minister. The following weekend, I was invited to minister at the Days of Glory Conference in Boston with a group of charismatic Catholics, hosted by Father Tom DiLorenzo and evangelist Maria Vadia. In those meetings, I began telling them how God was working at the Bible college in Birmingham. If we are willing to spread the fire, God will set us and others ablaze. Revival will come to your town if you will get revived and then join your fire with a corporate flame fueled by other believers.

I gave anyone attending the meetings in Boston who had not yet received the baptism of the Holy Spirit the opportunity to come forward and receive this gift. Then I asked the worship team to go to their instruments and play some anointed music as I ministered to the people. I was led to give the praise team a very simple instruction: "I don't want you to sing in English because people are receiving the Holy Spirit. If you sing in English, that will distract them." Waving my left hand toward them, I said, "Sing in the Spirit." They seemed to understand and soon began to sing. Their singing created a supernatural atmosphere, and I went around laying hands on those who had come for prayer. Every single one of them received their new spiritual prayer language, speaking in tongues, and it was a very powerful time of prayer.

The next day, Priscilla, one of the organizers of the Boston meetings, came to me in the restaurant of the hotel where I was staying and said, "The kids are really excited."

"What kids?" I asked.

As it turned out, she was talking about the worship team. They weren't really kids; they were adults, from about twenty to forty-five years old, I suppose.

"They're really excited," she repeated.

I said, "That's great."

"Oh, they're thrilled with this conference."

"Wonderful," I responded.

"No, you don't understand," she emphasized. "None of them had the baptism in the Holy Spirit—none of them. They had been seeking it and desiring it, but it wasn't until you looked at them, waved your hand, and said, 'Sing in the Spirit' that suddenly, instantly, they got baptized and began singing in heavenly tongues for the very first time. They are now worshipping in a way they have never worshipped before."

Well, needless to say, this excited me, too! Fire spreads.

A GATEWAY INTO THE SUPERNATURAL REALM

The *dunamis* power of the Spirit is at work right now. Let it explode in your life in such a way that it totally annihilates any spiritual darkness that has been set against you, anything that has hindered your progress in any area of your life and has seemed unmovable. *Dunamis* power is flowing right now to remove those blockages and bring you into a place of total freedom and liberation.

Several years ago, Bible teacher Billye Brim said to me, "Joshua, speaking in tongues is a gateway into the supernatural realm." And it's true. Speaking in tongues is often a gateway to every other supernatural gift of the Spirit. It's a doorway. I see it as a power portal. I see the *dunamis* opening portals for you to move into greater dimensions of operating in the Spirit, greater realms of supernatural expression, greater demonstrations of signs and wonders.

Pray in the Spirit. Stir up your inner man. Let that *dunamis* flow from you. When the *dunamis* begins to flow, there will be a sound, and that sound will be prayers or songs in tongues. It's the sound of the Spirit. Release the light!

Many breakthroughs are coming with this sound, breakthroughs in the area of relationships, breakthroughs in the area of ministry function, breakthroughs in salvation for those who have been so hard-hearted in the past, and breakthroughs of deliverance! Something is changing now. I prophesy it by the Spirit of God: *dunamis* breakthrough is happening. It is now being released in Jesus's mighty name.

Right now, God is giving us an opportunity to advance in His glory, to excel in His power, to move in the *dunamis* from one realm to the next as we become His chariots—the carriers of His fire, the releasers of His light. He wants to increase His goodness and His miracles in our lives, and this will happen as we focus our eyes on Him, seek Him, cleave to Him, and move with His Spirit.

HEAVENLY PURPOSE

After the outpouring of the Spirit that occurred among our Bible school students and the community at large, I was ministering in California, and I received a text from Jake, saying, "Okay, so I had an amazing encounter with the fire of God at church today! Holy Spirit hit me very mightily, and I literally felt like I was burning (in a good way). In this encounter, it was heavy, peaceful, and I felt the glory." He had now been speaking in tongues nonstop for weeks, and he was still on fire for God.

Jake also mentioned other things that happened to him at church that day, but one of them particularly stuck in my mind: "I clearly heard a very loud sound of a trumpet blowing in this encounter." He asked me what that meant, and I told him to read the following verse because God was giving him a message:

> *After this I looked, and, behold, a door was opened in heaven: and the first voice which I heard was as it were of a trumpet talking with me; which said, Come up here, and I will show you things which must be hereafter.*
>
> (Revelation 4:1 KJVER)

When you become a chariot of light, it positions you to access the open portal of heavenly encounter. Let us thank God for His fire that burns within us, and let us ask Him for fresh fire:

> Lord, we are not satisfied with yesterday's flame. We long to burn for You today. We want to burn stronger and brighter. Come and burn within us by Your Spirit. Your fire brings holiness. Your fire drives out all sin. Your fire purifies our lives. Your fire drives out all lukewarmness and spiritual coldness. Your fire enables us to do Your work. Your fire releases power for miracles. Your fire is contagious and will reach those around us. Burn in us. Make us Your chariots of light, for we long to bring many into Your kingdom of light.

God wants to ignite you in a new way today, to ignite you with revival fire and power. He wants to set you on fire with the flame of His Spirit and make you a sign and a wonder, a testimony of His goodness, His grace, and His mercy. Let Him light you up and set you ablaze. Let fresh fire come to your soul!

I can see you going into the streets carrying the flame, carrying God's torch, His fire, His light, setting you apart as a testimony. I can see you going into your neighborhoods, your communities, bringing the flame into homes and apartment buildings. This is the fulfillment of the words of Jesus that you will be His witness when the Holy Spirit has come upon you because it's in that place that power is released.

Give the Holy Spirit permission to flow through you as He wills. Feel the flow. Vibrate with the flow. Something is even now stirring inside you. Let it flow.

CONNECTING WITH THE FLOW

Some time ago, I learned an essential spiritual lesson for light warriors in a simple but enlightening way. I went into my bathroom to take a shower, but when I turned on the knob, there was hardly any water pressure. I thought, "This is very strange." I asked our girls to check their bathroom, and they said the water pressure was just fine in there. I wondered why this was happening. I could barely get enough water to take a shower. I decided to call a plumber later on in the day, but I got busy and didn't do it.

The next morning, when I went to take a shower, the water pressure seemed even weaker than the day before. I then left to conduct the business of the day, and when I came back home and checked the knob in my bathroom, this time, the water came out only in small drips. "This is crazy," I thought. This was serious. Now I would surely have to call a plumber.

Suddenly, the thought occurred to me that there might be a problem with the shower head. I fully removed the shower head, then turned the water on again, and, this time, the water came out full blast. In that moment, the Spirit spoke to me and said, "You can have power, but if your head is not right, the flow will be diminished. You can have everything accessible to you, but you need to be in right alignment, and it starts with the head." Needless to say, I went out and purchased a brand-new shower head, and the water flow is now perfect!

The space between your two ears represents the greatest battleground you will tread in your entire life. This is a mind war. God wants you to get your mind right about who you are. I'm talking about your identity in Christ. I'm talking about your heavenly identity, knowing who you are in God and what you have access to. You're not called to walk around weak and defeated. God has called you to stand up straight wherever He has placed you and to move in His light as He directs, letting His power flow. You are a light warrior—God's chariot of light!

YES, LET THERE BE LIGHT! CAN YOU FEEL THE SPIRIT'S POWER FLOWING THROUGH YOU AND CAUSING DARKNESS TO FLEE? YOU'RE WINNING THE SPIRITUAL WARFARE BATTLE BECAUSE YOU'RE A *LIGHT WARRIOR*.

CHAPTER 8

ASCENDING IN THE LIGHT

"I watched as thrones were put in place and the Ancient One sat down to judge. His clothing was as white as snow, his hair like purest wool. He sat on a fiery throne with wheels of blazing fire, and a river of fire was pouring out, flowing from his presence. Millions of angels ministered to him."
—Daniel 7:9–10 (NLT)

Heaven is the realm of God's light. Everything about heaven is filled with radiant light overflowing in abundance. Daniel saw the *"Ancient One,"* surrounded by millions of brilliant angels, sitting on *"a fiery throne with wheels of blazing fire,"* with *"a river of fire"* pouring out from His holy presence. In this one heavenly encounter alone, we see so much light! The Spirit desires to reveal His light to us in such a way that we're caught up into visions of God's glory beyond anything we've ever known before.

LIFTED INTO A DIVINE ENCOUNTER

I was in Birmingham, Alabama, during the very early morning hours of October 14, 2021, preparing to go to sleep, when I felt an unexpected urge to check my email. My phone had been charging all day, leaving me out of touch with people during the afternoon and evening. As I reviewed my inbox, I noticed an email from a ministry friend overseas, which had been sent earlier that afternoon. The email urgently requested my prayers for 1:00 a.m., central time, as his wife was scheduled for a special surgery at that exact hour. Miraculously, when I checked the clock, it was precisely 1:00 a.m. Moved by compassion and recognizing the divine timing, I knew the Spirit had orchestrated this moment to lead me into deep intercession for my friend's wife. Although I initially planned to pray from bed, the Spirit prompted me to get up for more intense prayer. I heeded this call and prayed fervently, receiving specific prayer points from the Lord. After praying, I sent an email of support to my friend, but, almost immediately, I was compelled to continue praying, sensing a divine urgency.

The prayer points were clear: believing that there would be no trace of cancer, declaring that there would be no complications in the procedure, asking Dr. Jesus to guide the hands of the doctor, praying for a quick recovery, and expecting a miracle testimony that would glorify God. The urgency I felt led me to move from my bedroom to the kitchen to pray out loud. As I prayed in tongues, the intensity of the intercession physically overwhelmed me. I was leaning against the kitchen counter with my eyes closed when my spirit was suddenly caught up into a bright room. Initially blinded by the light, my spiritual eyes eventually adjusted, and I realized I was above the operating room where the surgery was taking place.

I could see the surgeon, three medical attendants, and my friend's wife, who was glowing with radiant light on the operating table. Without being shown anything graphic about the operation, I was allowed to witness enough to intercede effectively. A melody filled my spirit, and I began singing prophetic declarations over my friend's wife:

Be made whole in your body.
No cancer shall plague thee,
No trouble befalls thee.

As I sang, I felt my awareness shift back to my physical body in the kitchen, and I continued to sing in tongues. Then, my spirit was once again lifted to the hospital room, now focused on the surgeon's hands. I was given another prophetic song to sing, directing the hearts and hands of the medical team:

I'm guiding hearts and hands,
I'm guiding hearts and hands,
I'm guiding hearts and hands,
Into My perfect work and plan.

This heavenly intercession gave me a deep sense of assurance that the surgery would proceed flawlessly. After a seemingly extended period, my spirit returned to my body, yet the urge to pray persisted. I continued interceding, and then, for a third time, I was spiritually transported to the hospital, and I repeated the initial prophetic song:

Be made whole in your body.
No cancer shall plague thee,
No trouble befalls thee.

After this final intercession, peace enveloped me, and I knew it was time to rest. Through email, I informed my friend that I was retiring for the night, and I received his heartfelt gratitude. He assured me that he would continue singing the Spirit-given songs—which I had related to him in the email—in the hospital. When I returned to the bedroom, Janet awoke, and I was able to share with her what had just transpired. She was delighted that God had meticulously attended to our friend in the night through this divine encounter.

Although I hadn't retired to bed until 3:30 a.m., I awoke at 6:30 a.m. refreshed by the Spirit's power, ready to lead worship at the Bible college. The spiritual journey had invigorated me, leaving me revived rather than tired. As I was preparing for the day, I received an email update from my pastor friend detailing the successful surgery and expressing profound gratitude for the prayers. He shared how the surgery had gone according to plan, with no trace of tumor cells, and with an optimistic outlook from the doctors. He wrote, "I believe that this assault from the enemy has now come to an end. Cancer is under our feet, and much glory and many miracles will come out of this all!"

I had also received an email from a prophet friend, saying that the Lord was preparing me for deeper encounters with Him. This reaffirmed to me the power of intercessory prayer and the importance of yielding ourselves to God's higher perspective. As light warriors, we've been provided with the best method for dealing with the spiritual battles we face. The Spirit has given us the heavenly strategy of light for spiritual warfare, and it's a winning strategy!

That morning, when I arrived at the Bible college, I prayed in the Spirit, receiving a new song for the students to experience the same glory I had encountered. The lyrics, inspired by the Spirit, came quickly:

> Whirlwinds, whirlwinds of glory,
> Swirling around and shifting the atmosphere.
> Whirlwinds, whirlwinds of glory,
> Lifting us up to see what You're doing here.
>
> Prophetic vision is my provision.
> Prophetic vision is my provision.
>
> Spirit, reveal Your heart and Your will.
> Spin us around to turn in Your wheel.

After I introduced this song to the worship team and the other students, we entered an hour of spontaneous worship and heavenly encounters, moving from glory to glory. (See 2 Corinthians 3:18.) This experience highlighted for me how one divine encounter leads to another, continually drawing us forward and upward in the light of Christ's vision for our lives.

PROPHETIC WORDS RELEASE PROPHETIC POSSIBILITIES

A couple of years ago, I began to experience moments during my public ministry when I would release utterances in heavenly tongues, followed by my giving their interpretation, delivering a precise message from the Lord. On at least five separate occasions, the Spirit conveyed to me insights about traveling in the Spirit. I believe that these prophetic words have been given for the body of Christ in these last days. These words are for the light warriors who are ready and willing to be used by the Spirit in extraordinary ways. The first instance occurred while I was preaching in Tomball, Texas, and this is what the Spirit revealed through me:

"Translations in the Spirit will become your norm. Transportations in the Spirit are a door that I am opening for you in My Spirit. Just step on in, let go, and let Me move. Let go and let Me carry you. Let go and let Me take you to the places I have prepared for you," says the Lord. "Do not be discouraged when you find yourself restricted in the natural, for in the realm of the divine supernatural, there's a moving that the world does not know about. There's a realm of access that has not been written about in times past. But you shall begin to write. You shall begin to reveal the movings and the methods of My Spirit, the way that I catch up My people in a moment and carry them to the place of My leading."[26]

A few months later, during a ministry session in Chandler, Arizona, on the first night of the Jewish feast of Pentecost, I received another word of prophecy that built upon the previous message:

Rely on My Spirit, lean into Me, and watch and see how I will begin to move you. Rest in My plans that I give to you, for I will cause you to navigate on roads that the enemy does not know about, I will cause you to move through tunnels that cannot be seen with human eyes, and I will begin to open up portals in My Spirit for you to travel from one place to another.[27]

Later the same year, while I was ministering in Kingston, New Hampshire, the spirit of prophecy came upon me once more, and I began to declare the following words:

There's a glory realm that's open tonight to you. A supernatural door of glory is being given to you. There's a portal in the Spirit that's being enlarged, and it's opening wide, and there's a voice calling, saying, "Come up, come up, come up. Come up, come up. Come up higher than you've been before. For I desire to show you My heart, I desire to reveal it to you. I desire to impart to you, oh yes, My will and My ways. And even as you surrender and yield yourself to Me," the Lord

---

26. Prophetic word spoken by Joshua Mills at Joan Hunter Ministries, Four Corners Conference Center, Tomball, TX, January 13, 2023.
27. Prophetic word spoken by Joshua Mills at David Herzog Ministries' Pentecost Glory Conference, Chandler, AZ, May 25, 2023.

says, "I shall begin to impart to you more and more and more and more, and you shall find yourself moving in a heavenly way. Moving with divine insight, divine wisdom, the guidance of My Spirit. It shall be in the Spirit, and I shall also move you from place to place in the flesh. You may be in one place and begin to pray, and suddenly you will find yourself praying in another place. And do not say, 'Oh, this is strange,' but say, 'Lord, what is it that You would have me do in this place? For I know and understand that I am on divine assignment.' And let Me begin to speak to you, and let Me begin to guide you. Let Me begin to give you the words to speak, and let Me show you the ones that need My touch. Do not allow fear to block your mission, but allow faith to arise so that you might successfully accomplish that which I have sent you to do, for even as I move you, and even as I translate you, know that I am the One that leads you, and I will ensure your safety in the journey. Rest in Me as I rest in you, and watch to see what I will do," says the Lord.[28]

This word was followed by another prophetic word a few weeks later while I was ministering one night in Los Angeles:

The Spirit of the Lord would say to you even tonight, "Even as I came upon Philip and caught him up in a moment and began to lift him from one place to another, so My Spirit is being released in this day to carry you into divine appointments, to carry you into ministry assignments, to carry you to the right connections at the right time. Behold, watch and see as I begin to move you by My Spirit. As you begin to feel My Spirit upon you, do not be surprised as I begin to do for you what you cannot do for yourself. Do not be surprised when, instantly, you begin to see yourself in a place that you did not walk to, in a place that you did not naturally travel to, but know that, in that moment, I have set you there for divine appointment, and surely My Spirit is upon you. And surely there's an anointing that I have anointed you with to preach the good news. Oh, yes. And there is healing in your hands and miracles that will begin to flow with abundance. Oh, begin to move with My Spirit as My Spirit begins to move you. For these are

---

28. Prophetic word spoken by Joshua Mills at Kingdom Awakening Ministries, Kingston, NH, June 2, 2023.

the last days. These are the end times, and I will have a church that is glorified."[29]

I've learned that when God speaks once, we must listen. If God speaks twice, we'd better get ready—because He's confirming some things. But if God speaks three or more times about a matter, there's an urgency to it, and it's time to activate our faith to immediately move into what He's speaking!

THE PROPHETIC OPENS THE DOOR

By releasing those prophetic words into the corporate atmosphere, the Spirit opened pathways of light for those who had "ears to hear" what He was saying. This created a spiritual network, an invisible yet very real route through which believers could access this flow. Those who were spiritually attuned found themselves linked to these pathways of light, enabling them to receive and respond to the prophetic utterances. On several occasions, I publicly read these prophetic words, and, each time, the atmosphere was charged with expectancy, creating fertile ground for supernatural experiences to manifest.

Not only did I personally experience a significant increase in heavenly encounters, but our ministry also began receiving numerous testimonies from others who had experienced them. These individuals reported profound and unusual experiences of "traveling in the Spirit," often during their nighttime dreams or even through vivid daytime visions. They described being divinely lifted and transported to minister to others in miraculous ways, feeling a heightened sense of God's presence and purpose. These testimonies confirmed to me that the prophetic words had established a tangible bridge between the supernatural and earthly realms.

BELIEVERS HAVE ACCESS TO SUPERNATURAL PATHWAYS

Believers having access to heavenly encounters and supernatural pathways of light is not something new but can be read about in both the Old and New Testaments. I believe that, in these last days, we will see the number of

---

29. Prophetic word spoken by Joshua Mills at In His Presence Church, Woodland Hills, CA, June 21, 2023.

such encounters greatly increase among the people of God. I've heard it said that "faith is the currency of heaven." I know that's true, and that's one of the reasons why I believe we will have more heavenly encounters in the days ahead. God's people are awakening with new faith to receive from Him the glory that's connecting them to heavenly realities. New faith is opening up new pathways of light. The Scriptures teach us that, without faith, it is impossible to please God (see Hebrews 11:6), and, in my experience, you don't really need to have *a lot* of faith to do really big things in the kingdom.

Jesus taught that faith even as extremely small as a mustard seed is big enough to move mountains. (See Matthew 17:20.) Anything that heaven offers is always available by faith, and that includes the realm of heavenly encounters. If mustard-seed faith can move mountains out of the way, then it can certainly translate your spirit from the earth to heaven and back again. Since the time of the Bible until now, spiritual seekers have received visions and revelations and have been caught up into heavenly realms. Think about ancient biblical figures like Jacob, Elijah, Zechariah, and Ezekiel, to name a few. They all had glimpses of the heavenly dimension. (See, for example, Genesis 28:10–19; 1 Kings 18:9–12; Zechariah 3:1–5; Ezekiel 3:10–15.)

TRANSLATED IN THE LIGHT OF HIS GLORY

In the New Testament, we see Saul (afterward called Paul), the most intense persecutor of Christians, being impacted greatly by *"a light from heaven"* that *"flashed around him,"* and by the words that Jesus spoke to him. (See Acts 9:1–18.) That one encounter shifted his destiny forever, and it was later followed by his experiencing another encounter in the *"third heaven."* (See 2 Corinthians 12:1–4.) Through the revelation of who Jesus is—including how this is revealed in His ministry, sacrifice, resurrection, and ongoing work on the earth—God's light is shining upon the earth and creating a supernatural doorway through which we can be translated into the heavenly realm. Look at what John had to say about one of his many supernatural experiences:

Then as I looked, I saw a door standing open in heaven.

(Revelation 4:1 NLT)

John saw a door. When speaking about heavenly doors, I like to use the word *portal* because it gives us a better visual of what this looks like in the Spirit realm. Normally, when you use the word *door*, people think about a rectangular wooden frame with bolts and hinges and some sort of doorknob, maybe even a little window opening in the middle. But, in the Spirit, I don't see heavenly portals in the same way. I see them as swirling openings of bright light. They are vibrant and filled with divine heavenly energy, and they present us with an invitation to step into something greater.

John continued to describe his glimpse into the glory realm, and not only did he see something, but he also heard something:

> *And the same voice I had heard before spoke to me like a trumpet blast. The voice said, "Come up here, and I will show you what must happen after this." And instantly I was in the Spirit, and I saw a throne in heaven and someone sitting on it.* (Revelation 4:1–2 NLT)

A door was swirling open in heaven, and a voice said to John, "*Come up here…*"! John saw the door and heard the invitation, and the Spirit wants you, as a light warrior, to see the door, too. Jesus is the open door, and He's beckoning you to come up. (See John 10:9.) A present-day invitation is being given to you by the Spirit of light. He's calling you up higher. You can only navigate according to the directional map that's been given to you. And that's the amazing thing about the glory realm. In the glory, you are given a higher perspective as you receive heavenly directives.

There is a very real spiritual battle taking place, but you are not created to fight in the same way that those who fight earthly battles do. In the glory, your victory has been settled; you're already an overcomer in Jesus. As a light warrior, you're being invited to daily rise into a place of heavenly revelation. On a continual basis, you must see the door standing open in heaven and choose to respond to the Lord's voice beckoning you to know Him on the throne in heaven, as the One seated in triumph. This builds within you confidence and faith, and it positions you to stay in the victory.

It is possible to experience heavenly encounters daily. I know that statement may stretch your faith as you read it, and that's the point. God is stretching us beyond what we've known in the past as He invites us to come up higher. The days ahead on earth will be filled with darkness and wickedness of all kinds, but we've been given the solutions in the glory realm. This is the realm of light. It's a victorious strategy for spiritual warfare. When the enemy wants to play games and make a mess in the natural world, we rise above it and receive heaven's divine plans from the throne room. In this way, we begin to bring heaven to earth, and that's what makes all the difference.

MY ANGELS CARRIED ME TO HEAVEN

Some years ago, late on a Wednesday night in October, I arrived in San Francisco by plane. I had been invited by Prophetess Peggy Cole to preach and minister at her prophetic gathering in Pacifica, California, along with other notable speakers. I was looking forward to these meetings, but nothing could have prepared me for the wonderful things I was to experience that week.

After landing, I picked up a rental car and drove myself to the hotel where I would be staying. Once I arrived, I was rather tired and ready for bed, so I lay down and quickly fell into a deep sleep. Yet, a few hours later, I was suddenly awakened by my three angels. You may have read about these angels in some of my previous books, including *Seeing Angels*. These are the predominant angels that always travel with me in life and ministry. I knew their names and assignments because I had met them on previous occasions, but it surprised me that they had awakened me with such urgency. It had been a long time since I had seen them, and now they had visibly come into the room on a mission. They proceeded to tell me that they had been commissioned by God to take me to heaven.

Immediately, I was in the Spirit, and my angels carried me to heaven. It sometimes happens that angels carry people to heaven in the glory realm. Whether I was in my body, or this was an out-of-body experience, I am not sure. The apostle Paul didn't seem to worry about it, and I guess I shouldn't be too concerned about it either. However, over the years, it has perplexed me as I've thought about it because it felt so real, and it felt like I was still in my body.

Many of the things that I saw, heard, and experienced that night when I was carried into heaven are unspeakable. I wouldn't be able to say enough to describe the beauty and magnificence of it all. These heavenly things are too holy to try to explain using earthly terms or comparisons. There are some things I saw that I know I'm not allowed to talk about, and there are other things that I am still processing in my spirit and may possibly be able to speak about at a later time, as the Spirit permits.

However, there is one thing in particular that I felt a release to share immediately upon returning to my hotel room later that night, and I want to share it here with you because it pertains to releasing the light.

A DIVINE REVELATION OF HEAVENLY LIGHT

While I was in heaven, I was taken to a huge room where the Lord presented me with a large, folded piece of paper. I can't tell you what the Lord looked like because I didn't see Him in a way that you would see another person, and yet I felt His presence and knew that it was He who was present with me. He placed the paper in my hands. On the outside of it were the words "Map of the Stars." It reminded me of the kind of maps you could purchase in a Hollywood souvenir shop to aid you in visiting the homes of movie stars and other famous locations.

I was instructed to open this folded paper, and, when I did so, I saw that on the inside was an outline of the state of California, which I recognized immediately. At once, tiny little lights began sparkling and appearing all over this map. I could see them as they were turning on. From North to South, these little lights appeared throughout the map of California like bright, shining stars. Then, all of a sudden, I saw bright clusters of these stars beginning to form over Southern California. "Wait a minute!" I thought to myself. "Los Angeles! I can see clusters of stars forming over Los Angeles. I can see stars forming all over the entertainment areas of Los Angeles!"

As I stood there astonished at all that I was seeing, the stars continued to appear, and they shone with great brightness. What I understood in that moment as I held this map in my hands was that the glory of God was breaking out all across the state of California, and that God was doing something supernatural in the entertainment industry specifically. These stars were bright portals opening from the heavenly realm, God's light directly impacting the earth. Later, as I prayed about this heavenly encounter, I came to understand that these portals prophetically represented actual people in these areas becoming ignited with the power and presence of God's light. The day after I experienced this heavenly encounter, the *San Francisco Chronicle* published a story about unusual lights being physically seen in the skies above the entire state of California![30] What an amazing natural confirmation of the things I had seen the night before while I was in the Spirit.

This heavenly encounter became a catalyst for our ministry to pursue God's heart for the media and the entertainment industry through prayer, praise, and large prophetic gatherings. We initially hosted a large night of worship at Paramount Pictures studios to take initial steps in activating what I had seen in the Spirit, and we later followed this with a Bible study held in a screening room at the Walt Disney studios in Burbank, with Disney employees and other entertainment people joining us. We also spent several years hosting spiritual seminars on the Warner Bros. Studios backlot. In addition, the Spirit has given us divine favor with notable celebrities and other cultural influencers to whom we've been able to minister. We've seen the spiritual impact that occurs when you follow the heavenly instructions provided through an encounter like the one I just described. Over the past twenty years, we have been a part of spiritual revivals across the state of California, and we have seen God's favor shining through the entertainment industry with more spiritual movies being made, Christian television programs bringing in the highest ratings, worship music winning the top music awards, and more. Heaven has invaded Hollywood, and we've only just begun to see all that God will continue to do. I share additional details about the unfolding of this encounter and further revelation that the Lord gave us for occupying prophetic promises in my book *Power Portals: Awaken Your Connection to the Spirit Realm*.[31]

A TEST FOR HEAVENLY ENCOUNTERS

In chapter 9, I will provide you with revelatory scriptural keys that will enable you to ascend into heavenly encounters, by faith, on a regular basis. These encounters will lift your vision higher and provide you with spiritual warfare strategies that work and ultimately advance you ahead of the enemy, so you can catch him in his tracks before he has any opportunity to thwart you.

---

30. Chronicle Staff Report, "Strange Lights Reported All Across State," SFGate, October 27, 2005, https://www.sfgate.com/bayarea/article/Strange-lights-reported-all-across-state-2575501.php.
31. Joshua Mills, *Power Portals* (New Kensington, PA: Whitaker House, 2020), chapter 9, "Establishing Places of Power."

In the glory realm of light, the enemy's tactics are exposed, and his evil plans are uncovered. As a light warrior, you will have a supernatural advantage for successfully moving forward in your call and ministry. Some of these heavenly encounters may come in day-vision form, while others may take place as you dream at night. Some may even feel so realistic that you would swear you were physically there. Regardless of the way you experience these heavenly encounters, I want you to know that they are legitimate, and you have no reason to fear them.

Sometimes, when people speak about experiencing an "out-of-body" phenomenon, they are referring to an occult practice by which their soul has self-willed a supernatural experience, and they begin to travel on the "astral plane." For a Christian believer, this practice is illegal and spiritually dangerous, and I can guarantee you, that is not what I am talking about here.

The difference between a false spiritual experience and a genuine one is the difference between the profane and the holy. The first relies on self (and the enemy takes advantage of this), while the second relies on God (and the Spirit responds to our spirit). We do not "self-will" these experiences; instead, we give ourselves to God's prophetic Word and hold fast to His promises, knowing that His plans are perfect for our lives. True faith is not about self; it's about trusting God. We pray, "God, Your will be done in my life," and we pursue His supernatural guidance. He has said that He is *"my glory, and the lifter of my head"* (Psalm 3:3), so I will allow Him to carry me by His glory and lift me into whatever experience is necessary for me to fulfill His calling on my life—that's His will.

Some people may argue, "Well, what if I'm being deceived?" I would encourage you to test every encounter against the truth of God's Word. In this way, you will be able to divide between the Spirit of truth and the spirit of error. Test the spirits. (See 1 John 4:1–6.) According to the Scriptures, you will be able to verify if your encounter is genuine by following certain guidelines. Does your encounter agree with these truths?

1. Jesus Christ has come in the flesh and saved us from our sins, according to His finished work on the cross of Calvary.
2. Jesus Christ is exalted as the one true God and is Lord over all.
3. In Jesus Christ, you are a child of God.

4. As His child, you are an overcomer through Jesus Christ.

5. God's Word is His final authority.

Many different encounters are available for believers. They are as diverse as the regions, mansions, and rooms of heaven, but, again, you will be able to solidly test your encounters using the above guidelines. Every spiritual encounter will confirm the Word and make it clearer to your heart, not contradict it. As we prepare to dig further into this revelation in the next chapter, let's pray together:

> Lord, we thank You for the impartation that's available right here and right now for heavenly encounters as You open pathways of light. Thank You, Jesus! We ask for divine vision to be imparted because we desire that our eyes would be enlightened to this supernatural realm of Your glory. Lord, I thank You for opening our spiritual eyes to see and our spiritual ears to hear—to see clearly and to hear accurately what You are revealing in this present day. God, I ask that You would remove all preconceived ideas that we might have about what You can do or how You can do it. We yield to Your Spirit completely. I boldly ask You to remove all limitations, hindrances, distractions, and blockages that might attempt to keep us bound to the earthly way of thinking. And I thank You, heavenly Father, for an ease in the glory flow of what You are revealing now. In Jesus's name, we thank You. Thank You, Jesus, for Your revelation glory. In Your powerful name, amen!

YES, LET THERE BE LIGHT! CAN YOU FEEL THE SPIRIT'S POWER FLOWING THROUGH YOU AND CAUSING DARKNESS TO FLEE? YOU'RE WINNING THE SPIRITUAL WARFARE BATTLE BECAUSE YOU'RE A *LIGHT WARRIOR*.

CHAPTER 9

ENTERING PATHWAYS OF LIGHT

Jesus taught us to pray, "*Your kingdom come, Your will be done on earth as it is in heaven*" (Matthew 6:10). Wherever you're living right now, Jesus wants you to see it as a place where heaven can descend and be manifested in a very real way. Over the years, I've had the privilege of living in various locations, and, in each place, we've prayed:

- In San Diego, California, as it is in heaven.
- In Spring Hill, Florida, as it is in heaven.
- In London, Ontario, as it is in heaven.
- In Langley, British Columbia, as it is in heaven.
- In Burlington, Ontario, as it is in heaven.
- In Birmingham, Alabama, as it is in heaven.
- In Palm Springs, California, as it is in heaven.

You can make this prayer personal, as well, for the location where you live:

- In _____, _____, as it is in heaven.

I am a disciple of Christ, and I believe that you are, too, and Jesus taught His disciples to pray in this way. I believe that, in the Spirit realm, this prayer gives permission for a heavenly whirlwind to form and swirl with God's light and glory. It's like a holy tornado that turns things around and gives us an upward pull. You see, when heaven comes down, we get caught up!

Recently, as I was ministering in the glory at a meeting, one woman received a powerful touch from the Lord. She later wrote me,

> I felt myself ascending in the light as we worshipped together. It was so different than anything I've ever experienced before. The higher I [was] lifted into the glory, the more I wanted to give God all the glory. The next thing I knew, I was standing before the throne of God, and, for the first time in my life, I felt His love filling me completely. After, when I came back into my body, I knew that I would never be the same again. I feel so much love and peace and goodness coming into my life. Plus, I don't have any pain in my body anymore, and I suffered for more than fifteen years with chronic pain. It is gone now, and I know that can only happen in the presence of the Lord.

We can expect these types of things to happen in the light.

One of Jesus's greatest recorded prayers is found in John 17:24:

Father, I desire that they also whom You have entrusted to Me [as Your gift to Me] may be with Me where I am, so that they may see My glory, which You have given Me [Your love gift to Me]; for You loved Me before the foundation of the world.

"*That they…may be with Me where I am.*" Where is Jesus located right now? Is He hanging on the cross and suffering in agony? Where is He now? Yes, we believers know that He lives within us, for the Scriptures declare that "*the kingdom of God is within you*" (Luke 17:21). But I want you to recognize that Jesus is seated at the right hand of the Father, even as He is seated on the throne of your heart. (See, for example, Acts 2:33; Hebrews 1:3; 12:2; 1 Peter 3:22.) Clearly, it's God's will for you to ascend in the light, for Jesus prayed that you would be with Him at the right hand of the Father—and I believe this includes the present time, as well as when we will be with Him forever in eternity. (See Ephesians 2:6.) There are various ways to enter into heavenly encounters, but they all begin through a personal relationship with Jesus

Christ. (See John 14:6.) Yet, remember, we don't just want an experience—we want *Him*. Our heart's desire must be to be with Him in a greater way.

We see different modes of ascension for heavenly encounters outlined in the Scriptures. Here are some instances:

- Jacob and Zechariah ascended through dreams and visions. (See, for example, Genesis 28:12; Zechariah 1:8; 3:1–5.) You, too, can be lifted through a dream or a vision.

- Elijah ascended in a whirlwind, and Ezekiel ascended through a *"stormy wind"* with a great fiery cloud. (Elijah was literally caught up in the whirlwind, while the heavens were opened in a supernatural storm for Ezekiel to be able to see into the glory realm.) (See 2 Kings 2:11–12; Ezekiel 1:1, 4.) You may have an unusual prophetic encounter in which you, too, are lifted in similar ways.

- Jesus ascended to heaven in a cloud. (See Acts 1:9.) We should expect to be lifted higher when we are immersed within the cloud of God's glory.

ENOCH WALKED WITH GOD

As we prepare to look further at the nature of heavenly encounters, I want you to consider this interesting Scripture about the prophet Enoch from Genesis 5:22–24:

> *Enoch walked [in habitual fellowship] with God after the birth of Methuselah 300 years and had other sons and daughters. So all the days of Enoch were 365 years. And Enoch walked [in habitual fellowship] with God; and he was not, for God took him [home with Him].*

"All the days of Enoch were 365 years"! Now, I want you to recognize that this was before the finished work of Christ, under a lesser covenant. How much greater glory do we have available to us today under the new covenant in Jesus's blood! The sustaining power of God was remarkable within Enoch's life and the lives of his descendants. But, the supernatural key here was that Enoch walked with God. Whenever you walk with God, supernatural things are bound to happen. Enoch positioned his life in such a way that God was

very close to him. He walked so near to God that, eventually, he just got completely engulfed within the power portal of God's presence and ceased to exist on the earth any longer. He walked so closely with God that he walked right into heavenly glory.

A HEAVENLY CHALLENGE

Some years ago, as I read the above passage about Enoch, I felt the Spirit challenging me concerning the number 365. He asked me, "Would you be willing to walk with Me three hundred and sixty-five days of the year, every year that you're living?" Of course, my answer was a resounding, "Yes, Lord!" Then, recently, when I was meditating upon these things in my heart, I could feel Him ask me another question: "Joshua, would you be willing to walk with Me in three hundred and sixty-five days of heavenly encounter?" It was another challenge, this one calling me even higher. I want to ask you the same question: "Would you be willing to walk with the Lord in three hundred and sixty-five days of heavenly encounter?"

Here, now, are four keys for ascension in the glory light.

ASCENSION KEY #1: INVITE THE GLORY

Since we know that it's the Spirit's desire for us to spiritually ascend, we can invite the glory of God by praying in the Spirit. This both prepares our hearts and aligns our motives to be synchronized with the heart of God: *"not My will, but [always] Yours be done"* (Luke 22:42). Remember, Billye Brim told me that tongues is the gateway for activating the other gifts of the Spirit and supernatural experiences. I believe it. I've found that the more I speak in tongues, the more I'm able to get out of my head and move into my heart (this is the location of the spirit). Praying in the Spirit is a key preparation for moving into deeper encounters and ascending higher in the light of God's glory.[32] As you pray in the Spirit, begin to recognize the manifest presence of God that fills you and surrounds you. This will help you to connect more easily with the next ascension key.

---

32. If you need assistance in creating an atmosphere of Spirit-filled prayers, I encourage you to stream or download our soaking album *Prayer Power*, which can be found everywhere digital music is available.

ASCENSION KEY #2: DIE TO SELF

This key may seem obvious, but there is only one way to get to heaven: you must die! Now, it's obvious that, as a believer, when you physically die, you will go to heaven. (In some ways, we could say that a believer never dies because they really go from a lower realm of living to a higher realm of existence.) The Bible tells us that *"it is appointed for men to die once"* (Hebrews 9:27 NKJV) and that to be absent from the body is to be present with the Lord (see 2 Corinthians 5:8). These Scriptures are talking about a natural death of the physical body, but that's not what we're focusing on here. It's more about what the apostle Paul mentioned when he said, *"I die daily"* (1 Corinthians 15:31). He was speaking about the very real sacrifice of dying to oneself each day. This is a choice that must be made, and only you can make it for yourself. Remember that Paul, who said this, also had encounters in the third heaven. Sacrifice is a key to heavenly encounter.

We can die to self by aligning our soul and body with our renewed spirit, which was quickened when we accepted Christ and received salvation. Our spirit, guided by the Holy Spirit, directs our souls and bodies to conform to godliness.

> *I have been crucified with Christ [in Him I have shared His crucifixion]; it is no longer I who live, but Christ (the Messiah) lives in me; and the life I now live in the body I live by faith in (by adherence to and reliance on and complete trust in) the Son of God, Who loved me and gave Himself up for me.* (Galatians 2:20)

We were crucified with Christ, and we were also raised with Christ to *"walk in newness of life"* (Romans 6:4, various translations). This walk in newness requires the sacrifice we have been discussing. There are two ways for believers to consecrate themselves in total sacrifice: (1) soul sacrifice and (2) physical sacrifice. Spiritually speaking, we completely bury the carnal desires of the soul and flesh, and we commit ourselves in totality to the work of God's Spirit in every part of us.

1. *Soul sacrifice.* This is where our mind, will, and emotions are fully given over to the purposes of God. In this way, we choose to be motivated by the impulses of glory instead of being motivated by our soul's natural desires.

> *Do not be conformed to this world (this age), [fashioned after and adapted to its external, superficial customs], but be transformed (changed) by the [entire] renewal of your mind [by its new ideals and its new attitude], so that you may prove [for yourselves] what is the good and acceptable and perfect will of God, even the thing which is good and acceptable and perfect [in His sight for you].* (Romans 12:2)

2. *Physical sacrifice.* This is where we commit our physical body to the Lord's service. We honor Him with our temple (body) and devote ourselves to Him completely as a form of spiritual worship. What begins in the spirit ultimately displays itself in physical manifestation.

> *I appeal to you therefore, brethren, and beg of you in view of [all] the mercies of God, to make a decisive dedication of your bodies [presenting all your members and faculties] as a living sacrifice, holy (devoted, consecrated) and well pleasing to God, which is your reasonable (rational, intelligent) service and spiritual worship.* (Romans 12:1)

Here are some other Scriptures to consider regarding these sacrifices: Luke 9:23–24; 1 Peter 4:1–2; Galatians 5:24; Romans 6:8, 11–14.

ASCENSION KEY #3: KNOW YOUR SPIRITUAL POSITION

This is another essential key to making a spiritual connection in the heavenly realm. You must first recognize your spiritual position in Christ and then call your entire being into alignment with it. Call yourself up into the light of Christ.

Coming into agreement with the apostle Paul's revelatory insight in Ephesians 2 will make all the difference. I would highly recommend that you study the entire second chapter of Ephesians. In this chapter, Paul states that when Christ ascended to sit at the right hand of the Father, we spiritually ascended with Him to be seated together with Him in the heavenly realms:

> *He raised us up together with Him and made us sit down together [giving us joint seating with Him] in the heavenly sphere [by virtue of our being] in Christ Jesus (the Messiah, the Anointed One).* (Ephesians 2:6)

It's clear that God desires for us to have a throne-room perspective because that's where we have been spiritually seated with Christ. Heavenly encounters are easier to receive once you understand that your spirit is already located in heaven. Now, it's just a matter of becoming aware of this, and awareness comes easily when you put into practice the next ascension key.

ASCENSION KEY #4: SOAK IN THE LIGHT

"Soaking" brings spiritual focus, and despite what you may have heard, it's scriptural to soak in the light of God's glory. Soaking is simply the idea of resting in the manifest presence of God and opening your heart to receive Him fully. In Psalm 46:10–11, the psalmist David penned these words: *"Let be and be still, and know (recognize and understand) that I am God.... The Lord of hosts is with us; the God of Jacob is our Refuge (our High Tower and Stronghold)."* When we soak in the glory light, we recognize the lordship of Jesus Christ, and we rest in His heavenly presence. The following are some of the benefits of soaking:

1. *Transformation.* Just as soaking in the sunshine can be beneficial for our physical and mental well-being, soaking in the glory light can transform us from the inside out. It can soften our hearts, make us more like Jesus, and change us in ways that we can't change ourselves. As we yield to God in the glory realm, we are transformed by His glory presence. (See 2 Corinthians 3:18.)

2. *Peace.* Spending time in the glory light can bring a sense of peace, calm, and serenity to our lives. In the light, the presence of Jesus is magnified over our problems, providing us with a heavenly perspective that brings rest. (See, for example, Psalm 17:15; 29:11; Exodus 33:14.)

3. *Joy.* Soaking in the glory light can fill us with joy that is beyond words. Many times, as we do this, spontaneous laughter will burst forth from our innermost being, or we'll feel an overwhelming sense of inner happiness. Being in God's light brings so much joy! (See, for example, Psalm 16:11; 21:6; Nehemiah 8:10.)

4. *Healing and deliverance.* Many people have experienced physical, emotional, and spiritual healing while soaking in the light of God's glory. Anointed music carries the ability to impart God's light into the very depths of our

being. As David played his anointed harp for King Saul, Saul received healing and deliverance. (See 1 Samuel 16:15–23.)

5. *Heavenly encounters.* Soaking in the glory light can lead to powerful encounters with God that can change our lives forever. Remember what James wrote: *"Draw near to God and He will draw near to you"* (James 4:8 NKJV). When you soak in the light, drawing near to Him with an open heart, you give permission for God's Spirit to encounter you in new and powerful ways. (See also Psalm 36:8; Ephesians 1:3.)

Many people enjoy soaking with praise and worship music each evening as they go to sleep. This creates a peaceful atmosphere for them to relax and posture themselves for daily heavenly encounters even as they sleep at night. Although your body needs natural rest, your spirit and soul can be alert and active, exploring heavenly realms throughout the night. The thing I really like about soaking in the light is that it's connected with rest. In a posture of rest, we're able to be more spiritually alert. Don't be in a rush but instead saturate yourself in the atmosphere of God's light.[33]

HOW TO POSITION YOURSELF TO SEE

I can feel the anointing so strong, flowing through me, as I convey this message to you. There is no doubt in my mind that as you follow these instructions and fully give yourself to the light of God's glory, you will find yourself ascending into heavenly encounters. The biggest challenge is to not force yourself to try to see anything. Again, the last ascension key, "Soak in the Light," is all about rest. In a posture of rest, it becomes very easy to receive. There is no struggling, no striving, no pushing, no pulling—just resting and receiving.

Occasionally, I like to go for a relaxing massage. There's a nice place in Palm Springs that gives a very good foot massage, which is especially nice to have after a long missionary trip during which I've done a lot of walking. I've found that every time I receive a massage, whether I'm expecting it or not,

---

33. As I mentioned earlier in this chapter, International Glory Ministries has soaking music available on all digital platforms. It's easily accessible for you, and it's a good way to get started in soaking in the light. Three albums that I would suggest you listen to are *Opening the Portals*, *Experience His Glory*, and *Receive Your Healing*. Each one carries a specific theme and unique anointing; you can choose which one you prefer, depending upon what you need at the moment.

my mind easily relaxes into a place of divine flow. As I lie back and rest, my soul begins to see in the Spirit. What I mean is that, suddenly, a spontaneous surge of ideas, pictures, and impressions begin to flow across the screen of my imagination. This is not forced; actually, it's the opposite. And the same thing happens, at an even greater level, when I follow the ascension keys that I've provided for you in this chapter. As you invite the glory, becoming dead to self and connected to your spiritual position, being seated with Christ in the heavenly realms, you begin to rise into heavenly awareness in the light.

As God's light begins to shine in your heart and lift you into heavenly encounters, you can expect His thoughts to infiltrate your soul. This means that God can fill your mind with new thoughts, He can realign your will to feel His desires, and He can move upon your emotions with holy laughter, purifying tears, ecstatic joy, a strong sense of loving devotion, and more. Without any effort of your own, you will begin to receive new ideas, feel new things, hear God's voice, and see what you've never seen before. You may even begin to taste or smell things in the Spirit realm.

A few days ago, while I was ministering in Los Angeles, the entire front half of the church began to fill with an overwhelming floral scent. This is one of the fragrances of Christ. It's very common for people to smell the scent of flowers, vanilla, cinnamon, myrrh, frankincense, cedars, burnt wood, or other aromas while having heavenly encounters in the glory realm. It's also common for people to taste honey or a sweetness of some kind on their lips, because this prophetically speaks of God's Word, like revelation, beginning to flow. Pay attention to these supernatural manifestations and appreciate them. Don't simply dismiss them as "just my thoughts" or "my imagination"—if you've positioned yourself before the Lord to receive, that's exactly what will begin to happen. In regard to entering through the heavenly doorway, remember what Jesus says in Luke 11:

> *So I say to you, Ask and keep on asking and it shall be given you; seek and keep on seeking and you shall find; knock and keep on knocking and the door shall be opened to you. For everyone who asks and keeps on asking receives; and he who seeks and keeps on seeking finds; and to him who knocks and keeps on knocking, the door shall be opened. What father among you, if his son asks for a loaf of bread, will give him a stone; or if he asks for a fish, will instead of a fish give him a serpent? Or if he asks for an*

> *egg, will give him a scorpion? If you then, evil as you are, know how to give good gifts [gifts that are to their advantage] to your children, how much more will your heavenly Father give the Holy Spirit to those who ask and continue to ask Him!* (Luke 11:9–13)

"How much more will your heavenly Father give the Holy Spirit to those who ask and continue to ask Him!" As you seek to enter into heavenly encounters, you can trust that God is not going to lead you astray. He's heard your request, and He is willing to open the door of encounter for you as you rest in His light. But, as He begins to introduce you to His heavenly realm through thoughts, ideas, and beautiful pictures, you must be willing to receive what you see, and then thank Him for it.

REVELATIONS IN THE LIGHT

When, by faith, we're yielded to God's spoken word, supernatural things begin to happen. He speaks, our spirits listen, and, in this way, we're positioned to be lifted into His heavenly purposes. We must learn how to ascend in the light of His glory. We can receive some further revelation about this from Ezekiel's prophetic encounters:

> *Now [when I was] in [my] thirtieth year, in the fourth month, in the fifth day of the month, as I was in the midst of captivity beside the river Chebar [in Babylonia], the heavens were opened and I saw visions of God.* (Ezekiel 1:1)

What I think is so amazing about this is that although Ezekiel was in captivity, he discovered a supernatural passageway to freedom. The Scriptures say that the heavens were opened, and he saw visions of God. Yes, that speaks to me right now. It doesn't matter what type of situation you're in at the moment. Maybe you feel trapped, captive, or bound. Maybe it feels like you're locked down and chained to a horrible situation. If the heavens are open, you can find a way of escape. Just begin to get a vision of the glory. Begin to get a vision of the open heavens right now. Yes, in your spirit, let the heavens be opened. Open heavens require an open earth. If you will open up right now, right here on the earth, you can experience the open heavens. Just say to God, "My heart is open. My soul is open. My mind is open. God, for You, I am completely open. My spirit is open for You. God, I am open to You and for You." Yes, it is possible for you to connect with that open-heaven reality. The heavens are open for you, too.

You might feel like you're trapped in sickness. Let the heavens be open for you with a vision of healing. The Spirit is bringing a vision of wholeness, a vision of Jesus as the Great Physician. Yes, He is the Great Restorer of your body, soul, and spirit. He is the King of Glory. Jesus is Lord over all. Be healed, in Jesus's name!

You might feel trapped in a terrible monetary situation, stuck in financial bondage, but, right now, a lifting is taking place. Reach higher! Be lifted up into a vision of the open heavens. See the overflowing abundance and limitless provision. There is no end to the goodness of God. He said, *"The silver is Mine and the gold is Mine"* (Haggai 2:8). Trust Him in this. Lift your hands in this atmosphere of glory and receive the showers of blessing that are raining down on you right now from the open heaven. If you can see it in the glory realm, then just thank God now for whatever you need. All of your needs are supplied according to His riches in heavenly glory through Christ Jesus. (See Philippians 4:19.) The heavens are open, so see Jesus. See Him exalted in your life. See Him as your King of Kings and Lord of Lords. Receive a vision of these divine realities because doing so is bringing you into divine alignment and moving you into position to ascend in the light.

I want to pray for you right now:

Lord, I thank You for releasing Your people into open-heaven visions to see You high and lifted up, to see Your angelic hosts in worship before You. Yes, Lord, to see the glories of heaven and to witness the marvelous wonder of Your glory. You are beautiful and holy and seated upon Your throne in victory and authority. May we see You in all of Your glory!

STEWARDING HEAVENLY ENCOUNTERS IN THE LIGHT

Whenever God gives us something, He requires us to steward it properly. This includes the realm of heavenly encounters. I want to conclude this chapter with some guidelines for how to be a good steward of encounters in the light.

GIVE THE GLORY TO JESUS

First, heavenly encounters are not given to bring attention to ourselves, and this is something that we need to remember. All the attention should be directed toward Jesus Christ; He is the focus. We're not to say, "Hey, everybody, look at me! Listen to what I have to say. I saw all these marvelous heavenly visions." As light warriors, we should always seek to shine the light of Christ everywhere we go. It's all for Him, because it's all about Him. Let's not be careless or flippant about the way in which we speak of heavenly matters. Encounters are precious and are to be deeply cherished; they are something holy to be held carefully and with dignity.

SHARE ENCOUNTERS AS THE SPIRIT DIRECTS

Second, such encounters are not to be hidden. They are not simply for us to say, "Okay, that was for me, and I'm not going to tell anybody about it. I'm just going to leave it alone." Of course, you might not be able to share everything, as I mentioned in the previous chapter concerning my own experience. Speaking about his third-heaven encounter, Paul said that he *"heard things so astounding that they cannot be expressed in words, things no human is allowed to tell"* (2 Corinthians 12:4 NLT). There are some parts of an encounter that you may be able to share now, while other parts you may need to save to be shared later, and maybe a few parts that you'll just hold in your heart and never share publicly. However, ultimately, heavenly encounters are given to you with the responsibility to steward them properly, including passing along the revelation to others.

Thus, there are moments when you might just need to sit with the revelation for a bit, contemplating and meditating on what God is showing you and speaking to you, but you must also be open to sharing it (or portions of it) with others as the Spirit directs. It's important to discern the appropriate audience, place, timing, and atmosphere as you plan to share these encounters. It's true that not everybody will be spiritually prepared to hear about some of the things you have seen, but there will be people who are ready, and they will be waiting to hear about your heavenly encounters. Your testimony can be the very catalyst that provokes them, too, into a greater spiritual awareness.

BE A LIVING EXAMPLE

There might be some things you see in the Spirit that you really don't have the words to express, or, again, things that you are not permitted to talk about. That's okay; every heavenly encounter you have should create a new depth of spiritual growth within you, which is the third point of being a good steward of encounters. In the heavenly realm, when we receive an impartation of the light, this illumination lifts us and changes our perspective. We need to hold on to that transformation and allow the encounter to make us more like Jesus.

When people see you and the life that you live, it should demonstrate the truth that you've been with Jesus in His light. While some details of your heavenly encounters may be just for you, the evidence of those encounters will be visibly apparent to those around you. The apostle Paul didn't need to talk about everything he saw because his life became a living example of the light he had experienced in heaven. It will be obvious to people if you've been in the presence of Jesus. You will carry and emanate that light. You will release that light everywhere you go. Paul wrote almost one quarter of the New Testament. This is a remarkable feat, especially considering that he had originally persecuted Christian believers and hated their message. It's obvious that he was changed by the light of God's glory through his initial encounter on the road to Damascus but also through his subsequent encounters with heaven.

WRITE DOWN THE REVELATION

Fourth, beyond being a verbal witness to others and demonstrating the change God has made in your life, I believe the Spirit will ask you to write down the revelation of your encounter or the prophetic message you've been given, describing what you saw in the glory realm. The prophet Habakkuk wrote, *"The Lord answered me and said, Write the vision and engrave it so plainly upon tablets that everyone who passes may [be able to] read [it easily and quickly] as he hastens by"* (Habakkuk 2:2).

I'm so thankful that Ezekiel's visions about the heavenlies were recorded so that we can read them today, and I'm grateful that John's revelations on the Isle of Patmos were recorded as well. These men saw the throne room of heaven with all its glory, and they wrote down portions of what they saw. Their encounters have been available for people to read or hear about from generation to generation. This is important because these revelations are life-changing. Since the revelations were physically written down, many others can now know about them and be blessed.

How might we *"write the vision"* if we have seen things that we don't necessarily have words to describe? If we have a picture of them in our spirit, we might be able to draw or paint them or depict them in some other way through the arts, or work with someone else to create a visual presentation of them. Or, if we are able to express portions of the encounters or visions, we might choose to make an audio recording as we speak about them or put them into song or poetic form. This can be as simple as pulling out our smartphone and making a recording using the voice-memo application. I do this all the time. When I receive a new song from the Spirit while I'm driving, I just pull over to the side of the road and park, then pull out my phone and record it in that moment. Why? Because I know that if I don't do that, I might lose it. At other times, a thought will cross my mind—for example, a new idea for a message or a book. Although, initially, the thought might not seem like much, I can still take it and use it as a seed, and it can become a springboard for further revelation to flow.

Making a record of the revelation doesn't need to be complicated. The most important thing is that you capture, in some way, what you've received from the heavenlies. Write down your vision because, as you move forward in the Lord and grow in Him, and He takes you from glory to glory, you may forget some of the important details. There is a reason that God gave us His Word in written form. He knew that people would forget it if it wasn't written down and recorded for reference.

In all of this, moving with the Spirit is essential. There is something very wonderful that happens when we take the heavenly deposit that God has given us and are willing to steward it well and share it with others. Our simple words (whether written or recorded), music, or artwork can inspire others with a multiplied harvest of glory.

Entering Pathways of Light 189

YES, LET THERE BE LIGHT! CAN YOU FEEL THE SPIRIT'S POWER FLOWING THROUGH YOU AND CAUSING DARKNESS TO FLEE? YOU'RE WINNING THE SPIRITUAL WARFARE BATTLE BECAUSE YOU'RE A *LIGHT WARRIOR*.

CHAPTER 10

SHIFTING ATMOSPHERES WITH PRAISE-LIGHT

"Make a joyful noise to the Lord, all the earth! Serve the Lord with gladness! Come into his presence with singing."
—Psalm 100:1–2 (esv)

Who is to make a joyful noise to the Lord? *"All the earth!"* (Psalm 100:1). That includes you and me. It includes us all—no one is excluded.

Through praise, our voice becomes a "soundwave" that releases the light! When you open your mouth, the light of Christ that is in your spirit is released into the atmosphere around you. In this way, you partner with the Spirit to make changes in your life and in the world wherever they're needed.

Did you know that one of the Hebrew words used in the Bible for praise (see, for example, Psalm 111:1) is *halal*, and that one of the meanings of that word is "to shine"? Isn't that amazing? The hiphil form of the word means "to flash forth light."[34] I think of it in this way: when we praise God, we are "flashing forth His light," dispelling darkness and shifting the atmosphere.

---

34. *Strong's*, H1984, Brown-Driver-Briggs, Hebrew Lexicon (public domain), Bible Tools, https://www.bibletools.org/index.cfm/fuseaction/Lexicon.show/ID/H1984/halal.htm.

Praise turns on the light! It releases a "light atmosphere" that scatters feelings of heaviness or gloom. In the atmosphere of praise, people feel lighter, more joyful, exuberant, energetic, and charged with faith for the things of God.

THE SPIRIT'S PRAISE PROTOCOL

The Holy Spirit has given us a protocol for receiving God's healing and delivering light that directly involves praise. That's why we're provided with this divine instruction:

> *Come into his presence with singing!* (Psalm 100:2 ESV)

This is the protocol of the Spirit.

When a person of greatness—for instance, a king, a queen, a president, or a prime minister—makes an appearance, there is a prescribed protocol that those in attendance must follow. This includes not only the way they are to act—what they can do and what they cannot do, what is expected of them and what is not allowed—but it also concerns how they dress and what they say or don't say.

Many years ago, Janet and I were praying some very specific prayers for America, and God gave me a dream. In this dream, I saw myself at the presidential inauguration. I was in back rooms, private rooms, areas that I would not normally have access to in the natural. After I saw this scene in the Spirit, we prayed into that vision, and God began to unfold the fulfillment of it little by little.

By faith, and because of what I had seen in the Spirit, we booked a hotel room in Washington, D.C., in advance of the inauguration. Then God began to bring us the needed connections. The assignment from the Spirit that we knew about was to pray the night before the event in one the ballrooms at the hotel and to sing in the Spirit throughout the night.

Through a miraculous divine connection, a couple of weeks before the event, we were provided with access to actually sit on Capitol Hill during the inauguration ceremony. Then, when we arrived in Washington and checked into our hotel, I received an email stating that we had also been invited to one of the presidential balls. These balls are by invitation only, and not open to the general public. I was to find myself in a room filled with the movers and shakers of Washington. However, along with that invitation was a protocol, a list of do's and don'ts. There's always a protocol to be followed.

Now, think about this: you and I have been given the honor to be in the presence of almighty God, the King of all kings, the Lord of all lords, the King of Glory, and Psalm 100 outlines for us the correct protocol for entering His presence: singing—and singing some more. When you're singing the praises of God, you have what He's looking for, and you give Him the honor He is due.

THE SOUND OF GOD

Praise is the voice of faith, and faith gives us access to divine illumination. *"Faith is the substance of things hoped for, the evidence of things not seen"* (Hebrews 11:1 KJV, NKJV). Just as light makes the invisible visible, faith allows us to perceive the reality of God beyond our physical senses. If you review the Scriptures looking for such instances, you will discover that many moves of God have been released into the earth through spiritual sounds. Here is the main point I want you to understand: the sound of God on our lips, especially in relation to praise, has the ability to shift atmospheres with His light.

A sound from anointed men and women is creative, just as the sound of God's voice created the world.

At the dedication of Solomon's great temple in Jerusalem, the singers and the trumpeters released their sound, and as that sound was released, a cloud of God's glory descended upon that place. Praise brings the glory.

When King Jehoshaphat was faced with formidable foes, his army was little more than a ragtag team. They were not only limited in number, but they also lacked equipment. They seemed to be doomed. But, wait—they did have something: they had a song. After King Jehoshaphat and all the people prayed earnestly to the Lord and were assured that He would fight for them and bring them the victory, a revelation came to the king, and he instructed his military officials in what to do to win the battle:

> *And when he had consulted with the people, he appointed those who should sing to the* Lord, *and who should praise the beauty of holiness, as they went out before the army and were saying: "Praise the* Lord, *for His mercy endures forever."* (2 Chronicles 20:21 nkjv)

The king ordered his generals to send out the praisers first. Yes, praise comes first. When we talk about the realms of glory, when we talk about moving from realm to realm, if we want to encounter the move of God, we simply have to be willing to give God what He's asking for, and that is praise. Light warriors are praisers! Praise comes first because praise is the language of faith. You cannot praise God without having faith; and, with your faith, you need to make a *sound* of praise.

Sending worshippers out first might have seemed to Israel's military officials like a foolish thing to do, but they did it anyway. The praisers went before the warriors, with their natural weapons. I can see those worshippers now with their singers, their musicians, their banners, and their flags marching boldly out in front. What happened as a result?

> *Now when they began to sing and to praise, the* Lord *set ambushes against the people of Ammon, Moab, and Mount Seir, who had come against Judah; and they were defeated.* (2 Chronicles 20:22 nkjv)

How did this remarkable miracle happen? The praises of God's people rising up to heaven activated something in the realm of the supernatural that caused warrior angels of light, angel armies, to be released from heaven. The seemingly impossible battle Jehoshaphat had faced became God's battle, the forces of heaven were sent out, and the enemies didn't know what hit them. (See 2 Chronicles 20:23–30.)

Who can win against the hosts of God's angelic armies? Our God is victorious every time. This means that you are not a loser; you're a winner. Why? Because you're on the winning side. God is for you; He's not against you. (See, for example, Romans 8:31.) You're destined to be the top, not the bottom. You're the head, not the tail. You're above and not beneath. (See, for example, Deuteronomy 28:13.) We are *"more than conquerors"* (Romans 8:37) through Christ Jesus.

What does it actually mean to be "more" than a conqueror? A conqueror is someone who has won a battle. So, how could you top that? Think about it. Do you ever watch boxing matches? There is big money to be made in winning a major match. There will surely be some bloodshed and a lot of pain and bruising, and there is also the danger of being knocked out and/or suffering some permanent damage. But many people do it because the money is so good. They are tempted to fight because the boxer who goes home with the purse can afford to take his wife out on a shopping spree to buy items by Louis Vuitton and Gucci.

That man is a conqueror—but his wife is more than a conqueror. Why? Because she ends up with the fringe benefits, the perks, the blessings. She is favored because of her relationship to the conqueror, and she doesn't have to bear the aches and pains of combat. Similarly, you are more than a conqueror in Christ Jesus. He won the battle, and you reap the rewards.

When King Jehoshaphat gave the order to sing, and his army moved out to battle, led by the worshippers, they didn't even have to fight—their enemy armies were set against one another and ended up slaughtering each other. (See 2 Chronicles 20:23.) That result would have been impossible in the natural. Why did they win against such overwhelming odds? Because the sound went first. And, as "more than conquerors" the Israelites also gathered many items of value left by the armies. The Israelites not only praised God before the battle, but they blessed and praised God following the victory. (See verses 25–28.)

In another example of the power of praise, this one from the New Testament, we see Paul and Silas being beaten and imprisoned in Philippi. They were not in prison because they had done something illegal or were dangerous to others. They had been preaching the gospel and doing good, but the fact that they had brought deliverance to a demon-possessed woman infuriated her masters, and these men stirred up the people and the officials against them. (See Acts 16:16–24.) You would think everybody would be very excited that this woman had, at last, been set free, but when you start moving in the divine supernatural, religious spirits get stirred up. Again, religious spirits tend to dismiss anything they can't control. Because the woman had been set free, her owners could no longer control her to make money from her fortunetelling, and they were angry. You must realize that not everybody will be excited when you set people free from the darkness, and sometimes you will be surprised by who didn't get excited: you thought they were for the works of God, but now you know better. It seems they were only using you. But God is always for you. Hallelujah!

At some point, we have to make a decision about whether or not we will take a stand for what is right, even when others become angry about it. Imagine being beaten and thrown in jail for doing good! It happens. You may very well find yourself in a situation in which you have done the right thing and yet you feel like you've gotten the wrong result. You look back over what you have done and can't see where you went wrong. You felt you were doing what the Lord had asked of you. So, why do you now feel like you're in prison? Please don't give up, and don't lose heart. God is doing something important. He is looking for people who will stand in His authority and stand with His truth—those who will be bold, strong, and courageous, moving in the divine supernatural. Remember, *"if God is for us, who can be against us?"* (Romans 8:31, various translations).

So, trust Him with the process. Don't stop praising Him! Here were Paul and Silas in prison in Philippi. It was the middle of the night, and their hands and feet were shackled. What should they do now? What *could* they do now? They could easily have sat in that prison complaining, but that's not what they did. They knew they were in God's will, in His perfect plan, even in that cell. I imagine Paul turning to Silas and saying, "Silas, I don't have a key in my hand, but we do have a key in our mouth. Let's sing praises to God."

Silas agreed, and they started singing songs, hymns, and spiritual songs. In this way, they sang and prayed and sang some more—right there in the darkness of their cell. As they did this, their sound of praise unlocked something in the heavenlies, and the atmosphere began to shift. Your praise will also change the atmosphere. Your sound will bring you into the very presence of almighty God and activate His heavenly host.

The sound Paul and Silas made caused a manifestation of glory to hit that prison, and suddenly the earth beneath the jail began to shake. The shaking was so violent that the prison doors were opened, and all the prisoners' shackles fell off. The result was that not only were Paul and Silas freed, but also the jailer and his family were saved. (See Acts 16:25–34.) This account is prophetic concerning what God is working in your own life. If you'll stay fixed on the main thing, if you'll recognize that God has called you for greatness—you are the head, not the tail; the top, not the bottom; above, not below—your victory will come, also. God's favor and blessing are upon you. He has anointed you for this moment. Release the light!

What you are facing is no mistake. God has set you in that situation as a light warrior, a light releaser, one who can shift the atmosphere. When you recognize this, you will see that it's not about you; it's about what God desires to do on the earth. Many people will be saved because of your release. Many will be saved because of your testimony. Many will be saved because of what God is working in your life—but the sound precedes the manifestation. Don't stop releasing the light through praise!

Think about Joshua and the battle of Jericho. God gave Joshua divine instruction, and it is very important to listen to divine instruction. What God speaks to you may be very different from what He speaks to someone else. The things of the Spirit are never cookie-cutter. It's not about just following a certain list, doing certain things, and then everyone receives the same result. Our God is very relational. Jesus Christ wants to have a personal relationship with you in which you hear His voice—having listened for His instructions—obey what He has spoken, and receive the release of His light.

Joshua followed these instructions from the Lord: the Israelite army circled the city wall of Jericho once each day for six days, while the priests played shofars, or trumpets, and the ark of the covenant was carried behind them. Then, on the seventh day, the army and priests circled the wall seven times in a row. After the seventh time, they released the *"long blast"* (Joshua 6:5) of the shofar, and the army gave *"a great shout"* (verses 5, 20). What happened? That wall came tumbling down. (See Joshua 6:1–20.) Light always prevails.

This incident reminds me of Psalm 44:3 (TPT):

> *Our forefathers didn't take the land by their own strength or their own skill or strategy. But it was through the shining forth of your radiant presence and the display of your mighty power. You loved to give them victory, for you took great delight in them.*

There is no barrier that's too tough for God to overcome, no situation that's too hard for Him to solve. With many of the situations we face in life, we say, "I have no idea how God could move in this circumstance. It feels so impossible." But we must always remember that, with God, nothing is impossible. With God, all things are possible. (See, for example, Mark 10:27.)

Of course, our receiving these impossibilities from God requires a partnership, a relationship, with Him. It requires our being yielded to Him, surrendering to and following His ways. Very often, in such situations, God tells us to be bold, to stand, and to release our sound. When we have done these things, He does the rest. We can do this by trusting in who God is and who we are in Him. After Psalm 100 encourages us to *"make a joyful noise to the* LORD*"* (verse 1 ESV) and to *"come into his presence with singing"* (verse 2 ESV), we then read:

> *Know that the* LORD*, he is God! It is he who made us, and we are his; we are his people, and the sheep of his pasture.* (Psalm 100:3 ESV)

"He is God!" Do we really know this? *"It is he who has made us, and we are his."* Do we really know this? These truths put everything into proper perspective. We're not God, but He is God. In other words, we don't make the rules; He does. He gives the instructions, and we simply follow His lead.

"We are his people, and the sheep of his pasture." Do we really know this? If you don't know it yet, allow the Spirit to bury this truth deep in your innermost being as you continue to praise Him.

THE PROTOCOL INCLUDES THANKSGIVING AND PRAISE

Psalm 100 then continues with more of the praise protocol:

> *Enter his gates with thanksgiving, and his courts with praise! Give thanks to him; bless his name!* (Psalm 100:4 ESV)

"Enter into his gates with thanksgiving." Can you picture it right now? A golden gate or portal is set before you, and God is saying that you can enter it if you use the right protocol, which is thankfulness. Enter His portal with thanksgiving. We must develop an attitude of gratitude.

I love the way *The Message* Bible expresses Psalm 100 in its entirety:

On your feet now—applaud God! *Bring a gift of laughter, sing yourselves into his presence. Know this:* God *is God, and God,* God. *He made us; we didn't make him. We're his people, his well-tended sheep. Enter with the password: "Thank you!" Make yourselves at home, talking praise. Thank him. Worship him. For* God *is sheer beauty, all-generous in love, loyal always and ever.*

I love all of this wording, but especially verses 2 and 4. Verse 2 says, "*Sing yourselves into his presence.*" That's the key: releasing the sound. And verse 4 says, "*Enter with the password: 'Thank you!'*" Now we know the password for access into God's presence. It's "Thank You." It's gratitude. It's a right heart attitude toward Him.

Today, we see so many new technologies being quickly developed. One of the newest ones enables us to utilize our voiceprint. Just speak, and we have instant access—to our cell phones, to our homes, and to other areas of our lives. Our voice commands can now literally unlock things in the natural.

But "voice activation" is nothing new. God has instructed His people to use it all along. We're only just now discovering its uses in the natural. Yet this is exactly what Psalm 100 is speaking about, in a spiritual sense. Speak gratitude and praise, and you can enter the gates and courts of the Lord. It is your voice that unlocks things in the Spirit. And I believe that in the same way that we each have individual, unique fingerprints, we each have a God-given sound that is unique to us; nobody else in all of human history has carried the same sound. It is a spiritual sound, given to those who are God's light warriors.

So, God has given you a unique voiceprint, and one of the reasons He has given it is so that you can unlock doors that nobody else can unlock. You hold a key that is specific to you, and it will open realms of glory that God has reserved for you. Can you see that in the Spirit?

We enter into God's gates with thanksgiving, into His portals with gratitude, and into His courts with praise. Verse 5 (esv) concludes Psalm 100:

For the Lord *is good; his steadfast love endures forever, and his faithfulness to all generations.*

God is worthy of all praise. Therefore, we must be thankful toward Him and bless His name. If there's anything the enemy will try to stop you from doing, it's blessing the name of Jesus. If there's something that makes the enemy angrier than anything else, it's when the name of Jesus is exalted and when God's name is lifted high among His people. If there's anything that makes the enemy jealous beyond anything else and sends him into a fit and a fury, it's when God's people recognize His greatness and, therefore, pay no attention to the enemy's distractions, annoyances, and hindrances but keep their eyes focused completely on Jesus.

MORE PROTOCOL FOR HEAVENLY ENCOUNTERS

In Psalm 103, David gives us another model for praising and extolling God, essentially describing how to live in the realms of glory. I want you to see this truth and receive it as your own. I don't want you to only experience glory realms when you're with others corporately in the church. This is an impartation that you can carry with you wherever you go that will literally shift the atmosphere of your life. You can find a new way of living in Christ Jesus. You can live in the authority and the victory that Jesus paid for.

David begins the psalm in this way:

> Bless (affectionately, gratefully praise) the Lord, O my soul; and all that is [deepest] within me, bless His holy name! (Psalm 103:1)

The book of Psalms is beautiful. Certain psalms can be sweet, and we enjoy some of them so much that we put their words on plaques and hang them up on the walls of nurseries. But the Psalms can also be powerful. David was a man of revelation. When he composed and sang psalms, it was not just from some pie-in-the-sky thinking. He was speaking out of his personal encounters with the Lord. He was a prophetic person, a man ahead of his time.

Light warriors are often way ahead of their time because they move in prophetic giftings. Don't be afraid that people will misunderstand you because you have something today that others will only come into in the days ahead. Because you saw it in the Spirit as you praised and worshipped God and were lifted into His presence, you're choosing to live in the reality of it today. When you see things in the Spirit, take hold of them and "pull them down." You can, in effect, live in your future right now.

David literally commands himself to praise God, to come back into divine alignment with faith. He directs himself to be repositioned with the Spirit of Truth. We all need to frequently check to see if we are still in divine alignment and to reposition ourselves with the Spirit as needed.

Next, David says,

Bless (affectionately, gratefully praise) the Lord, O my soul, and forget not [one of] all His benefits. (Psalm 103:2)

Here, David commands his soul—his mind, will, and emotions (including the way he feels and the way he acts)—to be established in the truth of the need to bless the Lord in all things. "Don't forget His benefits," he tells himself. Then he begins to name a few of them:

Who forgives [every one of] all your iniquities. (Psalm 103:3)

This speaks of our forgiveness for sin through Christ.

Who heals [each one of] all your diseases. (verse 3)

This speaks of the healing of our physical bodies.

Who redeems your life from the pit and corruption, Who beautifies, dignifies, and crowns you with loving-kindness and tender mercy; who satisfies your mouth [your necessity and desire at your personal age and situation] with good so that your youth, renewed, is like the eagle's [strong, overcoming, soaring]! (verses 4–5)

This speaks of a divine reversal of the effects of time and of stepping into the ageless realm of the glory. As David sang of the salvation that comes only through Jesus Christ, he was a thousand years ahead of everyone else in the natural timeline of things. He lived ten centuries before Jesus came to the earth to give of Himself on the cross for us. How could David sing such a song? It was because he had encounters with the Lord that gave him revelation of a truth that was unshakable and eternal.

David even foresaw the crucifixion of Christ. If you doubt that he did, go back and reread the Psalms, including Psalm 22:1. In some of David's psalms, he describes very specifically what Christ would accomplish through His crucifixion and resurrection. How did he do that? He was seeing through the eyes of faith. Peter, preaching on the day of Pentecost, and referencing Psalm 16, said of David:

> *He, foreseeing this, spoke [by foreknowledge] of the resurrection of the Christ (the Messiah) that He was not deserted [in death] and left in Hades (the state of departed spirits), nor did His body know decay or see destruction. This Jesus God raised up, and of that all we [His disciples] are witnesses.* (Acts 2:31–32)

Not only did David foresee the crucifixion of Christ, but he got the full picture: he also saw the resurrection. When you see things in the Spirit that others have not yet seen, you can sing a song that others are not yet singing. You can say something that others are not yet saying. Why? Because, again, you've already seen it prophetically; you've recognized it in the Spirit as you've entered into God's presence with praise and thanksgiving, blessing the Lord with all your being. And what you see in the Spirit, you can have. Once more, all you need to do is take firm hold of it, receive it, and then pull it down, making it your "now" reality. This is how you begin to change your atmosphere with praise-light.

You may still wonder how David could "see" something that had not yet happened in time. Time is a natural entity, but the realm of the Spirit, the realm of the glory, is eternal. Jesus Christ is the Lamb who was *"slain [in sacrifice] from the foundation of the world"* (Revelation 13:8). Before the crucifixion happened in time, it had already happened in the realm of the Spirit. Things first come from the Spirit, and then they manifest in the natural.

Thus, when God gives you a revelation about your family, your health, or your finances, look at it in the Spirit from that moment on. If you look in the natural, you will become discouraged and depressed. But when you look in the Spirit and see how God has destined things to be, that heavenly vision will drive you forward and create within you a new sound, a new song, a new praise. Then you can say something that others are not yet saying. For example, other people might look at your life and only see lack and insufficiency, but you're already seeing the plenty that is to come. When, in the Spirit, you see God's plentiful provision, you can declare it, and you can rejoice and thank God for it. You can praise Him in the midst of all that befalls you. When you do this, that praise suddenly changes the atmosphere, prophetically shifting your earthly reality.

David was singing about something others could not yet know—but he knew it. And because he knew it, he could command his soul to come into alignment with it.

Therefore, to shift atmospheres with praise-light, you have to take authority over your soul: *"Bless…the Lord, O my soul"* (Psalm 103:2). If you don't take authority over your soul, your soul will try to take authority over you. Make sure to take authority over your mind. That is the greatest war you will ever face in life. If you don't take authority over your mind, your mind can start to go into made-up scenarios, creating false situations, even accusations, and suddenly you go down a demonic trail of thoughts that have no basis in any truth or reality, and yet you have already decided the outcome will correspond with those thoughts. Next, you begin to walk in that demonic outcome in the natural because *"as he* [a person] *thinks in his heart, so is he"* (Proverbs 23:7).

Instead, let God fill the portal of your mind with His Word, His truth—and when His truth comes to you, begin to shout it out, and begin to speak about it to others. The greatest thing you can do for your future is to find a promise of God for your life and then begin to sing about it, talk about it, and share about it with others. Bring it up frequently and continue to live in that truth. Your praise changes the atmosphere!

PRAISE-LIGHT RELEASES HEALING FOR LIBERTY

A few summers ago, our daughter Liberty suffered a serious physical attack. Her tongue swelled up so badly that it was blocking her breathing. She spent more than twenty days in the intensive care unit at the Hospital for Sick Children in Toronto, and we stayed there with her night and day until she received the physical manifestation of her healing. Every day, when the doctor came in on his rounds, I would ask him if they had discovered what was wrong with Liberty. Invariably, his answer was something like, "We don't yet know why this is happening to your daughter." There seemed to be no natural cause for her condition and also no natural remedy.

After Liberty's tongue had swelled to many times its normal size, it actually turned black, and the doctors' reports were not good. Liberty tried to maintain a positive attitude through it all, but, as you can imagine, it was a very frightening situation. She couldn't pull her tongue back inside her mouth, and, obviously, she couldn't sing with it that way.

Liberty had been attacked like this once before, a couple of years previously. At that time, she had also been admitted to the hospital and was in the ICU, but God had healed her. We knew He would do it again, regardless of what the doctors said. We refused to accept a bad report and continued to hold on to the healing promises of God. Janet was fearless in this situation, and I also refused to accommodate any fears. Although we knew that God was going to do the healing, we also knew that we needed to be with Liberty to set the spiritual atmosphere with praise and release healing light in her room. You might wonder how we could do this in a loud hospital setting, with doctors and nurses bustling in and out of the room, machines beeping, and lights being turned on and off. Here's what we did: as we stayed by her side, we played our *Receive Your Healing* and *SpiritSpa* music albums nonstop, and we decreed God's healing promises from the Bible.

After the first time Liberty was in the ICU, I had gone into a recording studio with my friend Steve Swanson, and we had recorded the *Receive Your Healing* album. I had initially recorded it to bless other people, using the same anointing of the Spirit that had gotten our daughter out of the hospital, and the album had quickly gone around the world, ministering to millions of people. At the time I recorded it, I didn't realize I would need that album myself for a second time in the hospital with Liberty. I couldn't be in Liberty's room 24/7, so, when I had to go out to rest or eat, the album continued to play, and she was still able to hear me speaking God's Word to the anointed sounds of music.

In time, as we continued to change the atmosphere and express our faith in God through praise-light, Liberty fully recovered from this mysterious ailment.

There were three other families in the large ICU where Liberty stayed, and our presence there was like a missionary assignment. The music ministered to

Liberty, but it also ministered to the other families. From the beginning, we had asked permission from these other families to play our healing albums. It was, after all, a public healthcare facility, and we had all been assigned to that space. Thankfully, the families were receptive to the music and also to hear from us about God's healing miracles. As light warriors, we must recognize that wherever we find ourselves, we are supernaturally sent on divine appointments to release the light. *Shift atmospheres with praise-light!*

LIGHTNING FLASHES FROM THE THRONE

When you choose to praise God, you also choose to become a throne for Him. (See Psalm 22:3.) Revelation 4:5 speaks about lightning flashing forth from God's throne. When you praise God, in that moment, spiritual lightning flashes forth from your life. This shifts the atmosphere in a major way. Suddenly, things that were once dark are now revealed in a burst of light. That's why, many times, while you're praising the Lord, suddenly "the lights will come on" in your spirit and mind, and you'll receive an instant download of heavenly information. This happens to me very often when I'm in the midst of praise and worship, whether it is corporately in a public church service or on my own at home in a private setting. The physical location doesn't matter, but the spiritual location does. When your heart is lifted toward the heavens in such a way that it becomes a heavenly throne, you can expect a heavenly manifestation to flow from the glory realm into the natural realm.

The Urim and Thummim were used by the high priest in ancient Israel as a means of determining God's will. (See, for example, Exodus 28:30.) The Hebrew word *Urim* is the plural of a word that means "light" or "fire."[35] *Thummim* means "perfections."[36] Just like the Urim and Thummim, God's light shines on our hearts, and we are illuminated with understanding.

FOUR WAYS PRAISE-LIGHT CHANGES THE ATMOSPHERE

I now want to explain four different ways in which praise changes your atmosphere.

---

35. Strong's Lexicon, "224. Urim," Bible Hub, https://biblehub.com/hebrew/224.htm.
36. Strong's Lexicon, "8550. Tummim," Bible Hub, https://biblehub.com/hebrew/8550.htm.

1. PRAISE CHANGES YOUR SPIRITUAL ATMOSPHERE

As mentioned previously, everything begins in the Holy Spirit and flows from the Spirit into your spirit, and then into your soul, and from your soul into the natural realms—the physical, the financial, and so forth. Thus, first of all, praise changes your spiritual atmosphere.

We appreciate all the encounters God brings to His people from time to time, but, every once in a while, He catches one of us up into the glories of heaven, and they encounter God in His throne room in the third heaven, and it's glorious. They come back and report on their experience. When someone makes such a claim, we can discern in the Spirit whether it was a genuine encounter with the Lord or just someone's wild imagination. When it comes from the Lord, we say, "Wow, that's so amazing. It's awesome." And we often have a desire to be lifted into heaven's throne room also.

As I have sought the Lord about this desire, He has showed me that we can have it fulfilled every single day, although in a different way from what we may have thought. We're looking to be caught up and taken out of the life that we're dealing with, but Jesus taught us to pray in this manner:

> May your Kingdom come soon. May your will be done **on earth**, as it is in heaven. (Matthew 6:9–10 NLT)

Many times, we're trying to escape the earth, but, as I previously mentioned, God wants to invade it. If we will allow ourselves to be the portals He has created us to be, He will flow through every doorway of opportunity we give Him to change the atmosphere in our lives and in the lives of others. Instead of desiring a throne-room encounter in the third heaven, our desire should be this: "God, since You said that You abide in or are enthroned upon the praises of Your people, I choose to praise You in this very difficult and terrible situation. I will build a throne of praise right here and find myself in Your throne room so that Your Spirit can flow through me and meet this need."

When you begin to praise God and build a throne to Him in your life, what happens? I have read in the Bible about the throne of God and know some of what it looks like, and I have seen some of the glories of heaven. Over God's throne is an emerald rainbow (see Revelation 4:2–3), and green is the very first color mentioned in the Bible (see Genesis 1:30). It's a color of new beginnings and signifies a brand-new start. When God's throne shows up, there are new beginnings. There's a new start for each of us.

I believe that the rainbow over the throne is a sign of God's covenant promises coming into the atmosphere. Around the throne are the four living creatures, who cry, "Holy, holy, holy!" These creatures, individually having the face of a lion, an ox, a man, and an eagle, represent faces of glory that express the unique dimensions of God and His authority. To me, the lion signifies the Lion of Judah as He roars in victory. The ox represents the servanthood of God. When we want to see the greatest things of God come into our lives, we have to be willing to lay down our own agenda, our own preprogrammed ideas of what God's miracles or breakthroughs will look like, and say, "Lord, let Your glory come in whatever way You desire to bring it." The man represents not only the humanity of Jesus Christ, the King of Glory, but also Jesus's ultimate desire to release the light of His glory through His people, those who call Him Lord. The eagle represents God's supernatural vision, and His desire for us to see beyond the natural into the supernatural.

Around the throne, there are also angels. To establish God's throne in our hearts means to establish a place where God can sit and rule as King, reigning as Lord of our lives and commanding the heavenly hosts to work on our behalf as we fully submit to Him; where God's Spirit has liberty to work in and among us; and where we are given an ever-increasing glory perspective.

Many years ago, I discovered that the word *hallelujah*, from the Hebrew *halal*, doesn't just mean "praise the Lord." It's a command indicating that we must praise. When you say, "Hallelujah," the *jah* portion of the word refers to Yahweh, the Hebrew name for God. Yahweh must be magnified. Yahweh must be glorified. Yahweh must be praised. Hallelujah! Hallelujah! Hallelujah! Hallelujah!

When we begin to speak this word, it shifts atmospheres. Go through your home and build a throne with the word *hallelujah*. Go into your workplace, your business, and build a throne with the word *hallelujah*. Speak over your body and build a throne there for God with the word *hallelujah*. Praise changes your spiritual atmosphere. In praise, we celebrate God's mighty acts, His wonders. It's all about Him.

The psalmist declared,

Then I will proclaim your justice, and I will praise you all day long.
(Psalm 35:28 NLT)

Some people may ask, "How could we possibly praise God all day long? That just seems like an impossible feat." Our praise begins with singing, but that's just the beginning. It's important that we make a joyful noise, a sound, to the Lord, but the truth is, it doesn't end there. When people don't understand this, it can become a serious problem for them in their spiritual life. Some believers go to church on Sunday morning and sing for twenty minutes, and that's all the praising they do. But praise is what we should do because of who we are. God is expecting each of us to become *a living praise* in the earth. In this way, we will live our whole life as a praise to God.

I'm not trying to put you into a "works" mindset—into a structure of trying, striving, or attempting to do more for God. What I am saying is that freedom comes when we release the things of the earth and no longer allow them to hold us bound. We then say, "I am living my life for Jesus. I have decided whom I will serve. My life is not my own; it is a drink offering poured out for all those around me. I want to carry and release the glory everywhere I go. I am, therefore, a living demonstration of praise and worship, a living song for the Lord."

When I was ministering at a church in Gallup, New Mexico, I met the pastor's daughter, who was a doctor with John Hopkins Hospital in Baltimore, Maryland, and I asked her, "Do you think it's possible for the glory to change our DNA? I believe in the core of my being that this is a reality, and I've been saying it, but I don't have any scientific proof to make such a statement, only what I feel."

"Well," she said, "we've done a study showing that DNA can indeed change, so, about that statement, 'The glory can change your DNA,' I don't see any scientific reason why it couldn't happen."

I firmly believe that the glory changes our DNA. And if the glory can change our DNA, that means it can take a sad song and make it into a glad song. It means it can take a sorrowful song and make it a joyful song. It means that God can transform your whole life in the power of His Spirit. He can do something that nobody else could ever do for you, changing your story and your song.

Praise is the voice of faith and victory. If you're feeling spiritually dry, begin to praise the Lord and let the refreshing living waters overflow in your life.

The words of the godly are a life-giving fountain. (Proverbs 10:11 NLT)

I love that verse. Who are the godly? Those who are called unto God, those who are living in the glory and for the glory and who are allowing the glory to flow through them. Our words become a life-giving fountain, and we become a source of refreshing everywhere we go.

Refreshing waters change dry atmospheres, producing well-watered gardens. Hopeless atmospheres are filled with the hope of Christ. Atmospheres that have been filled with pain and despair are suddenly overflowing with the healing waters of God that pour through the praises of the righteous. Praise changes the spiritual atmosphere!

2. PRAISE CHANGES YOUR MENTAL ATMOSPHERE

Your praise to the Lord also has the ability to enhance, nourish, and renew your mind. We are commanded in the Scriptures, *"You shall love the Lord your God with all your heart and with all your soul and with all your mind (intellect)"* (Matthew 22:37). Hallelujah! We are to praise Him with all of our soul, all of our strength, all of our heart, and all of our mind.

Praise him for his mighty works; praise his unequaled greatness!
(Psalm 150:2 NLT)

All that is [deepest] within me, bless His holy name! (Psalm 103:1)

In faith, we sing and celebrate, which causes our minds to align with the mind of heaven. Let everything within us resound with praise to God, for this praise is changing the atmosphere, and He receives the glory. As the atmosphere begins to shift, the enemy can no longer control your mind. He can no longer have authority over that domain. When you choose to give God high praise, and your mind is brought into line with the thoughts of heaven, clarity comes.

"We have the mind of Christ" (1 Corinthians 2:16). Jesus's thoughts become our thoughts. His ideas become our ideas. His solutions become our solutions. In the glory, the blueprints of heaven, the pattern of heaven, and the coding of heaven are downloaded to our minds. In this way, breakthroughs can come from our minds into the earth.

God wants to remove all of our "stinking thinking," all of our limited mindsets, all thoughts of scarcity, all thoughts of impossibility, all doubt and unbelief. He wants to fill our minds as He shifts the atmosphere through our praise. When you praise God all day long, you press into the glory realm. When you find yourself facing a situation you don't know how to deal with, just press into that realm and say, "God, You know that I don't know what to say or do, but I recognize that You always know what to say and do."

Because I've ministered in more than eighty nations, I've preached on many church and ministry platforms. There are times when, before speaking, I will stand there and pray silently, "God, I don't have anything on my mind to say. I really don't know what to say." He always reminds me that He's God, and He knows what to say. I let Him speak to me, and I receive understanding about what to say next. I also follow the same practice in a very real way in everyday life.

Similarly, whenever you are in a situation where you don't know what type of praise to offer God, what sound to make, just pray in the Spirit. Let God speak through you. As He speaks through you, He will download to your mind what you need in that moment, and, in this way, He will give you the praise you need.

A husband and wife who are professors at the University of Kansas attended some of my meetings in St. Louis, Missouri, and they came to me with a testimony. They told me that, one day, they were working on a project that was due by midnight, and they were very concerned because they didn't have the solution they needed in order to complete the project. They decided to turn on some of our soaking music that is accompanied by praying in tongues. This created such a peaceful atmosphere that they prayed in tongues along with it.

Suddenly, the volume of the music began to increase. The wife thought that the husband was turning up the volume louder and louder in frustration because they so desperately needed to receive a solution. When she finally decided to go turn down the volume because it was just too loud for her, she realized that her husband hadn't been turning it up at all. The music was miraculously increasing in volume throughout the house. Then it dawned on her that they were experiencing a supernatural encounter: they were hearing the sound of angels singing in their home! Because this sound was filling the entire house, the wife decided to pray louder and speak in tongues louder as the angels worshipped the Lord so intensely. Within a few minutes, the revelation they needed dropped into their minds. They received their answer and were able to get the project completed on time. It was a real miracle! It is amazing how quickly praise can change your mental atmosphere.

3. PRAISE CHANGES YOUR EMOTIONAL ATMOSPHERE

Praise is able to change our emotional atmosphere, too, helping us not to fluctuate between high days and low days—being on the top of a roller coaster one moment and down at the bottom the next moment. I like roller coasters. I really do. I've enjoyed riding on roller coasters all over the world. However, some people live on a roller coaster of emotions, and it's detrimental to their health and a hindrance to fulfilling their God-given assignments. God wants to send them an emotional realignment. *Let there be praise-light, and let it bring balance to our emotions!*

Singing the Psalms can be an emotionally healing experience. When we read David's psalms, it's clear that, at times, he is being very vulnerable. He is brutally honest about where he is in his life, and he is not afraid to speak about it. He doesn't hold back. He just says it the way it is. Some psalms are designated as "Psalms of Lament," and Psalms 13 and 55 are two such examples. The dictionary defines the verb *lament* as "to feel or express sorrow or regret for."[37] When we put sound to our deepest emotions, not hiding from those emotions or pretending they don't exist, we open a supernatural door of invitation for Jesus Christ to step into the deepest and darkest places of our lives, and for His healing light to meet us at our point of need.

Sometimes, when we want to praise, the only thing we can do is offer God our groanings.

> O Lord, *hear me as I pray; pay attention to my groaning. Listen to my cry for help, my King and my God, for I pray to no one but you.*
>
> (Psalm 5:1–2 NLT)

---

37. Dictionary.com, s.v. "lament," accessed December 1, 2024, https://www.dictionary.com/browse/lament.

The Bible speaks about the groanings of God: deep calling unto deep, deep things within us calling unto the deepest things of God, inward cries and deepest sounds. God promises to receive all these sounds and answer us in the way that only He can. (See, for example, Psalm 42:7; Romans 8:26–27.)

When we submit our emotions to the Lord, God is able to bring us emotional stability and deep, authentic healing. Let praise-light change your emotional atmosphere.

4. PRAISE CHANGES YOUR PHYSICAL ATMOSPHERE

God's Word addresses matters related to health and wellness. Various Scriptures deal with the connection between God's plan and our physical well-being. (See, for example, Exodus 15:26; 23:25; Proverbs 3:7–8; 16:24.) One of the ways we can walk in divine wellness is by staying in tune with God's Word. We can stay in tune by hearing His Word, receiving His Word, speaking His Word, and singing His Word. All of these spiritual practices will help us to resonate with the spiritual frequency of divine health.

One evening, while I was ministering in Sydney, Australia, I just began singing one of the Psalms. We must be sensitive to times when the Spirit may want to sing through us. As I sang, the people joined in, and, before long, we were all singing a song we had never heard before. Then, we were all singing, "Holy, holy, holy," the same words the seraphim cry in Isaiah 6:3 and that the *"living creatures"* proclaim in Revelation 4:8. Our singing in this way brought an opening in the atmosphere, and God began to open realm after realm. Why? Because, guided by the Spirit, we had come into His presence with singing.

God wants to give you a new song to change your physical atmosphere. It's a song that has never been sung before. It's not an old song, and it's not a pre-rehearsed song; it's a song that changes the atmosphere because it is from God's light. Hallelujah! We sing the Word, and the Word opens new realms to us.

Proverbs 4:20–22 (NLT) reminds us:

> *My child, pay attention to what I say. Listen carefully to my words. Don't lose sight of them. Let them penetrate deep into your heart, for they bring life to those who find them, and healing to their whole body.*

When we receive the words of God, and not just hear them, from out of the depths of our heart, our mouth speaks and sings. We begin to sing by revelation the words of God that we received in our heart, and suddenly our physical atmosphere shifts.

Many areas of our physical well-being are realigned when we resonate with the frequencies of praise and worship. This is the anointing of God. This is who we were created to be. Once more, you were created to be a praise. You can say, "Praise is what I do because it's who I am. I release praise I because I am a praise in the earth."

When we praise the Lord, we look to Him as our Healer and turn our back on the work of the enemy: sickness, disease, pain, and any other physical suffering. God receives our praises, and He returns them to us as a healing flow of vitality. This flow of life streams through our physiological pathways, removing obstacles and filling our physical body with divine health.

The praise that God will direct us to release is a healing sound. It's a healing song, and, I believe, in many ways, it changes our physical health. The way I see it in the Spirit is this: as we release our praise, we release our breath. As we release our breath, we also release an incense, a fragrance, an offering to the Lord. As we release this to Him, He breathes it in the heavenly realms, taking it in with His nostrils, receiving our praise. But then, after He breathes in, He breathes out, and that *ruach*[38] breath brings life to us. He breathes over us the breath of life once again, and, in that breath, there is healing, there is wholeness, there is restoration. In His breath is everything we need.

I want to conclude this section with Proverbs 3:6–8 (NLT):

Seek his will in all you do, and he will show you which path to take. Don't be impressed with your own wisdom. Instead, fear the Lord *and turn away from evil. Then you will have healing for your body and strength for your bones.*

Your praise changes your spiritual atmosphere, your mental atmosphere, your emotional atmosphere, and your physical atmosphere. Praise changes every atmosphere, impacting it by the sound of the Lord that flows through you.

---

38. Hebrew word meaning "Spirit, wind, breath." Strong's Lexicon, "7307. ruach," Bible Hub, https://biblehub.com/hebrew/7307.htm.

Years ago, when I shared portions of this revelation at a meeting, a husband and wife named Glen and Ingrid, who owned a real estate business, were present. Later, they told me, "Your revelation about praise changing the atmosphere completely changed our life. We understood what you meant by it, but the Lord spoke to us and said, 'Speak differently to your employees. Where there has been chaos, where there have been problems, where the enemy has tried to get in and gain a foothold, begin to edify and lift up and encourage. Instead of focusing on what's wrong, begin to speak about what's right.' Praise changed the atmosphere in our real estate office. It has revolutionized everything."

Let God work this revelation through you, too, and see what God will do and how the atmospheres of your life will change as you release His praise-light!

YES, LET THERE BE LIGHT! CAN YOU FEEL THE SPIRIT'S POWER FLOWING THROUGH YOU AND CAUSING DARKNESS TO FLEE? YOU'RE WINNING THE SPIRITUAL WARFARE BATTLE BECAUSE YOU'RE A *LIGHT WARRIOR*.

CHAPTER 11

ACTIVATE THE GLORY LIGHT!

*"His appearance changed from the inside out, right before their eyes.
Sunlight poured from his face. His clothes were filled with light."*
—Matthew 17:2 (MSG)

More than twenty years ago, I stood at the front of the sanctuary of a church in Natchez, Mississippi, playing the keyboard and leading the congregation in worship during a morning service. As usual, I was scheduled to lead worship for half an hour before the evangelist with whom I was traveling in ministry got up to teach—but my heart told me that something unusual and significant was about to occur. My spirit was focused on the words we were singing, when there was a sudden shift in the spiritual atmosphere. In that moment, people began to move from their seats in unison, supernaturally drawn to the altar. Many of them fell to their knees, with their arms lifted in surrender and with tears streaming down their faces. I closed my eyes in worship, and the atmosphere started to pulse with an electric energy, a feeling that something further was about to happen. The presence in the room became indescribably strong yet gentle, and although my eyes were shut, I knew—I believe we all knew—that Jesus Christ had entered the room. A holy hush engulfed the sanctuary as we knelt or stood in the light of His glory.

Jesus's presence was undeniable. He was *there*. The Light was walking among us in a tangible way. The room felt charged with holiness, a purity that made my skin tingle and my heart race. I wanted to open my eyes, but I couldn't do so under the weight of His glory. I stood in silence while my spirit ascended to a space where earthly constraints seemed to dissolve. I later learned that the others who were present had the same experience. Time lost its meaning, and, suddenly, the sun, which had been high when we began, had dipped below the horizon, yet somehow it seemed like mere moments had passed.

When I finally opened my eyes, it was six o'clock in the evening. We had all been immersed in the light of Jesus for hours, yet it felt like the blink of an eye. Other people were now slowly coming into the sanctuary to attend the evening miracle service. As we gathered ourselves, the testimonies began to pour in—stories of supernatural healings, hearts mended, and spirits revived. All these results came about from a single, extraordinary encounter with Jesus.

Encounters in the light of Jesus are not simply emotional experiences; they are very real transformative moments that shape the course of our lives and ministries. They break generational curses, prompt our hearts to make a strong and renewed commitment to Christ and His kingdom, impart fresh anointings, and release blessings that ripple through time. In the book of Revelation, we see another beautiful picture of the throne of God, with *"the river whose waters give life"* (Revelation 22:1) flowing from it, and *"the tree of life"* (verse 2) on either side of the river, bearing fruit each month, whose leaves are *"for the healing and the restoration of the nations"* (verse 2). This imagery isn't just poetic; it's a promise of abundance, healing, and continuous fruitfulness for those who dwell in the light of God's presence.

EVERYTHING CHANGES IN THE LIGHT OF JESUS

The revelation in this book about being a light warrior has the potential to illuminate your life, producing profound supernatural healing and transformation. Not only does it have the power to bring about change in you, but it also contains the power to change everything and everyone around you—if you will embrace this truth and walk in it fully. You must put this revelation into practice to see that potential become reality.

As expressed throughout this book, this revelation is centered on the concept of light—not physical light but the spiritual light that emanates from the glory of Jesus. At the very core of this message is the fact that Jesus Christ *is* the Light of the World. What an amazing revelation! He is the Light of hope. He is the Light of healing. He is the Light of miracles. He is the Light of deliverance. He is the Light of truth. He is the Light that we all need!

In the imagery of the light shining from the menorah that was used in the temple in Jerusalem in ancient times, we see displayed the glorious revelation of who Jesus Christ is. It points to a spiritual reality with tangible implications for our lives. When we truly grasp this concept, we begin to see how God's light can penetrate every aspect of our being, bringing deep healing to our souls and even transforming our physical bodies. The Scriptures tell us that *"God is light and in Him is no darkness at all"* (1 John 1:5 NKJV). This foundational truth sets the stage for us to understand how light operates in the spiritual realm. Just as God spoke light into existence at the dawn of creation, He continues to speak light and life into our lives today.

When we receive and apply the revelation of the glory light, it brings us additional revelation of the power of God's light. It opens our spiritual eyes to see in a new way, and it opens our hearts to receive divine truth. This enables us to move into a higher glory dimension where healing and transformation flow with ease. We are called to be *"children of light"* (John 12:36, various translations), filled with the presence and power of Christ. And, as we embrace this truth, we become like lamps, radiating the light of God to those around us.

The transformation that occurs as we embrace the light of Christ is not just superficial. Hebrews 1:3 (NIV) describes Jesus as *"the radiance of God's glory and the exact representation of his being."* As we behold Him and allow His light to fill us, we are changed into His image *"from glory to glory"* (2 Corinthians 3:18, various translations). This supernatural change affects every aspect of our being. Ephesians 5:9 (NASB) tells us that *"the fruit of the light consists in all goodness, righteousness, and truth."* The light of Christ carries the very DNA of God, imprinting His nature and character onto our souls (mind, will, and emotions) and our physical bodies. As we walk in the light, we begin to manifest the very character of God and the realms of His glory in our lives.

In Isaiah 60:1–3, the prophet Isaiah speaks of the transformative power of God's light:

Arise [from the depression and prostration in which circumstances have kept you—rise to a new life]! Shine (be radiant with the glory of the Lord), for your light has come, and the glory of the Lord has risen upon you! For behold, darkness shall cover the earth, and dense darkness [all] peoples, but the Lord shall arise upon you [O Jerusalem], and His glory shall be seen on you. And nations shall come to your light, and kings to the brightness of your rising.

This passage, whose truths have come to life for Janet and me, paints a vivid picture of how God's glory light can lift us out of depression and difficult circumstances, causing us to shine brightly in a world covered by darkness. It's a call to action, to arise (we have to be willing to get up) and allow the glory of God to be seen in and through us.

The implications of this call are far-reaching. It means that no matter what darkness we may be facing—whether it's physical illness, emotional pain, or spiritual oppression—the light of Christ is more than capable of breaking through and bringing healing, restoration, and total deliverance. *This is the heavenly pattern for spiritual warfare God has given us!*

ACTIVATE THE REVELATION BY LOOKING TO CHRIST

How do we position ourselves to experience such glory? How do we activate this heavenly light strategy for spiritual warfare in practical ways in our lives and start living as light warriors? In this book, we have looked at many facets of receiving and imparting God's light, but it begins with a deliberate choice to pursue Christ above all else. This means reevaluating our priorities, setting aside distractions, and creating intentional space for such encounters.

It starts with turning our gaze toward Christ and recognizing that the Light of the World has come to dwell within us! (See Colossians 1:27.) We must stop focusing on the darkness all around us and embrace the light of Christ inside us. Jesus is not just seated afar off in the heavens somewhere; He is seated upon the throne of your heart. Just like a candle burning bright, your spirit shines with the light of His glory to bring illumination to every other area of your life. (See Proverbs 20:27.) But you must be willing to release this light. Ephesians 5:14 encourages us, *"Awake, O sleeper, and arise from the dead, and Christ shall shine (make day dawn) upon you and give you light."* As we awaken to this reality, we can begin to tap into the power of His light within us.

One practical way to do this, as I shared earlier in this book, is to understand and apply the power of our words.[39] Our voice becomes a soundwave for releasing the light of Christ from within our spirit. As we speak words of life from God's Word, they transmit the light. In this way, we shine God's light into the darkness around us. God's truth will change the words you speak, and your transformed words should lead you to take practical action.

Some other ways in which we light warriors can access and shine God's light that we've talked about include embracing the joy-light, releasing healing light by offering our whole selves to God's service, activating angels and disarming demons, moving as chariots of light with the fire of the Spirit, ascending in the light to receive visions of God's glory and divine revelation, and shifting atmospheres with praise-light. Review and apply each of these areas as you continue to train to be a light warrior.

Remember that praise is not just an action but a way of life. We *are* praise! As we choose to embrace a lifestyle of praise, we continually flash Christ's light for others to see so that darkness is dispelled and truth is revealed.

YIELDING FULLY TO JESUS

Some years after my experience of the glory in Natchez, Mississippi, I had another extraordinary experience that, once again, changed my life and ministry forever. Janet and I were leading a meeting in Beloit, Wisconsin, a small border town situated just north of Rockford, Illinois. The meeting was being held in a school gymnasium, and although the crowd wasn't overwhelmingly large—perhaps a hundred to a hundred and fifty people were in attendance—the Spirit's presence was very strong.

I had just begun preaching when I heard a voice calling my name, "Joshua." Instinctively, I looked up to my left—the direction where the voice seemed to be coming from—but I saw nothing. I tried to regain my focus and continue with my message, but then I heard the voice again, louder and more insistent this time: *"Joshua."* My eyes darted to the same spot, but still I saw nothing.

---

39. I go deeper into this revelation in my book *Power Portals: Awaken Your Connection to the Spirit Realm*.

Determined to press on, I tried to go back to my message, but the voice called out "Joshua" a third time.

That time, when I looked up, I saw something almost indescribable. At the very back of the gymnasium, to my left, stood a figure radiating an incredible brilliance—the light of Jesus Christ Himself. His face was shining more brightly than anything I had ever seen. And it was not just any light that radiated from Him; it was the light of His own glory. This wasn't merely a spiritual vision or an inner impression; Jesus was tangibly present, right there in the room, calling out to me. I saw Him with my own eyes.

This supernatural sight overwhelmed me to my core. My physical body could not withstand the intensity of His glory presence. Words escaped me; I could not describe what I was seeing or put into words what was happening. All I could do—and wanted to do—was yield completely to this divine encounter, to surrender completely to Jesus. I fell to the floor under the weight of His glory, unable to stand any longer. I lay there for a while, utterly enveloped in His glorious light, and it changed everything for me. In His light, I received an impartation for ministry. And in His light, I was energized and charged with His power.

As I remember it, I never did finish preaching that night. Janet later told me that she had stood up and gone to the microphone. Recognizing that the glory of God was in our midst, she had invited those present in the meeting to come forward to the altar area to receive their own personal touch from the Lord. Many people came forward and stepped into their own encounters with Jesus.

One thing I know for sure: encountering Jesus in the light of His glory left an indelible mark on my life. This encounter taught me a profound lesson about the nature of surrendering to God. It's not about receiving an occasional touch from the Lord or being satisfied with taking a small step of faith. True encounters with God's glory often require us to yield to Him completely. It's important to recognize that the journey into God's glory is ongoing. No matter how far we've come in our spiritual walk, there's always more to experience in Christ. Such growth requires our willingness to let go of what we think we know and to embrace new levels of yielding to the light of Jesus.

Like the apostle John in the book Revelation, we may find ourselves falling prostrate in the presence of Jesus's majesty. (See Revelation 1:12–18.) Yet surrender isn't only about physical posture; it's about allowing God to reshape our attitudes, realign our perspectives, and heal our wounds. Fully encountering Jesus's glory requires a deep—often costly—willingness to yield to Him continually. If we desire to carry His light, we must first yield to His light. Jesus is everything, and He calls each of us to that place where His light can transform us, just as it did for me on that unforgettable night in Wisconsin.

AN INVITATION TO STEP INTO THE LIGHT

In our fast-paced world, it's easy to become distracted and to lose sight of what truly matters. Yet, God is extending an invitation to each of us light warriors. It's a call to encounter something far greater than we've ever known. This invitation is to experience the glory of Jesus Himself, to pursue Him with wholehearted devotion, and to be transformed by the light of His overwhelming presence.

The pursuit of Christ is a gateway to everything we need. As the Scriptures remind us, *"In Him…all things were created"* (Colossians 1:16). This profound truth suggests that when we stay connected to Jesus, we are aligning ourselves with the Source of all creation. It's in this alignment that we find fulfillment, purpose, and abundant provision.

Right now, I want you to hear the gentle whisper of the Spirit calling you into deeper communion with Christ. This is a sacred invitation to step into the radiant light of His glory, where transformation awaits. As you yield in complete surrender, let go of the burdens and unnecessary weights that have held you back. Release the past, the fears, and the doubts; they do not serve you in this spiritual journey.

Open your heart wide, ready to receive the healing that flows from the very presence of Jesus. Envision the light of His love washing over you, penetrating the darkest corners of your being, bringing restoration and wholeness. Allow this healing light to illuminate the path before you, guiding you toward the fullness of His grace.

As you embrace His love, you will become a vessel through which that love can flow abundantly into the world. Your willingness to be transformed opens the door for others to encounter the same light and healing. Step boldly into this divine invitation, and let the Spirit empower you to shine brightly, reflecting God's love in every thought, word, and action.

Embrace this moment of surrender—it is a step forward into your destiny as a light warrior. The world awaits the light that you will release through Christ who lives within you. Move into His glory, and let His love flow through you, transforming not only your own life but also the lives of those around you.

YOU ARE A LIGHT WARRIOR!

As we conclude this book, my prayer is that you would embrace the glorious light of Christ within you. Remember that your true identity is found in Him. Allow His radiance to flood every part of your being. As you do, you will find yourself transformed, shining the love and power of God to a world in desperate need of His glory. You are an overcomer, and you can now make this light warrior's decree with boldness:

> I am a light warrior.
> I carry God's light.
> I know who I am in Christ: God's beloved child and an overcomer.
> Being a light warrior means that I am connected to a higher purpose because I live from the Light and for the Light.
> I make a difference in other people's lives by contributing to bring heaven here on earth.
> I shine with the shekinah glory. This is a witness for others to see God's glory manifest in the world.
> I am dedicated to spreading the good news of the gospel wherever I go, knowing that by doing so I am fulfilling my purpose and releasing the light.
> I am aligned with the divine mission to spread love and bring about positive change in the world around me. This brings me a profound sense of joy, knowing that my actions are led by the Spirit and are making a tangible difference.
> As a light warrior, I am a catalyst for transformation. I hold space for healing and growth both within myself and for others. I understand that true change begins from the Holy Spirit who dwells

within me, and I commit to my own personal development and spiritual growth so that, in turn, I can continually help others in their journeys.

I radiate gentle, healing light waves that uplift and inspire those around me. My presence is a beacon of light that illuminates the paths of others because I carry the brightness of God's Word and Spirit. This guides me and others toward true growth and spiritual advancement.

By continually growing in God, I become a conduit for His divine energy, allowing it to flow through me to touch the lives of those whom I encounter.

As a light warrior, I embody the essence of love, compassion, and understanding.

By embodying the love of God and compassion of Christ in all aspects of my life, I create a ripple effect that touches the lives of others in profound ways.

As a light warrior, I am a point of contact for healing. Radical miracles happen wherever I go because the God of breakthroughs lives inside me.

The light I radiate is a source of hope and strength, offering solace and support to those going through challenging times.

I am a listening ear, a comforting presence, and a guiding light in times of darkness.

I bring solutions to the world by promoting the unity and harmony of the Spirit. I recognize the interconnectedness of all human beings, as we are all made in the image of God, as well as the unity of all believers in Christ. I strive to foster a sense of oneness in all of my interactions.

Through my words, thoughts, and actions, I inspire others to love one another as Christ has first loved us. I encourage open dialogue and communication between people, seeking resolutions that honor God's divine plan and purpose.

I stand for what is right and advocate for justice, using my voice to speak the truth to both people and situations. I help to set the captives free by bringing clarity to chaos.

Restoration, deliverance, and inspiration flow from the glory light I carry.

I offer support and guidance to those who are in need, providing a safe space for them to express their emotions and find restoration with the Creator of all things.

Through my words of encouragement and Spirit-led actions, I help other believers to find their inner strength in God and to recognize the presence of His light within them.

My prayers, in alignment with God's words, open heavenly light portals and dispatch angelic warriors on divine assignment. Thousands upon thousands of light-wielding angels surround my life, working with me in the call of God.

The light I carry pushes back against all forces of darkness. All demonic curses are void and inactive because the Greater One lives inside me. I actively contribute to releasing true freedom and liberty into every atmosphere by the power of the Holy Spirit that radiates from my life.

I ensure that the light shines brightly in the most difficult of circumstances. I will not be manipulated or bound by enemy assignments. I break free by releasing the light. When I do this, all demons must flee.

I commit to continually putting on the full light armor of God, deepening my connection with the Spirit and expanding my capacity to be a vessel of His light. I'm girded with the belt of truth, I wear the breastplate of righteousness, my feet are prepared with the shoes of the gospel of peace, I am surrounded by the shield of faith, I wear the helmet of salvation, and in my hands I wield the light sword of the Spirit.

I embrace my role as a light warrior with gratitude and humility, recognizing the immense power and responsibility that comes with this calling.

I am a light warrior!

ABOUT THE AUTHOR

Joshua Mills is an internationally respected minister of the gospel, a worship leader, a recording artist, a keynote conference speaker, and the author of more than twenty books and training manuals. In addition to *Light Warriors*, his books with Whitaker House include *Creative Glory*, *7 Divine Mysteries*, *Power Portals*, *The Miracle of the Oil*, *Moving in Glory Realms*, *Seeing Angels*, and *Angelic Activations*.

Joshua is well-known for his unique insights into the glory realm and the manifestation of God's divine presence that he carries. Wherever he ministers, the Word of God is confirmed by miraculous signs and wonders that testify of Jesus Christ. Regarded as a prophetic forerunner in the body of Christ for proclaiming the knowledge of God's glory, he has ministered in more than eighty nations on six continents. He and his wife, Janet, who cofounded International Glory Ministries, have been featured in several film documentaries and on many Christian television programs, and they have ministered to millions around the world through their books, soaking worship music, and weekly online webcast *Glory Bible Study*.

Still, Joshua considers his greatest honor to be a husband to Janet and a father to their three children—Lincoln, Liberty, and Legacy.